GLOBAL CAPITALISM
AND THE CRISIS OF DEMOCRACY

GLOBAL CAPITALISM
AND THE CRISIS
OF DEMOCRACY

by

Jerry Harris

Clarity Press, Inc

© 2016 Jerry Harris
ISBN: 978-0-9860853-2-1
EBOOK ISBN:

In-house editor: Diana G. Collier
Cover: R. Jordan P. Santos

Library of Congress Cataloging-in-Publication Data

Clarity Press, Inc.
2625 Piedmont Rd. NE, Ste. 56
Atlanta, GA. 30324 , USA
http://www.claritypress.com

TABLE OF CONTENTS

ACKNOWLEDGMENTS

I would like to extend a special thanks to Marek Hrubec, Director of the Centre of Global Studies at the Czech Academy of Sciences, and to Dr. Ondrej Sevecek, a director of the Institute of Philosophy at the Czech Academy of Sciences, for granting me a Visiting Professorship at the Centre of Global Studies in the Institute of Philosophy at the Czech Academy of Sciences in Prague. Surrounded by knowledgeable colleagues, Prague was the perfect environment in which to think and write, and complete much of this book.

There is also a group of fine scholars, activists and friends from the school of global capitalism I would like to thank. Our shared research, conversations and insights made this book possible. So thanks to Georgina Murray, William Robinson, David Peetz, Jeb Sprague, Jason Struna, Leslie Sklair, Anthony van Fossen, and once again, Marek Hrubec. In Chicago, decades of political discussions with Carl Davidson, Lauren Langman, Bill Peltz, Mel Rothenberg, Dan Swinney and David Schweikart have proven invaluable. As always, my brother Paul Harris, helped to guide my development and thinking, starting with an explanation of baseball when I was five. And to my wife, partner, and technical editor, Veronica Seizys, without whom this book would never have been published.

TABLES AND FIGURES

Table 1.1 Average Real Hourly Wages of All Workers, by Education in the US, 1973 to 1997 (1997 US$)

Table 2.1 Indicators of FDI and International Production, 2014 and Selected Years, Value at Current Prices (Billions of Dollars)

Table 2.2 Population and Wealth of UHNWIs with $30 Billion-plus Assets, 2015

Table 2.3 Apple's Global Chain, Number of Subcontractors

Table 2.4 Apple's US Subcontractors with Off-Shore Fabrication Facilities

Table 2.5 Employment of Foreign and US Auto Manufactures

Table 2.6 Auto Corporations Transnational Index (TNI), 2004-2008

Table 2.7 Top Ten Maritime Flags as a Percentage of Gross Tons of Registered Vessels

Table 3.1 Green New Deals

Table 5.1 China FDI Inflows and FDI Stocks (US$ Billions)

Table 5.2 Financial Investments in Chinese SOEs

Table 5.3 China's Outward FDI* Stock, 2009-2014 (US Billions)

Figure 5.1 Transcontinental Railway Route from Brazil to Peru

Table 5.4 Chinese Acquisitions Targeting European Technology Companies in Europe

TABLES AND FIGURES

DEMOCRACY IN THE TWENTY-FIRST CENTURY: STATE, MARKET AND CIVIL SOCIETY

Can the power of democracy overcome the power of global capitalism? This is the burning question we face and the central concern of this book. Global capitalism and the emergence of a transnational capitalist class (TCC) are not just temporary developments, nor is neoliberalism simply a policy choice of politicians. We've entered a new era of the capitalist world system, one of greater economic and political centralization, less democratic participation, more austerity, and growing repression. Setting the historic stage for the contemporary crisis are three interconnected changes impacting social relations—global production, financial speculation, and the technological revolution.

We now find ourselves at a historic conjuncture that demands a rethinking of left concepts and strategy. When we say "another world is possible," what will that world look like, and how can we move towards a more just society? Democratic participation at all levels of social existence is key to our common future. It is not just attacks on democracy viciously launched by global capitalism, but also the failure of twentieth-century socialism that compels our concerns. Therefore, a critical examination of contemporary capitalism is necessary, as is that of our own past as well as present ideas and practice. After all, criticism is the first act of democracy.

A starting point is a reexamination of the relationships between the state, market, and civil society. These institutions have developed over centuries of human social interaction. Combined, they are three pillars of modern civilization that encompass governance, the economy, and society. Any political movement that hopes to organize society around its vision of how people should structure their shared existence needs to recognize the organic interrelationship of these fundamental associations. Historically neither the state, market, nor civil society have a permanent form or set function. They are ever-changing institutions. And so the attempt to design a structure and method of interaction are questions that each social system and ideology, real or utopian, have tried to answer.

For the last two hundred years dominant modern ideologies have been defined by capitalism, communism, and efforts to build real existing socialism. Anarchism is a third influential ideology, particularly among social movement activists, but it remains untested as a ruling political principle around which society may be organized. There are many varieties of these ideologies and different practices, but whether in practice or theory, they all have stressed the domination of one institution over the others.

Market Fundamentalism

Classic liberalism and today's neoliberalism attempt to organize society by elevating market relations to the center of human existence and values. Neoliberals view human nature as driven by the desire to increase one's own wealth within a competitive society, and therefore see the capitalist market as the pinnacle of human expression. The broad notion of human freedom is reduced to that of individuals acting within markets to accumulate more riches or choose different commodities. Competition between individuals and corporations is fundamental to this freedom. It is said to lead to the best outcomes because the best products and the best people always win. Social solidarity and collective action only interfere with individual freedom. Accordingly, the public sphere should be commercialized, particularly government oversight of social services and the environment. Consequently, whenever concerted democratic activity challenges the power of capital, neoliberals feel the need to take political action to defend individual freedom from collectivist solidarity.

Jeb Bush gave a clear articulation of this worldview when speaking to white conservatives about how the Republican Party would attract Black support. As Bush stated, "Our message is one of hope and aspiration. It isn't one of division and get in line and we'll take care of you with free stuff. Our message is one that is uplifting—that says you can achieve earned success."[1] Any attempt by government to reduce inequality is seen as giving away "free stuff," and that degrades personal efforts and dignity. When government creates a social safety net it supports undeserving losers who have failed to succeed in competition. Helping the poor only interferes with their taking the initiative to better themselves, and this perpetuates poverty. Worse still, attempts to regulate the market inevitably lead towards socialist and collective domination. Instead government social functions, such as education and health care, should be privatized because the market will guarantee their best performance. The state is ultimately reduced to protecting and supporting business as the central institution of society and the best guardian of individual freedoms. Likewise, the role of the military is to expand access to markets and resources, creating an open world for business.

The social allure of neoliberalism is its emphasis on consumerism, individual materialism and the promise of wealth. Within this ideological framework it becomes easy to define others as the enemy. All group identities, such as class, race, gender, sexuality, and nationality, become political targets because collective demands for social recognition and equality violate individual freedom and effort. Again Bush gives voice to this worldview: "Since the 1960s, the politics of victimization has steadily intensified. Being a victim gives rise to certain entitlements, benefits, and preferences in society. The surest way to get something in today's society is to elevate one's status to that of the oppressed. Many of the modern victim movements—the gay rights movement, the feminist movement, the black empowerment movement—have attempted to get people to view themselves as part of a smaller group deserving of something from society."[2] Thus for neoliberals, movements to end discrimination are a call to battle by undeserving groups attempting to steal wealth created by honest and hardworking individuals. Entitlement is theft, violating the efficiency of the market in determining who is deserving. With such political appeals neoliberals have built a hegemonic bloc constructed around a reactionary base attracting those with racist, sexist, and homophobic fears and resentment. Only in the upside-down world of neoliberals can living under oppression be regarded as a privilege that has "elevated" one's life with entitlements.

It is important to understand neoliberalism as an ideology rather than a set of policies whose supporters can be voted in or out of office. Ideology gives neoliberalism its depth, defining good and bad in the world, and the acceptable limits of debate. It is hegemonic within the transnational capitalist class, and the reason why neoliberalism survived and continues to rule even after the devastating effects of the economic crisis. It is the ideology of global capitalism to which all ruling parties are committed. One can advocate harder or softer policy adjustments, perhaps a bit of neo-Keynesian modifications, but the underlying belief system remains. Whether social-democrats or conservatives, Republicans or Democrats, dominant political parties are all committed to hard or moderate neoliberal policies. Their worldview is all encompassing, and for them, there is no acceptable alternative.

Communist and Anarchist Alternatives

Communism, understood here as the socialist countries of the twentieth century, stood in direct opposition to capitalism and market fundamentalism. But the determination to eliminate the market led to state centralization and bureaucratic planning. Within civil society independent organizations were curtailed and subject to party leadership. A diverse political democracy was seen as a threat to the party's hold on state power, and rationalized as an attack on the working class. Consequently, freedom was defined as economic security, and democracy was stigmatized as bourgeois individualism that undermined the common good. This wasn't a predetermined inevitability. The New Economic Policy in the Soviet Union during the 1920s offered an alternative path, and will be discussed in a succeeding chapter.

Anarchism argues the road to liberation entails doing away with government and markets, replacing both with civil society in which councils and communes organize social interaction. Although experienced at the local level, or during short periods of social rebellion, anarchism as a principle for social organization has never succeeded. Never having had the responsibility of power it's easy for some to romanticize its unrealized possibilities. But we will analyze its actual viability through its practice in contemporary social movements, as well as its stated theoretical vision.

In summary, capitalism elevates the market, socialism the state, and anarchism civil society. These limit their vision of society, and so set the stage for their failure. A society built around the absolute structural hegemony of any one institution creates what becomes an irresolvable contradiction leading to revolutionary upheavals. Such a society restricts the autonomy of fundamental institutions in ways that permanently deform their functions. The result is an authoritarian regime in which democracy becomes confined to an ever more constricted space, in order to maintain the hegemony of the social, class or political forces that control the dominant institution.

It is impossible to permanently suppress any historically central institution of civilization. The state, market, and civil society are not separate realms of social existence. They are aspects and functions of the same social relations. These institutions are so interconnected that the arbitrary repression of one or another is an attempt to strangle historical materialism. Fundamentalist ideologies have failed to build sustainable societies because the contradictions inherent in their projects eventually explode. Contemporary capitalism creates global poverty, environmental destruction, and political stagnation. State-centric socialism resulted in the failure and collapse of the Soviet Union and satellite states. And anarchism has never generated a political and social movement with enough power and popular support to create a sustained project.

The following chapters will explore these questions of ideology and practice, success and failure, democracy and repression, and the shape of contemporary society. Chapter one looks at the remaking of the working class, austerity, and its effects on democratic society. Chapter two analyzes global capitalism, the character of transnational corporations, the emergence of the transnational capitalist class, and their construction of a new world system through global trade agreements and institutions. In chapter three we will explore green capitalism as a possible alternative to financialization and neoliberalism, and the role the Left can play in building a sustainable economy. The fourth chapter tackles the relationship between nationalism and transnationalism through the conflict in Ukraine. It explores the importance of national sovereignty, and its limits under global capitalism. China is the topic of chapter five, in which we investigate the use of state power to merge the Chinese economy into an essential part of transnational capitalism, and transform social relations from the Maoist period. Chapter six looks at the New Economic Policy in the Soviet Union, its defeat, and the development of Stalinism that led to the failure of twentieth century socialism. This chapter will also critique anarchism with an analysis of Michael Albert's *Parecon*, as well as the negative effects of anarchist practice in the Occupy movement. The last chapter will address possible alternatives arising from contemporary social movements and experiences in building and sustaining cooperatives. Moreover, we will reexamine the relationships between the state, market, and civil society in the new theoretical perspectives of some of the most original and important contemporary revolutionary thinkers who are attempting to resolve the historic impasse of democracy.

Endnotes

1   Charles Blow, "Jeb Bush, 'Free Stuff' and Black Folks," *The New York Times*, September 28, 2015, <http://www.nytimes.com/2015/09/28/opinion/charles-m-blow-jeb-bush-free-stuff-and-black-folks.html?_r=0>.

2   Ibid.

Chapter One

THE DECLINE OF DEMOCRACY

"Top-down class warfare. That may sound simplistic,
but it's the way the world works."
Paul Krugman

For the global one percent capitalism has been a fantastic success. A handful of 80 billionaires have the same amount of wealth as 3.5 billion people, or the bottom half of the world's population.[1] Just below the palatial elite are the 1 percent who own 50 percent of the world's total wealth. Their annual income is greater than that of the remaining population of the world. The promise of capitalism was a global middle class. Yet workers in all job categories face insecurity, weak bargaining power, and a shredded social contract. For most of the world's middle class the direction is downward, not up. As for the poor, the treadmill of poverty has led nowhere.

Alongside the downward spiral of the economy are growing restrictions on democracy. Economic inequality is tied to political inequality. Greater wealth in fewer hands generates greater political power in fewer hands. The rich exalt the market as the supreme institution of civilization. They believe those who rule the market should rule the country, while civil society and government should be subservient to the market.

But while wealth and power have always been a part of capitalism, so too has popular democracy. Now, however, we have entered a new era characterized by a world system of integrated production and finance. The new transnational capitalist class has little use for democracy, the social contract, or any sense of national responsibility. We are at a crossroads between creating a society with greater participatory democracy or one of greater authoritarian rule. To fully appreciate our historic moment we need to understand the beginning of modern democratic practice, and its inherent social and political contradictions.

The Revolutionary Origins of Democracy

Democracy was born from two different conceptions and historic traditions.[2] The first developed in Athens, where small farmers broke the rule of large landowners and debt bondage to create a revolutionary experiment in participatory democracy. Their new rights were protected by a legal framework of citizenship and political equality. The other tradition stems from Rome and later the Magna Carta, in which feudal masters won the freedom to control their property and servants. As Czech scholar Martin Brabec explains, "The main road to modern democracy runs through oligarchic historical events—oligarchic Rome, Magna Carta, the Petition of Rights and Glorious Revolution, the American Declaration of Independence of 1776 and Constitutional Convention of 1787, not through democratic, popular traditions— ancient Athens, the Levelers, the Diggers, Chartists, Communards, and Russian workers and peasants in 1917."[3]

This split in political traditions was clearly present during the early debates over modern democracy and representative government. The clashing viewpoints were characterized by Jean-Jacques Rousseau and Edmund Burke. Rousseau proposed direct popular sovereignty based on the will of the people, advocating participatory democracy over elected representation. Burke called for limits on democracy, and argued representatives owed people nothing more than their independent judgment. For Burke the masses were political sheep, unable to rule, and backward, similar to Mitt Romney's characterization of 47 percent of the population as "takers."

While these two distinct traditions exist, there is also a democratic dialectic at work that binds the two together—a contradictory unity that exists within modern society, based on the historic revolutionary class alliances, which formed the new hegemonic blocs in both the American and French upheavals. The capitalist class always viewed the market as the supreme arbiter of society. Government's first and foremost task was to help expand and protect capital. But popular democracy, based upon an actively involved civil society, was a class compromise that originated in the revolutionary alliance necessary to overthrow aristocratic rule. Although property rights were always primary, triumphs of democracy such as the end of slavery, voting rights, civil equality, and the rights of labor were won through mass struggles.

As social theorist and activist Bill Fletcher Jr. has noted,

> The notion of citizenship remains a powerful concept and one which people insist on fighting to achieve. It demarcates freedom vs. slavery; it offers the formality of participation. Yet most importantly, citizenship offers legitimacy and visibility. Citizenship assumes that one's history and life are relevant to the larger polity and, by implication, that one shares in the larger historical narrative. The fight to define and achieve citizenship becomes a fight to define and achieve recognition of one's humanity.[4]

The sacrifice and efforts of farmers, laborers and the poor won a historic victory that changed the world. Citizenship, democracy and nationalism were born—ideas that defined the era of bourgeois democracy for the next 250 years.

Such democratic space was resented and contested by the ruling class. Nevertheless, the ideological and political basis for an expansion of democracy was implicit in the French and American revolutions. When Thomas Jefferson wrote that "all men are created equal," he meant white male property owners. But the farmers, craftsmen, and laborers who joined the Continental Army and suffered through Valley Forge believed equality was meant for them. When the famous French document on the Rights of Man hit the streets of Paris the poor read of "Liberty, Equality and Fraternity," and joined the revolution with visions of a new society where a better world was truly possible.

This tension between popular democratic rights and property rights established a dialectic from the very beginning of the French Revolution. The most radical stage of the revolution was led by an alliance between the Sansculottes and Jacobins. The political clubs of the Sansculottes consisted of the urban poor, workers, small craftsmen, and shopkeepers. They were implacable foes of the rich, and their social ideas included "government guaranteed work, wages, and social security for the poor man (and) extreme, egalitarian and libertarian democracy, localized and direct."[5] The Jacobins were led by the radicalized and revolutionary section of the intelligentsia and middle class, and were the most decisive bloc in the government, writing a constitution which included universal suffrage, the right to insurrection, the right to an education, and the right to work or relief. Moreover, democracy was to be participatory, and government was to serve people's happiness. France was also the first country to allow divorce by mutual consent. As Eric Hobsbawm notes, "It was the first genuinely democratic constitution proclaimed by a modern state."[6]

But the Jacobin period was short lived and overthrown by the Thermidorian Reaction in 1794. Its primary objective was to eliminate workers, the poor, and women from the political life of the country. This set off two short rebellions in which the poor invaded the National Assembly demanding the reinstitution of the Jacobin constitution. Shortly afterwards 4,000 members of the Sansculottes were arrested and the word 'revolutionary' was banned. With the Girondins, the party of the bourgeoisie, now firmly in control, the constitution was rewritten, limiting voting to white men of property, and eliminating the right to insurrection, work, relief, and education. Private property became a foundational principle, the very basis of society. Furthermore, the concepts of equality and fraternity were redefined. Gone was the radical social and political equality of 1793, now replaced by a state-mediated legal equality. The Sansculottes had given fraternity a particularly revolutionary meaning, implying not only brotherhood, but a hatred of the rich and the right to seize their property. Consequently, fraternity became another banned word and was removed from public buildings. It was now illegal to even publically talk about the Jacobin constitution.

The overthrow of the Jacobin period was an early eruption of contradictions that still exist today. Class conflict has been the author of history, writing chapter and verse on the struggle between property rights and popular democracy. This is been the central contradiction located in the origins of capitalism. Modern revolutionary leaders have also been influenced by these democratic principles of earlier insurrections. Malcolm X argued the Black liberation movement should demand human rights, rather than civil rights. Like Jefferson, Malcolm maintained people were born with "unalienable rights" that existed above governmental power. He criticized Dr. King for demanding civil rights, which Malcolm saw as limited and dependent on the benevolence of the state. Ironically, Malcolm was firmly within the democratic tradition first established by the slave owner Jefferson. Also influenced by early democratic philosophy was Mao Zedong, whose favorite philosophers in high school were Rousseau, John Locke, Thomas Jefferson, and Benjamin Franklin.

In the following quote the first modern capitalist economist, Adam Smith, speaks to the tradition of property and capital. With small changes in style, the words of Smith could be a keynote speech at Davos. Below, he gives voice to the fears that now haunt contemporary global elites, defining the classic view of property and government, once more in vogue among today's transnational capitalist class (TCC). As he wrote,

Wherever there is great property there is great inequality. For one very rich man there must be at least five hundred poor, and the affluence of the few supposes the indigence of the many. The affluence of the rich excites the indignation of the poor, who are often both driven by want, and prompted by envy, to invade his possessions ... It is only under the shelter of the civil magistrate that the owner of that valuable property, which is acquired by the labour of many years, or perhaps of many successive generations, can sleep a single night in security. He is at all times surrounded by unknown enemies, whom, though he never provoked, he can never appease, and from whose injustice he can be protected only by the powerful arm of the civil magistrate continually held up to chastise it. The acquisition of valuable and extensive property, therefore, necessarily requires the establishment of civil government. Till there be property there can be no government, the very end of which is to secure wealth, and to defend the rich from the poor.[7]

This was the original articulation of liberalism, as the term is used in its classic and historical meaning. There is the recognition of ingrained inequality, which leads to class conflict and the need for governmental force to protect wealth. The protection of property, as the supreme function of government, in turn meant the suppression of the working class. Smith articulated that the essential character of the social relations between labor and capital was one of power: the capitalist dialectic of property rights in constant conflict with popular democracy. Neoliberalism has simply reasserted fundamental capitalist relations, without the economic and social compromise of Keynesianism. This is why the term "neoliberalism" has come into use to describe today's conservatives. They have returned to naked liberalism, which historically meant the freedom of capital. Liberalism not for people, but for property.

The Transformation to Global Capitalism

For millions of people citizenship means democratic rights exercised within a sovereign geographic and politically defined territory. This has been the basis for the present world system, organized into sovereign nation states, and ruled by governments formally committed to democracy and the welfare of their citizens. But neoliberalism has undermined both sovereignty and democracy. As an ideology and political movement neoliberalism has dominated the landscape for the past thirty-five years, providing the narrative for global capitalism and the primacy of property. But everything is historically contingent, including the character of nation states. The myth of middle class capitalism, particularly its Keynesian moment, was only realized during the post World War II expansion when social democracy ruled Europe and liberalism reigned in the United States. This period was characterized by an expanding social contract, mass movements that won greater rights for women and minorities, and environmental demands that propelled governments into action.

This short thirty-year period, contingent on a number of overlapping conditions, allowed wealth to be broadly shared. In its early industrial age capitalism produced brutal conditions. In the 1800s satanic mills consumed the western working class, while imperialist armies occupied the Third World. The twentieth century was ushered in by the economic violence of the Great Depression, squeezed between two cruel and devastating world wars. The Golden Age of capitalism took off only after the end of World War II, thrust forward by the need to rebuild the world after the destructive frenzy of fascism. The United States, whose territory and productive base were untouched by violence, ascended to primacy as the world's unquestioned hegemon. The government sent veterans to college for free. Unions were in a position to demand and win decent wages and better working conditions. As a result the middle class expanded, the suburbs grew, and children expected to do better than their parents.

This Golden Age of capitalism unfolded because important factors coalesced, creating historic opportunities, among them:

- The US entered a sustained period without significant economic competition. US monopolies dominated a world in which the industrial and productive capacity of its rivals and allies were largely destroyed by war.
- The US enjoyed financial domination with the establishment of the World Bank and International Monetary Fund. The dollar reigned supreme as the only acceptable world currency, and controlled the Third World through credit and debt.
- New technologies expanded the market, industry, and jobs. Jet engines revolutionized air travel, and advances in electronics produced mass consumer products such as televisions and refrigerators.
- As a result of the depression and war there was a huge pent-up demand for consumer goods. The post-WWII strike wave gained higher wages and benefits for workers. Working class families were able to consume more, enabling many to live the American dream. A virtuous cycle of consumption and production became the engine of the US economy.

But even for the US superpower the above conditions did not last. By 1972 international competition had caught up to the US, and President Nixon was forced to let the dollar float against other major currencies. At the same time living standards peaked and the middle class expansion reached its limits, encroaching too greatly on corporate profitability. After 1972 living standards began their long decline for the majority of people. As deindustrialization took hold unions declined, wages stagnated, and debt became a major component enabling consumer spending. More importantly, particularly for the capitalist class, profits rates began to stagnate and decline by the mid-1970s.

With stagnation spreading the capitalist class began to reorganize itself. A new hegemonic bloc emerged, with Ronald Reagan and Margaret Thatcher spearheading the neoliberal revolution. As global capitalism took hold, the transnational capitalist class (TCC) gained political and ideological hegemony within the major industrial nations. This was followed by transnational elites coming to power in the global South and becoming part of the newly forming TCC. Once again capitalism found areas for expansion, facilitated by new digital technologies and globalization. Borders were opened to vast flows of capital, global assembly lines emerged in manufacturing, and state-owned assets were privatized. The days of Keynesianism and liberalism were over.

As with the post WWII expansion, globalization emerged through a number of historically contingent elements coming together in the same period of time. These were:

- A vast expansion of the labor market that doubled the number of workers available to capitalism. This included the opening of China, Russia, and Eastern Europe to global markets, offering transnational corporations access to 1.5 billion workers. Coinciding with deep cuts in the Western social contract, former socialist countries eliminated guarantees of job security, free health care, and birth-to-death benefits. Now workers in both the east and west were dependent on the market for survival.
- The revolution in information and communication technologies allowed capitalist corporations to construct a global command and control structure that functioned in real time. This made possible the assembly, coordination and use of vast amounts of data necessary to carry out transnational production, run global markets, and create cross border financial flows. Digital technology also built the physical infrastructure for financialization, elevating financial institutions to the center of power for the TCC.
- A coinciding revolution took place in transportation,

with the ability to move huge amounts of commodities in containers aboard massive ships. This allowed for the geographic expansion of capitalism, while reducing the time it took for commodities to travel to markets. In effect, the compression of time and space paralleled the time/space compression in information technologies and financialization, leading to a more rapid turnover of capital. This added to the speed and flexibility of global capitalism.

These factors all developed in the 1980s, opening an exit door from the stagnation and crisis of the national Keynesian system. David Harvey has noted capitalism resolves its periodic crises with the relocation of industry to lower wage regions where labor is poorly organized.[8] This often happens within nations, but globalization offered new horizons for spatial relocation. For example, the textile industry went through a spatial reorganization from northern states like Massachusetts to the South, from there to China, and now to Viet-Nam and Bangladesh. The car industry went through similar patterns, from north to south, and into developing countries. In an era characterized by the hyper mobility of capital, geographic relocation is faster and more widespread. This had a profound effect on the global South. Previously exploited for resources, countries now became sites for transnational production.
Hence, globalization is deeply rooted in capitalist logic that unfolds in an ever-more integrated structure of world production and finance that entails the remaking of the working class. As new areas of production are opened up, a new industrial working class is constituted, concentrated in factories and neighborhoods whose conditions give rise to struggle, organization, and consciousness.[9] At the same time older industrial areas are abandoned, unmaking the social relations that brought together the working class, their organizations, and communities.

Remaking the Working Class

Key to the reorganization of labor was the deconstruction

of what Guy Standing has called "industrial citizenship." As he writes, "Global capitalism is profoundly different from national industrial capitalism. There is a vast amount of evidence to show how labour relations and patterns of work, and systems of social protection, regulation and redistribution, have evolved in the globalization era, in the process generating a new class structure."[10] For Standing the most important sector of new class formation is the "precariat." The precariat are not just the working poor, but more importantly those lacking a secure work-based identity, always facing temporary job status, and lacking social or work-based benefits—essentially workers living a precarious existence, or as some call it, working the "gig economy." One indication of the growing precariat is a report by Economic Modeling Specialists International, whose research found that jobs employing US part-time freelancers and part-time independent contractors numbered thirty-two million in 2014.[11]

The remaking of the working class resulted in the erosion of hard-won rights and benefits gained through union struggles over many decades, benefits such as job security, health and safety regulations, protections against arbitrary firing and harassment, good wages supported by retirement funds and progressive taxation, the right to strike, and a host of negotiated rights and responsibilities codified in union contracts. Corporations began a sustained attack against these rights in the 1980s, introducing the Japanese model of lean production, flexible work rules, just-in-time production, and quality circles. Spreading to the US and Europe lean production undercut established rights and benefits. Workers were also hard hit by contract concessions as corporations demanded "give-backs" that included vacation days, sick leave time, protected job categories, and wage gains. Already suffering massive lay-offs, unions buckled under the threat of plant closures. With many of the best organizers purged in the Red Scare of the 1950s, unions had lost the will to fight. Their combative tradition had been reduced to faded photos displayed in the plush offices of union bureaucrats. As labor scholar Beverly Silver points out, "By the early 1980s, the shop floor gains of core labor movements had been largely overturned."[12]

After the mean and lean Japanese model, the next strategy for profit retention was to cut corporations down to their "core competencies." Once-stable jobs were outsourced, off-shored, or turned into temporary and part-time work. Everything was geared to produce a "flexible" workforce, with full-time work cut to the bare minimum. The effect hit high- and low-end labor, from adjunct teachers at universities to sweatshop labor in Indonesia. Labor economist Susan Houseman points out that "In the past, firms overstaffed and offered workers stable hours. All of these new staffing models mean shifting risk onto workers, making work less secure."[13] Exactly Standing's point.

Jason Struna offers another approach to understanding the remaking of the working class. Struna looks at the relationship between labor and capital in terms of their spatial location to global production. His main focus is the fragmentation of the labor process into "transnational production chains that contribute incrementally and cumulatively to the creation of commodities."[14] This process is the result of dismantling national economies and constructing a global production system. Struna argues that workers who labor in the network of global assembly lines are part of a new transnational working class. Even though situated in a particular nation, they are employed by transnational capital, working for borderless corporations, their affiliates and subcontractors. Therefore, the linked geography of production inherent in transnational relations of production defines their status, rather than workers' singular territorial position. Workers become component parts of the production chain sharing an internal relation to one another. In this relationship global production travels to the worker. Immigrant labor is another important category, in which workers travel to the point of production. This consists of both high- and low-end labor. On one side are global cosmopolitan managers and professionals. On the other are farm and industrial workers crossing borders to find a better life, moving by both legal and illegal means. The Gulf States are an excellent example of Struna's description. Migrant workers are more than seventy percent of the work force in Saudi Arabia, Kuwait, the United Arab Emirates, Qatar, Bahrain, and

Oman. Almost all are laborers from India, Pakistan, and Sri Lanka who work under harsh conditions deprived of all democratic rights.

Focusing on the TCC and the working class in Latin America is the richly detailed work of William Robinson.[15] Robinson contends one of the most important changes was replacement of the developmental strategy of import substitution, with maquiladora factories that brought foreign manufactures to the US/Mexican border. Stretching from the Gulf of Mexico to the West Coast, manufacturing jobs increased from about 120,000 in 1980 to over 1.1 million by 2004. This greatly increased the feminization of labor, as most new industrial workers were young women. Furthermore, through the use of special export zones, maquiladoras and female industrial labor spread throughout Central America. Robinson's analysis of productive relations in Latin America applies to conditions in much of the global South. Worldwide export zones employ 70 million workers in 130 countries.

Another major change was the reorientation of agricultural goods towards global export markets. For countries in Central America such products account for more than half of their export earnings. This economic sector is no longer owned or run by the old landed oligarchy, but by new capitalists tied to global markets through financial relationships and transnational corporations (TNCs). Some crops like coffee are traditional, but new commodities are grown on an industrial scale throughout Latin America. Some of these include cut flowers from Ecuador and Colombia, processed fruits from Chile, and soy from Argentina and Brazil. Industrial-scale farms are often owned by TNCs such as Archer Daniels Midland, making use of imported seeds and pesticides supplied by bio-tech corporations such as Monsanto. Consequently, the entire commodity chain is integrated into global capitalism, from machinery and technology, to the farms, to control over purchasing, processing and marketing.

The export of labor and remittances is also a key aspect of the transformation of the working class. These workers not only travel to the point of production as Struna describes, but maintain strong cross-border family and community ties to their homeland. Such transnational networks, responding to global labor markets, create a working class culture molded by this era's relations of production. Migrant labor is a global phenomenon with workers coming from a diverse set of countries that include, among others, Albania, Egypt, Jordan, the Philippines, Bangladesh, Nepal, Jamaica, and Mexico. Although some cross-border workers are high-end managers and professionals, most migrants constitute the lower rung of global labor, many outside of legal protections and brutally exploited. The World Bank reported remittances grew by 400 percent from 2000 to 2010, reaching $500 billion in 2011. Remittances to Mexico and Central America are larger than US aid. Combining both migrant labor and those who produce export commodities, these workers totaled 900 million by 2005.[16]

Saskia Sassen takes another direction to the remaking of the working class by analyzing the geography and spatial relations between and within global cities. Cities such as London, New York, Frankfurt, Hong Kong, Shanghai, and Sao Paulo form strategic alliances through their financial markets. Concentrated in these cities are large technological infrastructures with deep pools of labor and talent geared to the financial industry. As Sassen explains, "Each of these centers is the nexus between that country's wealth and the global market and between foreign investors and that country's investment opportunities."[17]

This "new urban economy" has propelled changes in the working class, social stratification, and urban geography. A high concentration of executives, traders, lawyers, accountants, information technology experts, management consultants, and media professionals are centered in financial districts. This creates the social basis for gentrification, high-end real estate for the very wealthy, and the expansion of office space. The new economic regime of financialization drains capital from industrial manufacturing. The result, as Sassen points out, "contributed to the decline of mass production as the central driving element in the economy (and) brought about a decline in a broader institutional framework that shaped the employment relation."[18] As old industrial relations decline many of the unemployed go into lower-end jobs serving the financial districts. Rather than well-paying stable work the new jobs are in building maintenance, private security, child care, limousine driving, restaurant work, and dog walking. Low-wage jobs drive the expansion of fast food outlets and cheap retail giants like Wal-Mart, reproducing yet more low-paid, part-time, and often temporary work.

The Social Impact of Globalization

As mentioned above, globalization meant that manufacturing jobs flooded low-wage countries. The Commerce Department reported that from 2000 to 2010 TNCs in the US shed 2.9 million jobs, while adding 2.4 million abroad. By 2012 US transnationals employed 23,110 million inside the US, but another 14,043 million workers in their foreign affiliates.[19] These global assembly lines stretch around the world. TNCs from the US employ 4.2 million workers in Europe, over 4 million in Asia and the Pacific, and another 2.4 million in Latin America.

US TNCs are not the only corporations expanding abroad. Affiliates of foreign transnationals operating inside the US employed 5.8 million workers, or about five percent of the total US workforce.[20] But looking at the numbers in manufacturing we see a more concentrated picture. In 2012 there were 12.2 million Americans working full and part time in manufacturing. Of these, 17.7 percent worked for foreign affiliates. The largest sector was in transportation equipment, motor vehicle production, and auto sales, where foreign corporations supplied 917,600 jobs. Another big sector was in finance and insurance with employment standing at 390,000.[21] This is the new geography of global labor, with workers subject to hierarchical class power that's centralized in massive transnational corporations.[22]

The restructured world economy has impacted US workers by lowering living standards and introducing new social pressures. Since 1979 median compensation rose only eight percent although productivity grew by 65 percent. By 2014 the total value produced by US manufacturers had recovered to pre-crisis levels, but employed millions fewer workers.[23] If wages had kept up with productivity, which was the Keynesian promise, a low-wage family making $25,000 today would have an income of $40,000. Instead 51 percent of American workers earn less than $30,000.[24] Overall the share of national income going to the working class has fallen to its lowest level since 1951.[25]

Of course the money hasn't disappeared, it's just gone into the pockets of the wealthy as labor's share of the wealth has diminished. In 1965 the average income for a chief executive was 20 times the typical worker; by 2013 the gap had grown to 296.[26] The highest paid CEO in 2009, Aubrey McClendon of Chesapeake Energy, made $100 million. That's $50,000 per hour, equal to what 60 million households earned annually.[27] In the same year 25 hedge fund managers each banked over a billion dollars in annual income. With such great inequalities the 400 richest Americans control more wealth than the poorest 186 million. These are members of the top one-quarter of the top one percent, just 250,000 Americans who run the most powerful corporations, financial institutions, and law firms. Centered in enterprises that employ more than 10,000 workers executives have enjoyed a pay increase of 140 percent. Workers in these same corporations have suffered an average five percent drop in income. As *The New York Times* points out, "The phenomenon is not limited to Wall Street...

Table 1.1 Average Real Hourly Wages of All Workers by Education in the US, 1973 to 1997 (1997 US$)				
Year	Less than High School	High School	Some College	College	Advanced Degrees
1973	11.21	12.82	14.16	18.60	22.67
1985	9.91	11.70	13.33	17.95	22.66
1997	8.22	11.02	12.43	18.38	24.07

Source: Economic Policy Institute analysis of US Bureau of Census, Current Population Survey data, 1998 <http://www.census.gov>.

this pattern is being repeated in countries where the political landscape is quite different from that of the United States, like Sweden, Germany and Britain."[28]

Noble prize economist Paul Krugman points to the attack on labor and unions as fundamental causes for the growth in inequality. Krugman argues that, "Competition from emerging-economy exports has surely been a factor depressing wages in wealthier nations, although probably not the dominant force. More important, soaring incomes at the top were achieved, in large part, by squeezing those below: by cutting wages, slashing benefits, crushing unions, and diverting a rising share of national resources to financial wheeling and dealing."[29]

An early example of what was to become a widespread phenomenon was the establishment of Kelly Girl temp service. Temporary work and part-time jobs became pillars of the new economy. Kelly Services ran an ad in the 1970s for the "Never-Never Girl," offering a deal that corporations couldn't refuse. The ad read:

> Never takes a vacation or holiday. Never asks for a raise. Never costs you a dime for slack time. (When the workload drops, you drop her.) Never has a cold, slipped disc or loose tooth. (Not on your time anyway!) Never costs you for unemployment taxes and Social Security payments. (None of the paperwork, either!) Never costs you for fringe benefits. (They add up to 30% of every payroll dollar.) Never fails to please. (If your Kelly Girl employee doesn't work out, you don't pay.)"[30]

The conditions of labor envisioned in the ad reflect a sociopathic disregard for the welfare of workers. Yet what was a limited amount of part-time and temp work in the 1970s has spread to about one-third of the workforce today. Adecco, the Swiss temp agency and one of the world's biggest, has 700,000 people it can rent out to corporations. What hasn't changed is the feminization of part-time and temp labor. Women work about two-thirds of such jobs.

Years of unemployment and limited benefits have taken their toll. The most devastating effects are found in a study by two Princeton economists, Angus Deaton and Anne Case. In their analysis of annual death rates among middle-aged white Americans with high school degrees, they found startling results: a 22 percent rise in deaths due to suicides, drug, and alcohol use.[31] This segment of the population was one of the hardest hit by the economic crisis, its household income falling by 19 percent. For white men raised on the myth of self-sufficiency, privilege, and identity defined by work the end of the American dream has had tragic results.

Old industrial strongholds like Gary, Indiana and Detroit, Michigan are shabby shadows of a by-gone age. The story of Detroit is well known, but communities across the US have gone through similar wrenching experiences. For a number of years I worked for US Steel in South Chicago along with over 6,000 other men and women. The entire community was structured around the mill—not just employment, but home ownership, small businesses, union baseball teams in the park, local politics, the future of your kids, and the security of your family. The profits of US Steel were tied to mass employment in the concentrated working-class neighborhoods surrounding the mill. Gas stations, grocery stores, and restaurants all depended on the circulation of the wages earned by steelworkers. The great integrated mills were built around a coordinated use of large-scale industrial technologies, creating a social structure of accumulation that permeated South Chicago. But new steel technologies and globalized production undercut the older integrated mills that gave identity to Chicago's working-class community. When the mills closed the community lost its character, the remnants offering only a vague picture of the past. Unemployment spread, stores went bankrupt, gangs grew, and the union hall became a fundamentalist church with parishioners seeking answers to life that capital could no longer provide.

As always in America race adds its own unique characteristics of oppression to the crisis of working-class existence. Even after the Civil Rights Movement segregation still brands education, housing, and health care. Moreover, institutional racism pervades the job market, policing, and the justice system. These conditions structure an iron cage of inequality that defines the daily reality for minorities. Bill Clinton's 1994 crime bill helped fund the hiring of 100,000 new police officers, provided close to $10 billion for prison construction, created 60 new death penalty offenses, and allowed children as young as 13 to be tried as adults.[32] Lacking an external enemy in the post-Soviet world, the war on drugs created an internal threat that helped to imprison over a million African Americans.

For minorities historically on the bottom, the 2008 crash resulted in deeper poverty and greater suffering. Following the 2008 crisis unemployment rates for African-Americans climbed to 16 percent, almost twice the rate for whites. Children in minority families continued to endure the highest rates of poverty in the developed world, 25.8 percent for African Americans and 23.2 percent for Latinos. Deindustrialization and globalization hit the African American and Latino middle class exceptionally hard. Jobs in steel, auto, and other blue-collar work provided union wages and security that helped build a core of stability in minority communities. As the industrial base shrank, minorities were pushed into jobs in the lower end of the service sector, often at minimum wage in part-time work. The net worth of households tells a story of generational job and housing discrimination made worse by the financial collapse. This has resulted in a startling difference in household wealth as of 2013—African-American households held a net worth of $11,000, Latino households $13,700, and white households $141,900.[33] Black and Latino youth, often locked out from even minimum-wage jobs, were criminalized in the press and targeted by police. The rise of the Black Lives Matter movement and the all-too-often video recordings of police murders have finally brought this crisis to public attention.

What happened in Chicago, Detroit, and Gary was not the result of mysterious market forces independent of human will. The reorganization of social relations between labor and capital served the new mode of accumulation, not only on the factory floor, but in the community as well. Attacks on labor were accompanied by attacks on government programs for the poor, "ending welfare as we know it," as Bill Clinton put it. Everything from food stamps to aid to poor families with children was slashed, making way for tax cuts for the rich. It's not that government is weaker, but that government has been reengineered to institutionalize, contain, and expand transnational social relations in favor of capital.

The remaking of the working class also resulted in the remaking of the state. With millions losing industrial citizenship, the government's function of providing a broad social wage had to be undercut to correspond to the new relations of production. In its place the market was elevated to be the unchallenged institutional power within global capitalism. Not just in the US, but worldwide. Institutions based in the public sphere, such as education and health care, were privatized and turned into profit centers for capital. Economic security that provided a dignified life was attacked as a socialist burden on individualism. Elections financed by the very rich became so media packaged they appeared as little more than consumer choices between similar brands. Citizenship was reduced to an option of lifestyles, or to the one you could afford. Even fundamental human rights were surrendered to the market, exemplified by the privatization of water. In perhaps the most disturbing development courts sanctioned the privatization of human DNA, which now can be patented for sales and profits.

A. Sivanandan, editor of the respected journal *Race & Class*, has observed,

> The transition of the welfare state to the market state, as a categorical imperative of globalisation, has altered the priorities of government from the social welfare of the people to the economic welfare of corporations, which in turn replaces moral values with commercial values: caring with indifference, altruism with selfishness, generosity with greed."[34]

The Left, from social democracy to the old communist parties, has responded by calling for a return to industrial Keynesianism, a relationship the capitalist class has abandoned and left far behind. The old identities and culture forged in mass production and concentrated working class communities has been largely atomized into a flexible, diversified, often temporary, and thoroughly globalized workforce. The ability to organize resistance lies largely in the accumulation of shared experiences, networks, and organizations of solidarity and historical memory, a culture and identity kept alive in communities and families. But in the US, Europe, Russia, and China such traditions are like ghosts still punching the clock at an abandoned factory. The dynamic Civil Rights organizations in the US have been reduced to ritualized quotes from Dr. King. Leningrad has been returned to its original aristocratic founder, and Mao's Red Book transformed into tourist memorabilia. The Left has reacted to neoliberalism as if it is a mere policy choice when in reality it is the political aspect of a fundamental project to reshape capitalism into a post-national world system.

Globalism, Nationalism and Remaking the Military

One area where the US has maintained global superiority is the armed forces. The US has the most powerful military in the world, and many on the left and right assert it's the foundation of superpower hegemony. But the US military has been largely unsuccessful since WWII. It was fought to a stalemate in Korea, and defeated in Viet-Nam, Laos, and Cambodia. With the Taliban alive and well in Afghanistan, and ISIS controlling large areas in Iraq, these wars cannot be considered victories in any sense. The US abandoned Somalia after Black Hawk Down, and retreated from Lebanon after terrorists blew up a barracks killing over 200 Marines. Victories in Granada, Panama, and Serbia are minor engagements to hang medals on. Where the US has been successful is in killing civilians and destroying the social and physical infrastructure of countries. In defeat the US left two million dead in Viet-Nam, with well over a million more in Iraq and Afghanistan. So even in failure, the military maintains its ability to terrorize and threaten countries throughout the world.

As globalization became the main feature of the world system, the military faced a reevaluation and debate over its organizational structure. This became particularly sharp when Donald Rumsfeld was Secretary of Defense, and staffed the Pentagon with neoconservatives devoted to extreme forms of neoliberalism.[35] Consequently, the military came under the sway of privatization, outsourcing, and the technological displacement of labor. At the Pentagon it was termed the "revolution in military affairs." One result was large sections of security responsibilities were turned over to private contractors. In the occupation of Iraq contractors from transnational corporations like Halliburton outnumbered US troops. Today the third largest employer in the world is G4S, a private security firm that employs 620,000 workers and is active in 120 countries, with $12 billion in revenues.[36] Alongside the privatization of war is the automation of war through technology such as combat drones. The worker citizen army of old is now a combination of volunteers, paid mercenaries, contractors, and automated weapons. Today only Wal-Mart and Foxconn are larger than G4S. These are the new monopolies of global capitalism; low-wage employers and security corporations have replaced unionized industrial giants in the steel and auto sectors.

Displacing the citizen soldier has important implications for democracy. A ruling class dependent on their citizens for victory in war required an expansion of the social contract to solidify national loyalty. After WWII free health care was established in Great Britain, social welfare grew throughout continental Europe, and Cold War liberalism shared wealth with workers in the US. The ruling hegemonic bloc was strengthened through an expansion of social benefits, in turn producing greater nationalism within the working class. But the working class, which was a dependable core ally against fascism, became a liability in the imperialist invasion of Viet-Nam. Opposition to the war was widespread among soldiers, the story beautifully told in the documentary "Sir, No Sir!" After their defeat in Southeast Asia the ruling class understood they could no longer depend on a draftee army. This problem coincided with stagnating wages and profits in the 1970s, compelling a new strategy of neoliberalism and globalization to solve the economic crisis. As a transnational capitalist class emerged and consolidated they applied what they learned in redesigning the economy to the military. Privatization, outsourcing, flexibility of the workforce, and a greater use of technology was used to remake the armed forces. In effect, the modern military was reengineered to serve neoliberal capitalism even as it maintained patriotism as a culture and ideology. This matched neoliberalism in the social sphere. Less dependence on the national workforce correlated to less dependence on citizens in the military.

Today nationalism is no longer a patriotic response to an endowed social contract, but a reactionary populism rooted in racism, fear, and anger. The results are seen in the neo-fascist campaign of Donald Trump and the rise of the far right in Europe. Great power nationalism has always contained racist elements situated in its support for imperialism. But in today's context, nationalism functions more than ever as the political and ideological tool of the far right, demanding economic protection for the white working class by targeting minorities, immigrants, and globalization. A sizeable section of this political reaction resides in the old South, or what some call the "neo-confederacy." It seems the past is like a zombie—you only think it's dead.

The TCC may manipulate nationalism for their own purpose, but they are playing with fire. Twentieth century fascism as an expression of reactionary nationalism was backed by the most important sectors of the capitalist class in Germany, Japan, and other countries. Today the big bourgeoisie is transnational and cosmopolitan, and labeled an enemy by the far right. A typical attack on global elites was expressed by Marine Le Pen of the National Front when she stated, "No longer right and left, but globalists and patriots."[37]

This is the irony of historical dialectics because the conditions for the far right were created by the transnational capitalist class itself. As Bill Fletcher Jr. astutely points out,

> Neo-liberal capitalism...appears to be civilized yet is anything but. It promotes the expansion *into the global North* the differential that existed between the global North and the global South. It is this reality that has been so difficult for populations in the global North to fathom. It was one thing to sit back, observe, and accept the treatment of billions of people in the global South as *sub*human. It is a completely different thing to import that into the global North through both the expansion of sub-citizenship and the denigration of the formal citizen.[38]

This contradiction has become evident as the TCC moves ever closer to its global project of creating authoritarian state structures, undermining national citizenship in its quest for a borderless world of exploited labor. In turn a reactionary nationalist blowback has been created that attacks immigrants, international labor, *and global capitalism itself* as the enemy.

Austerity and Democracy in Europe

Global capitalism is not solely a US project, but is promoted by a world-spanning TCC. In Europe, which had a more substantial social contract than the US, the impact and political upheaval has been intense. The depression in Greece has created suffering not seen since the 1930s. Conditions in Spain, Portugal, and Ireland are not much better. In Latvia 30 percent of the population was declared "severely materially deprived." Deep cuts into the social contract also affected millions in Germany, France, the UK, and other countries in the European Union (EU). A Pew Research Center opinion survey conducted in 2013 asked:

"Will children in your country be better off than their parents?" Only 28 percent of Germans, 17 percent of the British, 14 percent of Italians, and 9 percent of the French believed their children will be better off than previous generations.[39] EU governance institutions, acting as technocratic authoritarian bureaucracies, have made the working class pay for their own repression through harsh austerity policies. Neoliberalism did not solely arise from the swamp of conservative US politics. It's the policy of global capitalism common to political parties throughout the world. In the EU elite politicians and institutional technocrats may be European, but the bond holders, financial institutions, and corporations they represent include capitalists from every region of the world.

To enforce unpopular economic measures, democracy, even in its most basic electoral form, must be beaten down to uphold market principles. With a newly elected anti-austerity left government in Portugal, the elite think tank Rhodium Group quickly predicted that international bond rating corporations would prevent the government from enacting any popular legislation. Jacob F. Kirkegaard, writing for Rhodium, stated, "Ultimately, any new leftist Portuguese government would find that its most important constituents reside not in Portugal but in the credit analysis department of DBRS, located in either Toronto, New York, or Chicago (and owned by a consortium led by the Carlyle Group and Warburg Pincus)."[40]

Syriza's left victory in Greece faced similar problems. Syriza had overwhelming support from the Greek population to end austerity policies that drove the country into a cruel depression. But the European Central Bank threatened to cut off all funding to a nation whose GDP had already fallen by 25 percent, and whose youth unemployment soared to 60 percent. The Bank pretends to be independent and apolitical, but is run by Mario Draghi, a former investment banker with Goldman Sachs whose commitment to the TCC is absolute. The other major players—the European Commission and the IMF—are similar institutions. When Syriza called for a national referendum on demands made by their EU overlords the anger among bankers and elites was apocalyptic. A challenge to their dictates through a democratic election was viewed as the ultimate betrayal by the Syriza radicals. Leading European neoliberals were quick to discard popular democracy when the referendum rejected more austerity. As German finance minister Wolfgang Schaeuble said, "Elections change nothing. There are rules," and the president of the European Commission, Jean-Claude Juncker, added, "There can be no democratic choice against the European treaties."[41] All this came to bear in one humiliation after another for the Greek people and its government. When the parliament passed a bill to ease the humanitarian crisis by offering medical care to those too poor to seek help, creditors were quick to reject the "unilateral" act by the supposedly sovereign government. As one EU official stated, "The Greek authorities are obliged to discuss all actions, including social policies, with the creditors before adopting them."[42]

Ultimately the government was forced to accept more austerity in order to access loans to pay off debt owed to transnational financial powers. Krugman summed up the situation well, writing, "The campaign of bullying—the attempt to terrify Greeks by cutting off bank financing and threatening general chaos, all with the almost open goal of pushing the current leftist government out of office—was a shameful moment in a Europe that claims to believe in democratic principles."[43]

Globalization, Taxes, and Mobility

Today's ruling class has a character different from past nationally-based ruling elites. Their fortunes have become so completely entwined in global accumulation that many see no reason to finance their own state. Taxes in their view are to be paid by the working class, not the rich. Their wealth is to be left untouched. And so a global chain of tax havens has been created where the rich deposit their wealth free from the grasp of any government. Records leaked from just three off-shore tax havens in the British Virgin Islands, the Cook Islands, and

Singapore revealed information on more than 120,000 companies and nearly 130,000 individuals from more than 170 countries. In the Caribbean the Cayman Islands is host to three-quarters of the world's hedge funds. The McKinsey Consulting Group estimates that from $21 to $32 trillion dollars of hidden wealth is hoarded in tax havens. Aiding these activities are global banks such as Barclays, UBS, and Deutsche Bank, all deeply involved in helping their clients hide their money.[44]

Further evidence is seen in reports from US transnationals. Challenging rational belief these corporations state that 43 percent of their overseas profits are generated from tax havens like Luxemburg and the Isle of Man. Yet only seven percent of their foreign investments, and just four percent of their foreign workers, reside in tax havens. In many cases their corporate headquarters is no more than a brass name plate on an empty office door. In 2012 US TNCs reported $80 billion in profits in Bermuda, greater than their combined profits in China, Japan, Germany and France.[45] Wal-Mart is a good example of how the largest TNCs in the world use tax havens. Wal-Mart has 22 shell companies in Luxembourg with $64 billion in assets, paying less than one percent in taxes. Yet not one Wal-Mart store exists there.[46] Oxfam reported even larger figures for General Electric, which uses 118 tax haven subsidiaries stashing $119 billion abroad. Yet another example comes from the UK where the average tax bill on the medium income of $40,000 is $7,800. Nevertheless, Facebook, which operates in the UK, paid taxes that only totaled $6,274 in 2014.[47] Australian scholar Anthony van Fossen completed a detailed study of tax havens which accounted for 70 different sites around the globe. He estimated that 19 percent of the wealth of high-net-worth individuals was in offshore financial centers as of 2009.[48] Continuing exposure of offshore records, such as the Panama Papers, reveal even greater amounts.

Corporate tax haven strategies hit developing countries particularly hard. A commonly used scheme is to channel foreign direct investments through tax haven subsidiaries. About 30 percent of all cross-border TNC investments are carried out using this method. Profits from the investments are then registered in the off-shore tax havens rather than the country where production takes place. Because of this scheme, the United Nations estimates a loss of $100 billion of annual tax revenues to developing nations[49]—monies badly needed for national development and social services. In addition to the various above schemes is the "inversion tax," a perfect illustration of the global capitalist system. This takes place when a TNC in the US buys a foreign corporation in order to pay lower tax rates in the country of their newly-owned affiliate. It has nothing to do with corporate synergy, it's simply a strategy to lower their tax obligations. The largest inversion took place through the acquisition of the Irish company Allegan by the pharmacy giant, Pfizer. Commenting on the inversion, well-known corporate raider Carl Icahn noted how the deal would erode the US tax base, hurt the US economy, and destroy thousands of US jobs. He then goes on to say, "I have spoken to many chief executives who confirm they are planning to follow Pfizer's lead...They are completely justified. Chief executives have a fiduciary duty to enhance value for their shareholders."[50] Not only is there a lack of national concern or responsibility, instead we have the full-blown advocacy of profits before national loyalty. Such thinking reveals that transnational capitalists are a self-conscious class, openly rationalizing the pursuit of their own interests above all else.

The common practice of hiding profits and wealth, and sharing information on how to pursue and structure tax havens, has become inside knowledge among global elites. It creates a class culture, one of shared assumptions about rights and techniques of control over personal and corporate wealth, while discarding concerns over social and national responsibilities. They have created new territorial space where governments cannot touch their riches. Their ultimate desire is to reduce government to an instrument that simply helps to organize, promote, and protect global capitalism. In their view, when governments seek to arrange a class compromise it only results in the welfare state. So government's historic role, even though it favored the interests of capitalists above all others, is now attacked as a barrier to the cold efficiencies of market relations.

Capitalists have not only moved their money, but also their residential locations. An interesting compliment to Sassen's work on global cities is the mobility of the ultra-rich between the world's top urban centers. Looking at primary and secondary homes, but excluding hotels, the Knight Frank research group reports that,

> Los Angeles' multi-millionaire population gyrates between a little over 11,000 to just under 6,000 through the year. Dubai, Cape Town, London and Miami also see significant volatility in their wealthy populations...Our calendar of global events looks at the key locations where the wealthy cluster through the year—through the lens of private jet travel. Networking with the wealthy will take you from Davos in January, to the Masters in Augusta in April, Monaco Grand Prix the following month and the Aspen Ideas Festivals in June before ending the year at Art Basel in Miami.[51]

In summer London and New York have peak populations of the ultra-wealthy at about 33,000, shrinking to just 11,000 in winter. Hong Kong experiences the same seasonal shift, from a high of 24,450 individuals to a low of 8,680. Spring favors Paris where 9,480 of the 0.001 percent flock, only to plunge to just 2,800 in February. Rio, Sydney, and Cape Town, being in the southern hemisphere, have the opposite flow. Knight Frank also ranked cities that "matter most to the world's wealthy, based on where they live, invest, educate their children, grow their businesses, network and spend their leisure time."[52] The top five included London, New York, Hong Kong, Singapore, and Shanghai. As part of their research Knight Frank looked at city residents and those who lived within two hours of transport. London had 4,900 residents, but could be reached by another 16,000 living in

Europe. New York registered 5,600 residents with 8,300 within two hours. For Paris the split was 1,500/19,000 and for Shanghai 1,500/6,300.

Such mobility attests to the fact that the ultra-rich have shed their national ties and become global citizens. As Sassen points out, global cities are essential nodes in the world economy. Van Fossen does the same for global tax havens, and Knight Frank reveals a network of world cities as the preferred territorial space for the rich. Together they expose the new class spatial relations of globalization.

Gramsci and Class Hegemony

We've discussed the historic development and contradictions of democracy, but it's also important to situate history in a theoretical context to help structure and inform our understanding. Perhaps Italian Marxist Antonio Gramsci best understood the political and cultural class relationships within capitalism. According to Gramsci the ruling class constructs a hegemonic bloc of class sectors around economic and political modes of accumulation. The hegemonic bloc not only includes dominant sectors of the capitalist class, but also sectors of the middle and working class as well. Power is based on both consent and coercion, using forms of democracy and economic well-being, but also threats of unemployment, prison, and political repression. In advanced capitalist countries consent is the most preferred tool of control, enforced by cultural and ideological hegemony. As Marx pointed out, the culture of the ruling class becomes the culture of the masses. Class hegemony sets the limits on acceptable political ideas and dialogue while establishing materialism and consumerism as the dominant forms of cultural expression. But the iron fist emerges to repress the poor, as well as mass movements that may threaten capitalist power on any number of fronts. And so there is the constant use of police violence in poor communities, the school to prison pipeline, mass arrests at demonstrations, and the threat of greater repression.[53]

Gramsci's lessons can be seen today when the hegemonic class incorporates the needs and interest of other classes into their structure of power. The working class desires a house, a car, and television, and the capitalist class wants to sell them to you. The working class wants good health care and good schools, and the capitalist class needs a healthy and educated workforce. The working class wants some say over political policy and the capitalist class offers elections that create greater legitimacy, stability and flexibility for the system. Moreover, social movements situated in civil society penetrate the state by demanding greater rights. As German scholar Ingo Schmidt points out, demands for greater social services and benefits make "claims on public funding, which are ultimately tied to the state's capacities to collect taxes or sell bonds to private investors."[54] When the state incorporates such demands from labor, women, and minorities a two-way process of consent takes place, solidifying the hegemonic bloc. Protest movements consent to be part of the system, and government consents to expand the field of democracy and human rights. Through such contested political process the state retains its legitimacy and stabilizes its class power.

But during periods of crisis it becomes more difficult to keep the social contract intact. Consequently, social and governmental institutions begin to lose legitimacy and class hegemony is shaken. For oppressed minority communities, whose needs are never fully incorporated, the crisis hits harder and rebellion is quicker to develop. As discontent deepens democracy must be restrained in the hopes of curtailing social turmoil. But repression often results in greater rebellion. Ruptures inside the ruling class may then occur over how best to solve the crisis. This can lead to the construction of a new hegemonic bloc, one that seeks to stabilize class rule by incorporating popular discontent and rebellious social forces under elite reformist leadership. For those who continue to demand more radical change there are harsher measures of political repression, jail, and police murders. The dialectic between dissent and incorporation, and between coercion and consent, has successfully functioned in the US for some 240 years.

This form of rule is not a conspiratorial strategy thought up in a Washington DC think tank, or some elite retreat at Jackson Hole or the Bohemian Club. It arose out of the concrete relationships created by the bourgeois democratic revolution as an organic response by the capitalist class, a relationship that originated in the class alliances that made possible the revolutionary seizure of power, creating a democratic dialectic that produced a social compromise conceding political space to the popular masses. This historic relationship generated both consent and coercion as a constantly shifting expression of class contradictions and the balance of power—a dialectic based in historical materialism.

It's important to recognize the difference between the normative repression inherent in bourgeois democracy and fascism. Fascism is the failure to maintain the historic democratic dialectic, a crushing of the bourgeois democratic compromise in favor of outright dictatorship and coercion. In response to a deep structural crisis a new hegemonic bloc is formed, antagonistic to both the working class and elements of the capitalist class itself. In WWII a Popular Front, between the working class and sections of the capitalist class committed to bourgeois democracy, defeated fascism. And although challenged by McCarthyism, democracy and the social contract were reaffirmed and extended in the 1960s.

The social contract, which developed over many decades of struggle and compromise, took place under the leadership of a national capitalist class, territorially rooted to a nation-centric state. With the development of global capitalism the national structure of accumulation and class power, which created this hegemonic bloc, was disrupted by new transnational relationships between labor and capital. As explained above, globalization ushered in the remaking the working class to conform to the new modes of transnational accumulation. As a result the role of the state was changed to help construct and contain the emerging relations of production. Shredding the national social contract was part of a realignment of forces. A new hegemonic bloc materialized under the leadership of the TCC that no longer saw a need to compromise with its working class, in effect, expelling the working class from the transnational hegemonic bloc.

The new bloc developed a popular base with promises of expanded consumerism, and individualized wealth based in stock market speculation. This base was mainly limited to the middle class, in particular those favored by the new economy. Both the Democrats and Republicans, and in Europe the conservatives and social democrats, promoted and defended globalization and financialization. But when the bubble burst the middle class saw their speculative wealth disappear, and the economic safety net caught only the rich. As the crisis spread the social base shrank and inequality expanded. Neoliberalism had only one answer to the crisis—greater austerity backed by an ideology that becomes more fossilized with each developing social disaster. Yet neo-Keynesianism has been unable to mount an effective alternative, trapped by its own belief in a more "just" globalization. Without an answer to be found within the confines of global capitalism the crisis goes on unresolved.

Political conditions have now begun to swing out of control. This was first seen in the left emergence in Latin America in Venezuela, Bolivia, and Ecuador, as well as anti-austerity governments in Brazil, Argentina, Paraguay, and Uruguay. In the US the crisis in political legitimacy is seen in the campaign of socialist Bernie Sanders, and Donald Trump and the Tea Party's disruption of the Republican elite. In Europe both the left and right grow stronger, from Syriza, Podemos, and Jerry Corbyn's Labor in the UK, to Golden Dawn and Marine Le Pen on the right. The hegemonic bloc of global capitalism is weakening even as it furiously works to incorporate what it must, and isolate what it can.

Under such conditions the ruling class has turned to greater coercion to make the working class comply with the demands of transnational accumulation. As social tensions intensify coercion comes to dominate consent as the main form of rule. Mass surveillance grows, with the security state selling its technocratic panoptic measures as necessary to protect "our freedom and civil liberties." Suffering immigrants escaping poverty and war are targeted as racial, cultural, and religious enemies. Property rights and the market continue to further crush the social contract, and neoliberalism continues as the dominant ideological expression even as it fails.

The TCC seem trapped in a world of their own making. Transnational corporations have a natural hierarchal, authoritarian, and technocratic structure. This organizational DNA is ingrained in the ideology of the TCC, and rules over global governance structures. Consequently, the IMF, World Bank, WTO, and global trade treaties override democratic and popular decisions made at the national level. There is no better example than the Greek tragedy. We may be facing a time in which the bourgeois democratic revolution has run its historic course. As Greek scholar and activist Andreas Karitzis observes, "Neoliberalism is not an economic policy; it's an ambitious strategy of fundamentally transforming the physiognomy of modern societies and subjectivities as well, of ending once and for all the democratic and emancipatory wave that emerged in human history after the French Revolution."[55]

The heritage of our contradictory democratic tradition is still part of our current political life. Global capitalism seeks to reduce democracy, shoving civil society into the market place and out of the realm of political and social power. And yet democratic space is forced open by movements such as Occupy and Black Lives Matter. When the power of coercion becomes ever more intense people take to the streets in opposition. Insurgent electoral campaigns attract mass support, new political organizations emerge, and alternatives are envisioned. Free speech, the right to assembly, and the use of civil liberties are put into motion to resist repression. The Gramscian dialectic is still at work.

Conclusion: Capital and Democracy

The problems of global capitalism are deeply rooted in the very structure of rule. Although the working class achieved political democracy, it lacks control over production and economic decision making. Consequently, the capitalist class that owns and runs corporations and financial institutions set wage and benefit structures and daily working conditions, plus determine levels of employment and unemployment, part-time and temporary work, and the outsourcing of jobs. They control dominant technological systems such as communications, the Internet, military weaponry, transportation, and energy, and have hegemonic control over the production of culture. They dominate the housing market, and command the flow of capital. Their factories and never-ending search for resources degrade our environment and cause global warming. Politically they affect taxation, legislation, and regulatory structures, and finance major parties throughout the world. They determines the quality of air you breathe, the water you drink, and the food you eat. They are the ruling class.

Within this context mass democracy has limited space, constructed as little more than a suggestion box for constricted reformism. The contradictions between democracy and economic power have become so glaring that critics from within the system have begun to forcefully speak out, since fear of rebellion lies not far over the horizon. Pope Francis surprised many when he castigated the values of market fundamentalism. As he stated,

> As long as the problems of the poor are not radically resolved by rejecting the absolute autonomy of markets and financial speculation and by attacking the structural causes of inequality, no solution will be found for the world's problems or, for that matter, to any problems... Today everything comes under the laws of competition and the survival of the fittest, where the powerful feed upon the powerless... Consequently, (the rich) reject the right of states, charged with vigilance for the common good, to exercise any form of control. A new tyranny is thus born, invisible and often virtual, which unilaterally and relentlessly imposes its own laws and rules.[56]

One might hope for such a statement from a spiritual leader, but leading economists, some of whom were once outspoken neoliberals, have also expressed concern. Mark Carney, Bank of England governor, spoke to the absolute power of free markets saying, "Just as any revolution eats its children, unchecked market fundamentalism can devour the social capital essential for the long-term dynamism of capitalism... All ideologies are prone to extremes. Capitalism loses its sense of moderation when the belief in the power of the market enters the realm of faith. In the decades prior to the crisis such radicalism came to dominate economic ideas and became a pattern of social behaviour."[57]

Pope Francis and Carney speak to the destructive domination of the market over government and society. And both point to the hegemony of neoliberalism and its central ideological position within the capitalist class. But why does this ideology have such a deep hold on the ruling elite? Krugman offers a simple and direct answer, "You can't understand the influence of austerity doctrine without talking about class and inequality. The austerity agenda looks a lot like a simple expression of upper-class preferences, wrapped in a facade of academic rigor... What the top 1 percent wants becomes what economic science says we must do."[58] Joseph Stiglitz, another Noble prize winning economist, puts it more succinctly, "wealth at the top of the ladder arises from exploitation."[59]

Both economists speak to the basic class nature of inequality under capitalism, and why market fundamentalism is so ingrained in ideology, economics, and government policy. It arises out of capitalist social relations and the structure of hierarchy and power within the system. The mediating role of democracy, trapped in its present formalistic and narrow space, can never tame the drive towards inequality. Just as cycles of expansion and contraction are permanent features of the economic system, so too is the political struggle between social justice and the concentration of wealth and power. We are trapped in the capitalist dialectic of growth and collapse, endlessly repeated but never resolved.

We now stare into the twin disasters of economic crisis and

environmental catastrophe that is like some Janus-faced monster of global capitalism. Only a new democratic revolution can take us beyond the dead-end we face. It's time to break the consent/ coercion dialectic, and complete what the bourgeois democratic era began, sans the bourgeoisie. Popular and protagonistic democracy is now on the historical agenda.

Endnotes

1   Mona Chalabi, "Meet The 80 People Who Are As Rich As Half The World," January 18, 2015, <http://fivethirtyeight.com/datalab/meet-the-80-people-who-are-as-rich-as-half-the-world/>.

2   Ellen M. Wood, *Peasant-Citizen and Slave: The Foundations of Athenian Democracy* (London: Verso, 1988); "Landlords and Peasants, Masters and Slaves: Class Relations in Greek and Roman Antiquity," *Historical Materialism*, 10, 3 (2002): 17-69.

3   Martin Brabec, "Recognition of Laborers as Citizens: first worker democracy versus liberal capitalist democracy," *Perspectives on Global Developments and Technology*, Vol. 14. No. 1-2 (2016).

4   Bill Fletcher Jr., "Neoliberalism Has Created New system of Dual Citizenship for the Poor and the 1%." *Alternet* (May 29, 2015).

5   E. J. Hobsbawm, *The Age of Revolution 1789-1848* (New American Library: New York and Toronto, 1962), 86.

6   Hobsbawm, *The Age of Revolution 1789-1848*, 93.

7   Adam Smith, *The Wealth of Nations, Book 5, Chapter 1, Part II*, (1776) <https://www.marxists.org/reference/archive/smith-adam/works/wealth-of-nations/book05/ch01b.htm>.

8   David Harvey, *The Limits of Capital* (Verso: London, 1999).

9   Beverly Silver, *Forces of Labor: Workers' Movements and Globalization since 1870* (Cambridge University Press: New York, 2003).

10   Guy Standing, *The Precariat: The New Dangerous Class* (Bloomsbury: London, 2001), vii.

11   Noam Scheiber, "Growth in the 'Gig Economy' Fuels Work Force Anxieties," *The New York Times* (July 12, 2015).

12   Silver, *Forces of Labor: Workers' Movements and Globalization since 1870*.

13   Scheiber, "Growth in the 'Gig Economy' Fuels Work Force Anxieties".

14   Jason Struna, "Toward a Theory of Global Proletarian Fractions." In

The Nation in the Global Era: Conflict and Transformation, edited by Jerry Harris (Brill: London & Boston, 2009).

15   William I. Robinson, *Transnational Conflicts: Central America, Social Change, and Globalization* (Verso: London, 2003); *Latin America and Global Capitalism* (The Johns Hopkins University Press: Baltimore, 2008).

16   William I. Robinson, *Global Capitalism and the Crisis of Humanity* (Cambridge University Press: New York, 2014).

17   Saskia Sassen, *Cities In A World Economy: Second Edition* (Pine Forge Press: Thousand Oaks, 2000), 104.

18   Sassen, *Cities In A World Economy: Second Edition*, 135.

19   Bureau of Economic Analysis, "Activities of U.S. Multinational Enterprises in 2012," <http://bea.gov/scb/pdf/2014/08%20August/0814_activities_of_u%20s%20multinational_enterprises.pdf>(August, 2014).

20   Bureau of Economic Analysis, "Activities of U.S. Affiliates of Foreign Multinational Enterprises in 2012," <http://blog.bea.gov/2014/11/21/activities-of-u-s-affiliates-of-foreign-multinational-enterprises-in-2012/> (November 21, 2014).

21   Bureau of Economic Analysis, "Table II.G 1. Employment of Affiliates, Country by Industry," (2012)<http://www.bea.gov/international/pdf/usdia_2012p/Group%20II%20G1%20to%20G5.pdf>.

22   Struna, "Towards a Theory of Global Proletarian Fractions," 230-262.

23   Alicia Parlapiano, Dewan Shaila, and Nelson D. Schwartz, "The Nation's Economy, This Side of the Recession," *The New York Times* (June 14, 2014).

24   Social Security Administration, (2014), <https://www.ssa.gov/cgi-bin/netcomp.cgi?year=2014>.

25   Steven Greenhouse, "The Mystery of the Vanishing Pay Raise," *The New York Times* (October 31, 2015).

26   Mishelelise Gould and Josh Bivens, "Wage Stagnation in Nine Charts," <http://www.epi.org/publication/charting-wage-stagnation/> (January 6, 2015).

27   David Schweickart, *After Capitalism* (Roman and Littlefield: Lanham, Maryland, 2002), 92.

28   Nelson D. Schwartz, "Economists Take Aim at Wealth Inequality." *The New York Times* (January 3, 2016).

29   Paul Krugman, "Twin Peaks Planet," *The New York Times* (January 1, 2015).

30   Erin Hatton, "The Rise of the Permatemp." *The New York Times* (January 27, 2013).

31   Gina Kolatanov, "Death Rates Rising for Middle-Aged White

Americans, Study Finds," *The New York Times* (November 2, 2015).

32   Patrisse Cullors, "Why #BlackLivesMatter is Disrupting the Political Process: To Transform America's Systemic Hatred of Black People," *Washington Post* (August 18, 2015).

33   Joseph Stiglitz, *Rewriting the Rules of the American Economy* (Roosevelt Institute, May 12, 2015).

34   A. Sivanandan, "Race, terror and civil society," *Race & Class*, Vol. 47, No. 3 (2006).

35   Jerry Harris, "The U.S. Military in the Era of Globalisation," *Race & Class*, vol. 44, No. 2 (2002); "Dreams of Global Hegemony and the Technology of War," *Race & Class*, Vol. 45, No. 2 (2003); "US Imperialism After Iraq," *Race & Class*, Vol. 50, No. 1 (2008).

36   William Langewiesche, "The Chaos Company," *Vanity Fair* (March 2014).

37   Adam Nossiter, "National Front Party in France Is Dealt a Setback in Regional Elections," *The New York Times* (December 13, 2015).

38   Fletcher, "Neoliberalism Has Created New system of Dual Citizenship for the Poor and the 1%".

39   Gideon Rachman, "The west is losing faith in its own future," *Financial Times* December 9, 2013).

40   Jacob F. Kirkegaard, "Portugal's Risky Experiment," <http://rhg.com/notes/portugals-risky-experiment> (November 13, 2015).

41   Gavin Hewitt, "The dangerous game," <http://www.bbc.com/news/world-europe-31082656> (February 1, 2015).

42   Angelika Papamiltiadou, "EU Approves E1 bn Loan Tranche To Greece Under Conditions," <https://mninews.marketnews.com/content/eu-approves-e1-bn-loan-tranche-greece-under-conditions> (December 17, 2015).

43   Paul Krugman, "Ending Greece's Bleeding," *The New York Times* (July 5, 2015).

44   Rick Gladstone, "Vast Hidden Wealth Revealed in Leaked Records," *The New York Times* (April 4, 2013).

45   Rob Davies, "US Corporations Have $1.4tn Hidden in Tax Havens, Claims Oxfam Report," *The Guardian* (April 14, 2016).

46   Americans for Tax Fairness, "The Walmart Web: How the World's Biggest Corporation Secretly Uses Tax Havens to Dodge Taxes," <www.AmericansForTaxFairness.org> (June 17, 2015).

47   Kimiko De Freytas-Tamura, "Welsh Town Leads a British Revolt Against the Tax System and Corporations," *The New York Times* (February 21, 2016).

48   Anthony van Fossen, "The transnational capitalist class and tax havens." In *Financial Elites and Transnational Business: Who Rules*

the World? (Edward Elgar Publishing Limited: Cheltenham UK, 2012).

49   United Nations Conference on Trade and Development, *World Investment Report 2015 Overview* (United Nations: New York, 2015).

50   Carl C. Icahn, "How to Stop turning U.S. Corporations Into Tax Exiles," *The New York Times* (December 14, 2015).

51   Liam Bailey, "Cities that matter," in Knight Frank, *The Wealth Report* (Knight Frank, London, 2016), 38.

52   Ibid, 37.

53   Antonio Gramsci, *Selections from the Prison Notebooks* (International Publishers: New York, 1999).

54   Ingo Schmidt, "Counteracting Factor: The Unmaking and Remaking of Working Classes in Europe," *Perspectives on global Development and Technology*, Vol. 14, No.1-2 (2015).

55   Andreas Karitzis, "The Politics of the right and the Dilemmas of the Left," *The 2016 Socialist Register* (2016).

56   John Nichols, "The Pope Versus Unfettered Capitalism," *The Nation* (November 30, 2013).

57   The Guardian, "Bank of England governor: capitalism doomed if ethics vanish," *The Guardian* (May 27, 2014).

58   Paul Krugman, "The 1 Percent's Solution," *The New York Times* (April 25, 2013).

59   Joseph Stiglitz, "Conclusion: Slow Growth and Inequality are Political Choices. We Can Choose Otherwise," *Washington Monthly* (December 2014).

Chapter Two

GLOBAL CAPITALISM AND CLASS POWER

"Now we can sit in London and New York and say
society isn't crumbling, the restaurants are beautiful,
I can live my life, but that doesn't mean it's smart,
or safe or moral... A divided society against itself will not
stand and it doesn't matter if you're in the top 1%
or 0.001%. If the society around you is crumbling,
you're in a bad place."
Lady Lynn Forester de Rothschild

It's clear that economic globalization and growing constrictions on democracy are twin aspects of the same process. But what does this say about the contemporary character of the capitalist class? This new world order is theirs, conceived, designed, and built by their hands. The widely circulated narrative that globalization is just the natural result of market forces is nonsense, as if market forces were some supernatural force free of human agency. To understand the character of the transnational capitalist class we need to investigate the system they've constructed over the past 30-odd years.[1] Their world outlook, their daily activity, and their deepest material desires are all bound to their project of globalization.

A good starting point is to distinguish between the

old international system of nation-centric economies and the contemporary global structure. Here we are mainly describing the developed nations, and not those of the former Third World. The old system was built inside national borders, and the protection of local and regional markets helped define modern nations. This territorial space was the basis of wealth and power, and corporations became embedded in a set of national regulations and protectionist mechanisms. The national market was the domain of home-based monopolies, guarded by the state, and ultimately the military. Corporations always looked beyond their national borders, and a large international market developed in which exports played an important role, but most production and assets were retained in the home country. Competition was characterized by internal competition between national champions, and through the export of goods and their monopoly over resource extraction from Third World countries.

This system laid the basis for nationalism, and enough wealth and production to pay for the social contract. The advertising slogan of General Motors (GM) is a concise expression of the entire arrangement—"What's good for GM, is good for America." Well, perhaps not all of America. There was always poverty and those in the minority community were locked out of the social contract, but the majority of GM's employment, assets, and sales were in the US. And with union membership those jobs meant home ownership, college for the kids, and a vacation at Disneyland. The dialectic between property rights and democratic rights was working to the advantage of the majority.

The Transnational Capitalist Class

But globalization has a different structure. Power and wealth are built around global finance, production, and markets. Rather than being primarily dependent on a national working class, capital makes use of worldwide labor. And this labor force doesn't just dig for coal and copper. It manufactures cars, develops technology, and works in finance. It is this transnational system that determines the current character of capitalism and gives the TCC its political power. No longer are national circuits of accumulation key to class formation. Instead global accumulation patterns have led to the emergence of a remade capitalist class. These globalized activities take place in various forms. Among the most important are: global assembly lines, foreign direct investments, value chains, networks of sub-contractors, foreign subsidiaries, tax havens, cross border capital flows in debt, stocks, derivatives, securitization, money and equity markets, investments from sovereign wealth funds, merger and acquisitions, joint ventures in production, research and development, global cities, networks of elite policy institutions, cross-border corporate board membership, and the new relations of production between capital and labor.

Another key difference with the nation-centric economy is the character of exports. The WTO reported that 70 percent of global trade is now in intermediate goods and services—commodities used in products that are exported once again. Most of this trade is intra-firm, sub-contractor to sub-contractor further down the value chain, until the final product is assembled in China or another final destination. In the old system most exports from industrialized countries were already completed commodities, built and assembled in the home country and sent to foreign markets. Information technology also plays a key role in organizing the flow of these physical commodities as well as financial assets. As the *Financial Times* observed, this vast global supply chain is "linked via complex cloud-based IT systems that shepherd everything from the ordering and movement of parts to the payment of invoices and are linked to new forms of trade financing."[2]

The TCC lives and thrives in this economic ecology. They not only design, construct and lead, but fight politically and culturally to bend the world to their mode of production and their vision of society. Globalization is not just a way to make money, it's an all-encompassing ideology of how the world should work. As William Robinson and I wrote in 2000,

A transnational capitalist class (TCC) has
emerged as that segment of the world bourgeoisie
that represents transnational capital, the owners
of the leading worldwide means of production as
embodied in the transnational corporations and
private financial institutions. This historic bloc is
composed of the transnational corporations and
financial institutions, the elites that manage the
supranational economic planning agencies, major
forces in the dominant political parties, media
conglomerates, and technocratic elites and state
managers in both North and South."[3]

The transformation of national contingents of the
capitalist class into sectors of the TCC took shape in the 1970s,
with corporations locating more of their assets, production, and
employment abroad. Instead of national protection, the TCC
fraction sought liberalization and the integration of global markets.
As they gained political influence the state apparatus was used to
restructure laws and regulations over trade and the flow of capital.
Major economic projects were successful launched, such as the
North American Free Trade Agreement (NAFTA), the European
Union (EU), and the World Trade Organization (WTO).

We covered part of this story in the first chapter,
particularly how changes impacted the working class. To link
these developments to the TCC we can briefly restate a few facts.
Labor needed to be made more flexible to fit the new mode of
production. In the early 1980s this meant deindustrialization in
the heartland, mass layoffs, breaking unions, and weakening the
social safety net. Neoliberalism became the political policy of
the TCC, ushered in by Ronald Reagan and Margret Thatcher.
In symbolic and important strikes Reagan broke the air traffic
controllers union, PATCO, and Thatcher broke the miners' union
in the UK. Corporations expanded the use of temporary and part-
time labor, and a 40-hour-plus workweek for full-time employees,
spreading it throughout the economy. Virtually every major

company instituted outsourcing and offshoring as key competitive strategies. The dismantling of the Keynesian welfare state, tax cuts for the wealthy, and austerity for the poor increased class inequality not only economically, but also in the concentration of political power. During the same period in China, Deng Xiaoping dismantled the massive system of collective farms, propelling millions of socialist peasants into coastal cities to work in foreign sweatshops.

The changes in labor relations set off many political and social battles that continue today. But the struggle is not only between labor and capital. It is also between national and transnational capital fractions. All the old social forces who benefit from privileged tax arrangements, subsidies, and regulatory protection fight to maintain their position. These two fractions have been vying for control of state institutions since the 1970s, but by the 1990s local contingents of the TCC gained a hegemonic position in most countries throughout the world. They controlled key areas of state policymaking, especially central banks, finance and foreign ministries, and government branches that link countries to the global economy. The process is ongoing and not every victory is won by TCC fractions. Nor has conflict and contradictions between nations disappeared; combined and uneven development still characterizes the world system.

Yet there continues to be a historical movement in a direction favorable to transnational capital. This is propelled by a dialectical process between the demands of transnational economic forces and local, regional, and world-level governance—in effect, between the economic base and the state and social superstructure that house the new relationship between capital and labor. As manufacturing became parceled out to links in a global chain, a push for financial liberalization took place so capital could freely flow between borders. Changes in state regulations and institutional limitations were required, and were instituted. Financial liberalization resulted in greater movement of capital, which enabled more cross-border investments, speculation, mergers, and acquisitions. This propelled the global system forward, and as it grew there were more efforts to tear down borders limiting trade. Subsequently, new trade pacts such as the Trans Pacific Partnership and the Transatlantic Trade and Investment Partnership appeared. New global investment banks were created, like the Chinese initiative to found the Asian Infrastructure Investment Bank, which was swiftly joined by 57 nations. World regulatory bodies grew in influence and power. The International Monetary Fund (IMF) and World Bank took control of debtor nations throughout the world. And the WTO has been given the power to override national laws that inhibit transnational corporations (TNCs) from entering protected markets. Each expansion of the global economy impels further changes in governance and new social relationships, which in turn provide the grounds for the further growth of transnational capital. And on it goes. The entire process has created the outlines of a transnational state, with world-level bodies such as the G7 and WTO, regional bodies like the EU, and local governments tasked with merging the national into the global.

Joseph Stiglitz provides a good description of the process of structural changes:

> Inequality has been a choice. Beginning in the 1970s, a wave of deliberate ideological, institutional, and legal changes began to reconfigure the marketplace. At the vanguard was deregulation, which, according to adherents, would loosen the constraints on the economy and free it to thrive. Next were much lower tax rates on top incomes so that money could flow to private savings and investment instead of the government. Third were cuts in spending on social welfare, to spur people to work. Get government out of the way and the creativity of the marketplace—and the ingenuity of the financial sector—would revitalize society. Things didn't work out that way...Today we can look back and see the toll of these 'reforms': the

> worst economic crisis in 80 years, slower growth
> than in the preceding 30 years, and an unbridled
> increase in inequality... 'deregulation' is, in fact,
> 'reregulation'... a new set of rules for governing
> the economy that favor a specific set of actors."[4]

Stiglitz doesn't name those actors, but we can—the transnational capitalist class.

Even with the worst recession since the Great Depression the transnational economy has still grown. The widespread protectionism in the 1930s has seen limited use since the 2007-08 crisis. And transnational economic factors, such as foreign assets and sales of foreign affiliates, continued to grow faster than their domestic counterparts. Significantly the global South has continued to close the gap with the North, with TCC fractions rapidly growing in the former Third World. In 2014 China was the largest destination for foreign direct investments (FDI).

Table 2.1 Indicators of FDI and International Production, 2014 and Selected Years

Value at Current Prices (Billions of Dollars)

Item	1990	2005-2007 pre-crisis average	2014
FDI inward stock	2,198	13,894	26,039
FDI outward stock	2,254	14,883	25,875
Income on inward FDI	82	1,024	1,575
Income on outward FDI	128	1,445	1,486
Cross Border M&A	98	729	399
Sales of foreign affiliates	4,723	21,469	36,356
Value added of foreign affiliates	881	4,878	7,882
Total assets of foreign affiliates	3,893	42,179	102,040
Exports of foreign affiliates	1,444	4,976	7,803
Employment of foreign affiliates (thousands)	20,625	53,306	75,075

Source: United Nations Conference on Trade and Development, *World Investment Report 2015 Overview* (UNCTD: New York 2015).

Among the top ten destinations were five in developing countries. Additionally, nine of the 20 largest investor countries were located in the South. Overall the emerging Global South represents one-third of all FDI outflows, up from just 13 percent in 2007. Asia now invests more than any other region.[5] In Table 1 we can see the strength of the capitalist expansion.[6]

To help clarify reading the data, in the last row employment figures if written in a sentence would read 20.6 million, etc., and total assets of foreign affiliates in 2014 would read $1.2 trillion.

Finance and Technology

Globalization has been characterized as the financialization of capitalism, because of the tremendous growth in size and power of international financial institutions. Accordingly, a good place to start a more detailed look at the TCC and its institutional power structure is with an examination of global finance.

As finance capitalism came to dominate the world economy the assets of transnational financial institutions grew from $2 trillion in 1980 to $196 trillion in 2007. By 2011 the top 25 global corporations by assets were all financial institutions, controlling the shares of 40 percent of the world's TNCs.[7] Foreign ownership of these assets was 48.8 percent, or $92.6 trillion, revealing the enormous cross-border flows that characterize the merger of TCC interests.[8] Information technology plays a key role in the organization and centralization of capital through the redesign and extension of the tools of financial production. Computers, fiber optics, servers, and algorithms paved the way for the concentration of money into the largest financial institutions. In a convergence of history and technology, the capitalist class was hit by a deep structural crisis in the 1970s causing falling rates of profits. But in this same period information technology was being developed and deployed. Seeking a way out of the crisis capitalists seized upon information technology as a means to restructure capitalism. Financialization was the solution and information technology provided the tools of construction.

Financial institutions occupy a strategic place in class formation and power. These institutions act as organizing centers for the investment of capital and the extraction of surplus value. An ongoing circulation of global accumulation flows through international financial institutions, with capitalists from every continent investing their money. As money comes in it is organized into various investment funds that cover virtually every type of economic activity in the world. Not just stocks and bonds, but debt, money markets, bundled mortgages, securitizations, derivatives, equities, and so on. Financial products have exploded over the past three decades offering a vast choice of opportunities and risks. Financial firms such as BlackRock, J. P. Morgan, Cerberus, Barclays, and UBS develop products and market them to the wealthy. As capital floods in, capital floods out. Investments look for money-making opportunities throughout the world, sometimes guided by human money managers, at times by algorithms. As profits are realized, mostly from the surplus value produced by laboring men and women throughout the world, the capital is recentralized into the financial firms and distributed out to their TCC investors. This activity is a key factor in the transnational economy, creating a structure with class agency that gives formation to the TCC.

Economist Costas Lapavitsas explains the deep structural relationships between technology, financialization, and the relations of production in his analysis of contemporary capitalism. As he states,

> Financialization has to be understood more deeply, as a systemic transformation of capitalism, as a historical period...think in terms of the forces and relations of production. We've got to think in terms of the deepest material development of capitalism, things like the technological revolution that has taken place in the last four decades, the transformation of work, and similarly basic factors of the economy. When we look at the

technology, for instance, it is obvious that there has been a revolution in terms of information technology and telecommunications...What it has done is to boost finance, and to transform the way in which finance and real accumulation interact. It has also transformed labor, the way we work. The deepest roots of financialization, then, must be sought in the transformed interplay of the forces and relations of production.[9]

The deep and systemic transformations Lapavitsas refers to result in trillions of dollars flowing through the global economy every day. To grasp this rate of circulation compare one million seconds, which runs just 12-and-a-half days, to one trillion seconds, which covers 36,000 years. The Foreign Exchange Market trades $5.3 trillion each day. This is just money that buys and sells other currencies through arbitrage or speculation. Arbitrage is the difference in price that exists at the same moment in time, but in different global markets, perhaps, for example, due to a mismatch in the price of the Euro between Frankfurt and Sao Paulo of one-tenth of a penny. Algorithms are written to search out these differences and make trades at lightning speed. So Goldman Sachs, owner of one of the most powerful algorithms, may buy $100 million Euros in Frankfurt and sell them in Sao Paulo where the price is just a fraction more. All within a second or two, or even less. That's a million dollars in profit. And so it goes all day long, turning money itself into a commodity to be bought and sold. Algorithm trading, which accounted for 20 percent of all currency transactions in 2001, hit 74 percent in 2013.[10] Worst still was a practice uncovered in 2014 known as "Banging the Close." London posts a daily benchmark rate that sets currency values at 4:00 PM known as The Fix. But traders at major banks were colluding to push the price up or down at one second to 4:00, using computer speeds to illegally defraud the market.

To manage, account for, defraud, or profit from such enormous sums would be impossible without the abilities of information technology systems. The financial markets simply would not exist as they do based on the telephone lines of the 1970s. Information technology is the nervous system of the global financial economy, and the transnational capitalist class swims in these electronic circuits of global accumulation.

We can also obtain a picture of the transnational capitalist class and the importance of international financial institutions by examining individual wealth and how it's invested. The big picture shows 13.7 million people who hold $66 trillion in wealth.[11] But the Knight Frank Wealth Report breaks down the data on top earners, reporting 187,500 people with $30 million to $100 million who hold a total of $19.3 trillion dollars. In the next category of "ultra high net worth individuals (UHNWI)," there are 22,294 with $100 million to one billion. While at the very top are 1,919 billionaires.[12] Over the past decade the fastest growth of the UHNWIs has been in emerging economies. Azerbaijan led with a growth rate of 444%, followed by India at 340%, China at 330%, Angola with 318%, and Russia with 195%. In comparison the rate of growth in the US was 32%. In Table 2.2 we can see the breakdown of wealth by regions.

Table 2.2 Population and Wealth of UHNWIs with $30 Million-plus Assets, 2015

Region	Population	Wealth Billions ($)
North America	69,283	6,928
Europe	46,191	4,619
Asia	41,072	4,313
Latin America & Caribbean	9,492	997
Middle East	8,910	980
Russia & CIS	6,105	702
Australia/Asia	3,795	417
Africa	2,620	301

Source: Knight Frank Research, *The Wealth Report 2016* (Knight Frank: London, 2016).

Credit Suisse states, "The wealth portfolios of (these) individuals are likely to be similar, dominated by financial assets and, in particular, equity holdings in public companies traded in international markets."[13] Tracking these flows everywhere and every day are the new tools of financial production. Allocating funds, analyzing markets, making decisions, and informing choices, computers, servers, routers, fiber optics and algorithms whirl away in their electronic matrix of reality.

Another study, by the Swiss Federal Institute of Technology in Zurich, provides key insights into the dominance of international financial institutions by tracing ownership of TNCs. Investigating a database of 37 million companies and investors, the study examined shareholding networks, focusing on a core group of 147 predominantly financial institutions that control the most important corporations of the entire network.[14] These financial institutions represented 47,819 individual and institutional shareholders from 190 countries holding principal positions within the world's largest 15,491 TNCs.[15] This extensive study underlines the central role played by financial institutions in global capitalism, as a conduit for TCC investments and accumulation.

BlackRock, the world's largest asset manager with $5 trillion, provides another telling example of how cross-border capital flows are essential elements in the transnational economy. In the first three months of 2014 retail investors poured $14 billion into BlackRock funds, $9.8 billion from foreign sources.[16] BlackRock has investments in about 14,872 companies around the world. Of those 11,072 are outside the US.[17] If we look at just one of their funds, BlackRock Variable Series Funds, Inc., we see $6.3 billion invested in 475 common stocks in 34 countries, $729 million in 95 corporate bonds covering 24 countries, plus investment vehicles in 16 different currencies.[18] BlackRock is headquartered in the US, and using a nation-centric analysis one would label BlackRock a US champion. But in reality BlackRock is a global financial institution in the service of the TCC. A look at KKR, one of most powerful global hedge funds, tells us the same story. By 2006 half of its funds were situated outside the US.[19]

One of the most telling statements on financialization was issued by Bain Capital, the hedge fund of Mitt Romney. Bain reported that by 2010 financial assets reached $600 trillion, a growth of 200 percent over 2007. This is ten times the value of the global output of all goods and services. As the report notes, the "relationship between the financial economy and the underlying real economy has reached a decisive turning point."[20] This "decisive turning point" indicates the rupture between socially necessary labor time and the creation of wealth. This has a profound effect on the relations of production. Information technology gives the financial industry the ability to make billions with little human labor. When the point of production is inside a computer, and labor is done by an algorithm, it undermines the bonds that tie capitalists to their national working class.

Another advantage financialization has over manu-facturing is the ability to repackage and sell the same commodity again and again. For example, debt can be sold any number of times, as in the bundling of mortgages that led to the 2008 crash. Or one can take out insurance on bundled mortgages without any ownership, simply betting on whether mortgages will be paid or defaulted. Such markets need minimum human labor, but vastly expand financial assets and debt. With cars, televisions or hamburgers, once sold, only more production can replace the commodity. To create another one or two billion in value, living labor, and a lot of it, needs to be employed.

Obviously hundreds of millions still work at the behest of capital, but the ruling class has never been as free of the laboring class as in the current era. The millions made by Henry Ford depended on workers walking through the factory gates and onto the assembly line floor. Without that daily human labor Ford had nothing. Both workers and Ford understood this. It's the reason why workers formed unions and went on strikes, and it's the logic behind Ford raising wages to $5 an hour. This contradictory relationship bound capital and labor together to produce the social contract.

Today finance dominates manufacturing, and the speed of the new technologies has played a part. The velocity of capital to invest or withdraw funds can drive stock prices up or down, and enforce neoliberal efficiencies. For example, the withdrawal of billions within hours helped precipitate the devastating Asian crash of 1997. With such power, holders of stocks, bonds, equities, securities, and derivatives can determine the corporate decisions that affect the lives of workers everywhere. Owners of capital, whose use of direct labor is minimal, now drive the real economy where the vast majority of labor works.

To better understand the role of technology and speed we can examine high frequency trading, which accounts for between 50 to 65 percent of all daily trades on the thirteen US stock markets. Just nine banks control 70 percent of all US stock trades. Credit Suisse is the largest, followed by Morgan Stanley, Bank of America, Merrill Lynch, Goldman Sachs, J. P. Morgan, Barclays, UBS, Citi, and Deutsche Bank.[21] While orders to buy and sell are logged by humans, the actual work where profits are produced is carried out by algorithms, servers, switchers, routers, and the quality of glass in your fiber optics. The faster the software and hardware the more competitive a firm becomes. Fiber optic cables transmit data at about a billion feet per second—speed enough to circumnavigate the earth 7.6 times a second. Algorithms are programmed to find, buy, and sell orders. This search takes place in milliseconds and microseconds, that is one thousand to one millionth of a second. Some of the profits come by front-running orders, a practice many consider illegal. This means firms obtain advanced notice of trades by a few microseconds, use the information to buy stocks, increase the price, and then sell as the original orders are processed in the following second. Consequently, orders themselves, and the information they carry, are turned into commodities worth billions.

Building the physical architecture takes real labor and significant amounts of money. The former chief technical officer at Goldman Sachs reported that as early as 2006 their trading strategies were done by "50,000 servers just doing simulations," and he noted many more have been added.[22] Citadel spent $300 million to run fiber optic lines from Chicago to New Jersey and rents out access for $10 million per firm. In return Citadel's CEO, Kenneth Griffin, had an income of $800 million in 2013.

Once the physical infrastructure has been built it only takes a small group of highly skilled programmers to write the software algorithms. Brad Katsuyama, around whom the best seller *Flash Boys* is based, created an entirely new trading exchange (IEX) with its own algorithm with just 25 employees. IEX created a system that slows all trading by 350 millionths-of-a-second—time enough to prevent high frequency traders from jumping orders. Algorithms are not just fast, but smart. They can recognize a broker's trading pattern, decide when to buy, how much to buy, and how much to pay. Programs making these decisions replaced thousands of traders with a single black box. But the space warehousing servers has expanded because high frequency traders will pay millions to co-locate in the same building. The closer the better. Each microsecond counts. The shorter the route taken by the connection between computers, and between the computers and the stock markets, the less time it takes for the data to travel. So high frequency trading firms access orders before anyone else by nestling inside, or close by the computers where trades are carried out. The names given to the algorithms speak to the cutthroat nature of the competition—Ambush, Nighthawk, Raider, Dark Attack, Dagger, and Slicer are some of the titles. Credit Suisse called its algorithm program Guerrilla complete with an image of Che Guevara. Firms that only specialize in high frequency trading have no clients, and at the end of each day they aspire to hold no stock. Such methods enabled Virtu Financial to make money 1277 days out of 1278 days of trading, results once thought impossible.[23]

Technology has always been about competitive leads, whether the English long bow or Henry Ford's assembly line. But contemporary financial technology is a difference in kind, working at speeds no person can ever match, and without real-time human control or direction. Profits are being acquired more on the power and speed of an algorithm, and less on the competitive advantage of a skilled and productive workforce. True, algorithms are written by skilled labor, but never in history could the work of five people produce a technology that, once in operation, would continue without human oversight and produce billions in profits.

Marx saw the compulsion for speed linked to the development of capitalism as a global system. He argued this created a unique time and space relationship. In the *Grundrisse* he wrote,

> ...while capital must on one side strive to tear down every spatial barrier to intercourse, i.e. to exchange, and conquer the whole earth for the market, it strives on the other side to annihilate this space with time, i.e. to reduce to a minimum the time spent in motion from one place to another. The more developed the capital, therefore, the more extensive the market over which it circulates, which forms the spatial orbit of its circulation, the more does it strive for an even greater extension of the market and for greater annihilation of space by time.[24]

Remarkably, Marx's phrase the "annihilation of space by time" is a commonly used concept by computer engineers and scientists referring to the speed and connectivity of information technology. Marx pointed out how the faster circulation of capital accelerated the turnover of profits, which then propelled the further expansion of capital. For example, cotton bought in South Carolina and transported to textile mills in England spent weeks in the holds of sailing vessels. The capital invested in the cotton could not be freed until sold to the industrial capitalists in Manchester. Only then could profits be realized and reinvested. In a more modern example consider steel mills, in which there is a large amount of capital invested in machinery. Those investments can only be realized with the production of steel and its sale in national and global markets. Eventually sales produce enough profits to expand capital beyond the original investment in the mill's physical assets. If the speed of the sailing ships, or the speed at which labor produced tons of steel increased, so would the circulation of capital and hence profits. With the speed of algorithms the circulation of capital explodes. Investments in computers and software are realized much more rapidly, and global space is reduced to microseconds.

While Marx could never have envisioned a market operating in microseconds across thousands of miles of geography, his perception of the internal driving logic of capitalism holds true for contemporary finance capital. Marx revealed a fundamental impulse that today impels the use of information technology towards high frequency trading, and the establishment of global stock markets operating in real time counted in nanoseconds. Thus information technology performs two essential tasks: it reduces the need for labor, and speeds the circulation of capital. Both increase the power and dominance of finance capital.

Such technological abilities also have ideological and cultural impacts. Algorithms have become financial avatars, doing battle at superhuman speeds and acting as alter ego stand-ins for Wall Street traders. The effects have produced the vicious driven individualism that makes the shallow fantasies of Ayn Rand the ideological fountainhead for financial capitalists. Creating billions with almost no connection to labor elevates the individual to seemingly Atlas-like abilities. These are great men conquering the miracles of the free market. As Goldman Sachs CEO Lloyd Blankfein once proclaimed, we "do God's work."[25] Evidently doing "God's work" involves a deep amount of fraud and corruption. Fifteen of the world's largest financial institutions have set aside more than $214 billion to pay legal fees and fines resulting from the 2008 crash. The other side of being God's financial agents is disdain for those who aren't. Romney gave expression to this when he labeled 47 percent of Americans "takers," while lauding hedge fund capitalists like himself as "job creators." Such an ideology justifies taking hundreds of millions, even billions, as an annual salary while advocating austerity for workers.

Global Assembly Lines and Apple

When Jeff Immelt, the CEO of GE, was asked what he was most proud of, he answered, "If I took just one thing to focus on in terms of being proud, it would probably be the global footprint. We've gone from a company a decade ago that was 70% inside the United States to a company today that's 65% outside the United States... If you look over the last decade, not just at G.E. but at other large companies, the biggest secular change in the last decade is this opening up of the global market. Companies need to be confident competitors in every corner of the world. That's what we are at G.E."[26]

Immelt's remarks are a concise expression of the worldview of the TCC. There are no national flags for transnational corporations, and they are proud of their global identity. Competition isn't between national champions, whose success is translated into territorial benefits and loyalty. Rather, world-spanning corporations fight each other to dominate their industrial sector. Territory is not conceived as borders, but as markets to be occupied. Borders are problems for refugees and immigrants, not for corporations and capital.

The integrated character of global capitalism can be seen in the statistics put together by the US Bureau of Economic Analysis (BEA). The BEA looks at both foreign investments in the US, and US investments abroad. At the end of 2011 US corporations and investors had a total of $21.13 trillion abroad. Breaking that down we see $4.2 trillion in foreign stocks, ownership stakes in foreign businesses that totaled $4.7 trillion, and money in bank and brokerage accounts valued at $4.3 trillion.[27] By the end of 2014 US foreign assets had risen close to $25 trillion.[28]

In turn we can look at the data for foreign corporations and individual investors crossing borders into the US. The largest investments were in US Treasuries, which attracted $5.1 trillion.

Treasuries were considered a safe haven from global economic turbulence and received funds from private investors, foreign central banks, and state institutions such as sovereign wealth funds. Ownership stakes in US companies were $2.9 trillion, and $4 trillion worth of assets were in US bank and brokerage accounts. Altogether, in 2012 foreign-owned assets in the United States totaled $25.16 trillion.[29] At the end of 2014 the total had risen to $31.6 trillion.[30] Another indication of the rise of global assembly lines and cross-border manufacturing are statistics from the Compustat 500. This is a dataset of the top 500 companies in North America by market capitalization. In 1950 only four percent were foreign-incorporated firms, by 2010 this had increased to 48 percent.[31]

Taken together the above cross-border flows are over $56 trillion. Yet this enormous sum doesn't take into account foreign corporations and investor activity outside the US. For example, included in the above totals are US capital flows of $65.8 billion into China, and Chinese investments into the US of $9.5 billion. But foreign investments from other countries into China, as well non-US investments to the rest of the world, are not included. So the sum total of global cross-border investments is actually a good deal more than $56 trillion. Such sizeable figures give us a general overview of TCC cross border flows, as well as investments in global manufacturing. These circuits of accumulation are the life blood of contemporary capitalism.

Li & Fung, the Hong Kong garment TNC, is a good example of global assembly line organization. Li & Fung owns no factories, no sewing machines, and no fabric mills, but takes orders from the world's biggest clothing retailers. What the corporation does offer is 15,000 suppliers in over 60 countries working for the lowest wages. In 2012 they had $21.8 billion in revenues. Because of their size, they can set wages and conditions throughout the industry. As chief executive Bruce Rockowitz stated, "We definitely are part of bringing prices down, there's no question about that, because we are arbitraging factories and countries all the time."[32] Such global arbitrage, and the speed at which it takes place, is an expression of the new transnationalized relations of production. But not only is Li & Fung's unskilled and semi-skilled labor globalized, so too is its managerial staff. Its 830 senior executives come from over 40 different countries, half of whom have worked in two or more countries.[33]

The fact that Li & Fung's senior executives are a global core of cadre, attests to the class character of the TCC. Immelt gives us further insight into elite class formation. As he explains, "I think leadership has a very short shelf life, and so every few years, we look outside the company to see what others are doing: What's Google doing? What's the U.S. Military Academy doing? What are they teaching at the Communist Party School in Beijing? What is McKinsey teaching its people? I'm paranoid about keeping up-to-date with attracting and retaining great leaders from Bangalore to Boston and everywhere around the world."[34]

To get a better understanding of the nature of global manufacturing we can investigate some details concerning the auto and electronics industry. When it comes to computers and electronics Apple is an iconic corporation. Apple's founder, Steve Jobs, is upheld as an example of unique American entrepreneurship and innovative thinking. In 2015 Apple was worth more than $760 billion; only 18 countries in the world had a higher GDP. But Apple isn't just larger than most countries, its production is also deeply situated in global assembly. Apple has about 80,000 employees, with just over 50,000 in the US. But Apple's global

Table 2.3 Apple's Global Chain, Number of Subcontractors					
Asian Countries	**#**	**Western Countries**	**#**	**Latin America**	**#**
China	330	US	75	Mexico & South America	9
Japan	148	Germany & Austria	13		
South Korea	38	UK	9		
Taiwan	35	France & Italy	7		
Malaysia	26	Belgium & Netherlands	6		
Philippines	23	Czech Republic & Hungary	6		
Thailand	19	Israel	5		
Singapore	18				
Viet-Nam	10				
Total	**647**	**Total**	**121**	**Total**	**9**

Source: Finance online, "The iPhone Saga," <http://financesonline.com/uploads/iPhone-infographic.jpg>.

sub-contractors employ about 1.5 million workers, creating an immense supply chain that stretches around the world. While most design occurs in the US, parts are made everywhere. In Table 2.3 we can see Apple's transnational network of production, i.e. subcontractors working with contracts directly from Apple. But even this only offers a partial picture, because many companies in the supply chain send work to other sub-contractors.[35]

Apple has 75 subcontracts in the US, but these companies in turn have offshore facilities around the world. Some examples are provided in Table 2.4.[36]

Table 2.4 Apple's US Subcontractors with Off-Shore Fabrication Facilities	
US Firms	Location of Subcontracting Firms
Avago Technologies	Italy, Malaysia, Singapore
Broadcom	China, Malaysia, Singapore, Taiwan
Corning	France, Japan, Taiwan
Cirrus Logic	China
Fairchild Semiconductors	China, Malaysia, Philippines
Maxim Integrated	Philippines, Thailand
Omni Vision	Taiwan
Qualcomm	China, Taiwan
RF Micro-Devices	China, UK
Skyworks	Mexico
Texas Instruments	Germany, Japan, Malaysia, Mexico, Philippines, Scotland

Source: Finance online, "The iPhone Saga,"
<http://financesonline.com/uploads/iPhone-infographic.jpg>.

Apple's transnational structure has a large presence in Asia. So it's worth investigating the supply base in some detail. In Japan LCD panels are made by Sharp and Japan Display, Sony makes the iSight 8mp camera, Toshiba supplies flash memory, and TDK works on inductor coils. Work in South Korea includes Samsung producing both the A6 and A7 chips used in iPhone models, LG makes LCD panels in addition to smooth swipe-and-zoom controls, and Samsung manufactures iPhone's microchips. From Taiwan comes more chips, flash memory, and

DRAM. China supplies the rare earth minerals necessary for key functions such as the color screen, circuitry, and speakers. And of course China also provides factory workers who assemble 85 percent of all iPhones. Production takes place in Taiwanese-owned Foxconn factories. The horrendous working conditions at Foxconn have become a global scandal. Their young employees live in crowded barracks, working six days a week, often 12 hours a day, for about $102 dollars a week. Conditions were exposed when a number of their workers, distraught over poor living and working conditions, committed suicide by jumping off the factory roof. The corporation now hangs canvas under the windows. The Taiwanese-owned corporation manufactures about 40 percent of all consumer electronics in the world, also producing for Amazon, Dell, Hewlett-Packard, Motorola, Nintendo, Nokia, Samsung, and Sony.[37]

An abbreviated look at Europe shows the French-Italian company STMicroelectronics, which operates in Switzerland, designs the smartphone's gyroscope. For wearable technology NXP from the Netherlands makes M7, a mixed-signal chip. Additionally, Bosch in Germany makes accelerometers for the iPhone, and AKM produces the electromagnetic compass.

The last part of Apple's global strategy is to keep the majority of their profits outside the US. They do this through a number of tax-evasion maneuvers, and by registering their intellectual property in low-tax countries. Because knowledge has no physical location it can be registered anywhere. This is officially called "intangibles-based transfer pricing schemes." Although only 4 percent of Apple's labor force is employed in Ireland, in 2013 the company registered 65 percent of their worldwide profits there. This allowed Apple to pay a tax rate of only 2 percent.[38] Apple's strategy is to shift profits between networks of subsidiaries that span the world. Many have no official employees and simply occupy empty office space with an Apple nameplate. Because of this arrangement Apple claims these subsidiaries are stateless, and therefore exempt from taxes, record keeping laws, and the need to file tax returns.[39]

In the first quarter of 2014, Apple kept $88 billion abroad and only $12 billion at home. But Apple isn't alone in this practice. In fact, it's widespread among many TNCs. In 2014 Microsoft kept $91 billion abroad and $9 billion in the US. Google with its "Don't be evil" corporate slogan, had $58 billion abroad with $42 billion at home. Some others corporate giants following suit include Cisco, Oracle, eBay, Starbucks, and Qualcomm.[40] This costs the US government billions in tax revenues, resulting in less money for environmental protection, health, education, and other such services.

GM's Transnational Production

If Apple represents America's electronic technology, the auto represents US industrial might. Cars have a particularly strong national identity. General Motors, Ford, and Chrysler are seen as uniquely US corporations. As *The New York Times* noted, "GM factories churned out…muscle cars with taut, sculptured body panels that were rolling displays of American DNA."[41] But if GM was once a pure American product, its contemporary family has become a diverse mixture of global identities. Today GM employs 212,000 employees spread across six continents working in 396 facilities, speaking 50 different languages. As GM states, "Whether in Detroit, Frankfurt, Sao Paulo or Shanghai our brands make an emotional connection to our customers."[42]

When the economic crisis hit in 2008, President Obama moved to save GM and Chrysler. The auto industry was too important to let fail as had Lehman Brothers. But exactly what is meant by a US auto industry in an era of globalization? Are we talking about corporations committed to maintaining good paying American jobs? Newly-hired GM assembly line workers make just $10.50 an hour, barely over minimum wage. Do we mean an industry pledging allegiance to protect and build the national economy? After the bailout auto employment for the Big Three plunged from 435,000 to 171,000. Are these corporations expected to depend mainly on their sales, employment, and assets in the US? Today the balance of these are in foreign countries. Or does the definition simply mean US headquarters linked to an assumption of national economic loyalty? As so often stated in the corporate community, loyalty is first and foremost to the stockholders, many of whom invest from outside the US.

When it came to taking government support GM didn't limit itself to appealing to Washington. Threatening plant closures, GM pulled in money from seven different governments. The biggest bail-out was from the US for $49.5 billion, but others included $10 billion from Canada, $5.5 billion from Australia, $3.45 billion from the UK, over $2 billion from Germany, and more from Spain and Sweden. As for Chrysler, their US bailout turned majority shares over to Fiat in Italy.

As a leading industrial giant the globalization of GM has had a particularly harsh effect on the US working class. Of the 300-plus world-spanning facilities run by GM 38 are in the US, and only ten of those are manufacturing plants.[43] Blue collar union jobs have always been at the heart of the working class, with auto

Table 2.5 Employment of Foreign and US Auto Manufactures

Foreign Employment (thousands)		US Employment (thousands)	
Toyota	30,000	GM	77,000
Honda	26,000	Ford	65,000
Nissan	10,000		
Hyundai	8,000		
Chrysler	39,000		
Total	**113,000**	**Total**	**142,000**

Source: Kelsey Mays, American-Made Index: Which Automakers Affect the Most U.S. Workers?

playing an outsized historical role. In 2015 GM reported 50,300 US hourly workers (those most probably in unions), down from 70,000 in 2009.[44] On a global scale GM employs 40,000 workers laboring in 35 manufacturing facilities.[45] But this is only about 25 percent of their global workforce.

Another way to view transnational production is to look at the footprint of foreign car production in the US. The figures in Table 2.5 are considered "direct employment," counting workers at assembly, drivetrain, stamping, casting and tooling plants, and research and design facilities. Most articles on the auto industry refer to Chrysler as one of the big three US manufacturers. But ownership is in the hands of Fiat, and so in the table Chrysler is counted as a foreign employer. Chrysler's successful advertising campaign plays on their twin identity with the clever slogan, "Imported from Detroit." Almost a reverse image of GM's "what's good for America" ad, each slogan representing different eras of national and global production.[46]

While GM and Ford retain a larger workforce, the overall picture shows foreign car makers with significant presence. In 2013 about 46 percent of total US car production was manufactured by foreign producers, and that's counting Chrysler as a US company. The majority of foreign production takes place in non-union plants in the south. Transnational competition not only takes place abroad, but inside the US as well.

It is instructive to look at the global footprint of GM, because it reflects characteristics similar to all auto TNCs. We can begin in Europe where GM acquired Opel in 1929. Opel produces 26 models in 12 plants located in Germany, Austria, Hungary, Poland Spain, UK, Italy, and Russia. GM also owns Vauxhall, which originated in Great Britain and has 24 models. Throughout Europe GM employs 34,500 workers. Germany is the home base of Opel and employed 25,000 workers before the 2008 crisis. The labor force has now shrunk to 16,000, German blue collar workers hit as hard as their US counterparts.[47]

China is now the biggest market for GM, and the company has significant facilities throughout Asia and the Pacific. Starting in China we see GM has ten joint ventures and two wholly owned foreign enterprises, as well as some 58,000 employees. Models are sold under Buick, Cadillac, Chevrolet, Opel, Baojun, Wuling, and Jiefang nameplates. The largest joint venture is with Shanghai General Motors Company in which GM allied with SAICMOTOR. They operate six auto plants producing 20 different models with sales in China going over 1.5 million per year. Another key joint venture is SAIC-GM-Wuling Automobile Company, also with sales registering better than 1.5 million a year. Besides other manufacturing alliances, GM does research and development at the GM China Advanced Technical Center. The center is part of GM's global engineering and design network, doing work on advanced design, vehicle engineering, powertrain engineering, and OnStar technology.[48]

Other important locations in Asia include India and South Korea. GM produces eight different models of Chevrolet for the market in India, operating two manufacturing facilities. Additionally GM has a factory making engines, and a world-class design and engineering center in Bangalore.[49] In South Korea 16,500 workers are employed by GM. Operating four production plants, GM makes 12 different models exporting more than 1.8 million vehicles to 150 markets throughout the world. One of every four Chevrolets sold globally are made in South Korea. Important research and development also takes place in South Korea, where GM's global small- and mini-car architectural development teams are located.[50]

GM also has substantial facilities in Thailand, Indonesia and Australia, as well as Kenya and Egypt. Lastly, Latin America needs to be mentioned as GM has established production plants in Mexico, Argentina, Brazil, Chile, Colombia, Ecuador, and Venezuela.

Without their extensive global assembly line GM could not exist as an auto manufacturer. Nor could any major player in the auto industry. As US and European national car markets went into decline during the economic crisis, the transnational character of all auto TNCs became even more pronounced. In Table 2.6 we can see some key figures for major auto producers. The TNI or Transnational Index used by the United Nations is based on the ratio between foreign assets, sales, and employment compared to national figures in the same categories. Note that in the years between 2004 and 2008 each auto corporation increased their transnational character.

Mainstream media, and many on the left, still portray the world system in terms of nationally contained economic units, with corporate champions flying flags with patriotic colors. But a serious look at the data clearly shows that TNCs are deeply committed to global production, financially connected to other global players, and base their corporate strategy on world-wide accumulation. Such patterns hold true for every major industry. This is the structural manufacturing basis of global capitalism.

Table 2.6 Auto Corporations Transnational Index (TNI), 2004-2008

Corp.	World Rank[1]	Foreign Assets[2]	Total Assets[2]	Foreign Sales[2]	Total Sales[2]	Foreign Employed	Total Employed	TNI % 2008	TNI % 2004[3]
Ford	9	102,588	222,977	75,853	129,166	134,000	213,000	55.9	48.7
GM	31	40,532	91,047	73,587	148,979	145,229	243,000	51.2	34.0
Toyota	6	183,303	320,243	143,886	226,221	123,580	320,808	53.1	49.0
Honda	23	96,313	130,236	89,689	110,317	165,589	186,421	81.4	68.5
Daimler AG	13	87,927	184,021	103,070	133,435	105,463	273,216	54.5	29.2

Source: *World Investment Report, 2009*. United Nations Conference on Trade and Development (UNCTD) (United Nations: New York and Geneva), 228; Notes: [1] World Rank is by Total Assets; [2] US$ (millions); [3] *World Investment Report, 2006*. United Nations Conference on Trade and Development (UNCTD) (United Nations: New York and Geneva), 280.

Globalization Hits Detroit

What has globalization meant for auto workers and their city? Detroit was known as the Motor City, and people loved their cars like they love their iPhones today. Both commodities are iconic symbols of American culture and life. But what's good for GM is no longer good for American workers. Life on an auto assembly line was never easy. Progress was always a process of two steps forward, one step back. But through labor struggles and a nationally rooted economy, working class Detroit achieved a better life. Facing up to challenges was part of a worker's existence, and why you joined a union. Employment went through cycles of hiring and lay-offs, a natural result of recessions and recoveries generated by the inherent functioning of the capitalist market. When a factory shut down and moved, it went to the suburbs, not to China. Workers also faced technological advances that resulted in the reorganization of the labor process and lay-offs. For example, Ford's immense River Rouge plant, where 85,000 had worked in 1945, employed only 30,000 by 1960. Nevertheless, mass employment still characterized the industry.

But an added dimension began to take shape in the late 1970s when globalization came to impact production patterns. This was a structural change, and a permanent deindustrialization took hold. Off-shoring to global assembly lines meant booming post-WWII Detroit would never return. By the time the financial crisis hit in 2008 the city was already on the downside of its history. And when the speculation in mortgages went bust, putting the economy into deep freeze, it pushed GM and Chrysler into bankruptcy. Global capitalism delivered a one-two gut punch to auto workers. First was global manufacturing, the next global speculation.

The Great Recession and bankruptcy may have been the hardest blow, but the decline of Detroit played out over decades. In the 1950s it was a city of two million. As factories moved to the suburbs and down south the population eroded, losing many of its white residents who followed jobs out of the city. After the Black rebellion in 1967 that left 43 dead and over 7,000 arrested, more whites fled. Then came the North American Free Trade Agreement (NAFTA), with Michigan losing more than 63,000 jobs as a result of the trade treaty. Between the years 2000 to 2010 with the auto industry in bankruptcy another 200,000 abandoned the city, reducing Detroit to a population of 700,000.

With plants closing, some moving south and others out

of the country, the United Auto Workers Union (UAW) faced a huge decline in national membership. In the 1970s the UAW had 1.5 million members; by 2015 it retained only 400,000. But the union's problems went beyond off-shoring and changing technology. The leadership was unable to organize the thousands of auto workers employed in the US south. This failure pushed working conditions for northern union members into reverse, taking away gains made over 60 years of struggle. When Obama bailed out GM and Chrysler the federal government mandated that new labor agreements in the north had to match the standards set in the non-union south. This was enforced with a no-strike clause that was in effect for more than five years. Consequently, German, Japanese, and South Korean auto manufacturers who had located almost exclusively in the anti-union south, helped to force lower labor standards on American workers in the north.

Deindustrialization in Detroit had a particularly devastating effect on the Black working class.[51] Industrial unionized jobs were a key element in building a black middle class of blue collar workers, not only in auto, but throughout the Midwest with steel jobs in Gary, Cleveland, Pittsburg, and Chicago. Other industrial jobs employed African Americans from Buffalo to St. Louis. Black workers often constituted a militant core that helped give unions their clout in the face of corporate attacks. And often Black workers constituted a radical push inside the unions forcing them to fight for greater equality and more integrated leadership. This was certainly true in Detroit, where Black workers were important in every major labor battle from the 1930s onwards. The 1960s emergence of the League of Revolutionary Black Workers in auto plants throughout Detroit had an immense effect on the entire Black community.[52] The collapse of industrial jobs meant the collapse of income that had paid for homes, cars, and college for the kids. *The New York Times Magazine* reported, "As a consequence of the economic crisis (of 2008), 20,000 black autoworkers were either laid off or took buyouts from the Big Three…with a disproportionate number of those coming from the Detroit area."[53]

Factories have been one place in America where minority and white workers intermix on a daily basis. Neighborhoods continue to be largely segregated. And so work and unions have played a major role in actual physical integration—unlike the arm's-length integration one can experience by watching beer commercials, buddy action movies, or sports. Frank Hammer, former president of UAW Local 909 at Chrysler spoke on the effects of factory shut-downs.

> This city, and the region, is one of the most segregated in the country. The factories became the places where black and white workers would coalesce and come together. Not where they lived, but where they worked. One of the consequences of the plant closures is that black and white workers no longer have a place where they rub shoulders each day, know each other on a personal basis and work together in solidarity. With the increased plant closures, the possibility of unity between black and white workers has been hampered and reduced.[54]

Today Detroit is 85 percent Black, with an estimated 20,000 homeless people in a city filled with vacant homes. Median income is $26,000, less than half of the US national average, and 39 percent of the population lives below the federal poverty level. Large sections of the city have nothing but empty lots and deteriorating buildings. Yet another 60,000 residents are threatened with eviction because they can't pay property taxes. As if citizens had not suffered enough, city officials threaten to turn off water if you fall behind in your bills. In response the United Nations, which states access to water is a basic human right and part of international law, sent representatives to Detroit who spoke on the dangers of a humanitarian crisis. Even formal democracy no longer functions for city residents. The Republican governor of Michigan took over administration of the city, delegating a special representative to oversee Detroit's budget—very much like the IMF taking control of a country's economy if too far in debt, or the European Central Bank destroying any semblance of economic independence in Greece. Detroit has been reduced to the status of an impoverished Third World city.

The tragedy of Detroit is that viable alternatives exist. Hammer speaks to one important example.

> A few years ago, one of the Ford factories that produced Lincolns closed in the suburbs. Two companies wanted to buy the factory. One of them made wind turbines, and one of them made solar panels. The union was making concessions, the state was making concessions, the city was making concessions. Everybody was on board: 'Yes we want this here. We'll do everything we can to make this happen.' The only reason it didn't happen is because the Department of Energy, the federal government, would not guarantee a five-hundred-million dollar loan. The plan collapsed, the factory was taken down. Now it's produced abroad.[55]

Global Capitalism and Transoceanic Trade

A key feature of transnational capitalism has been the revolution in oceanic transportation necessary to accommodate the circulation of global commodities. The first major technological change was the use of containers, replacing workers stocking individual goods on ships. This process was one of intensive mechanization and automation that resulted in a large reduction of port labor. At the same time more commodities were shipped in a shorter period of time. As the global shipping industry expanded, faster massive bulk carriers were built linking transnational production through deeper and more extensive ports. About 90 percent of all commodity exports travel by ship, and revenues are considerable. During periods of high demand oil tankers will earn about $110,000 per day.

In the nation-centric world system cargo ships flying national flags were attached to their states. World shipping symbolized the influence of imperialist powers such as the UK, France, and the US. These fleets were often financed or subsidized by their governments, and came under national regulations and taxes. Flagged industrial cargo shipping projected national interests into the international arena, often transporting raw materials from their colonials, or carrying finished goods to compete in international export markets. But transnationalization has ended this world transportation system, replacing it with flags of convenience (FOC).

In his study of the cargo industry, Anthony van Fossen links the rise of FOC to the decline of national capitalism. As van Fossen points out, "Flags of convenience are crucial to the trade networks that have created global capitalism."[56] FOC ports have grown at a rate that outpaces the world economy by 1000 percent. This new transnational cargo system is part of neoliberal economic restructuring, allowing ships to carry flags from tax havens that offer secretive offshore ownership. These ships most often move goods produced in industrial export zones, that in turn function as tax havens for manufacturers. As in the finance industry, such a complex system of movement and exchange is organized by the new technologies in telecommunications and information.

In 1965 about 14 percent of gross tons transported by world fleets was done by ships under FOC. By 2014 that had increased to almost 75 percent. In Table 2.7 we trace the impact of FOCs, and the change from national shipping to transnational shipping.[57]

FOC has also resulted in a neoliberal regime that has reduced environmental safety and costs, minimized financial regulations, weakened certification of ships and mariner competence, and undercut fair employment laws and wages. Finally, maritime laws in tax havens have transformed an organized national seafarers' workforce into a low-wage global labor pool. The top ten countries supplying seafarers are, in order of size: China, Turkey, Philippines, Indonesia, Russia, India, US, Ukraine, Malaysia, and Bulgaria.[58]

Table 2.7 Top Ten Maritime Flags as a Percentage of Gross Tons of Registered Vessels

December 1965		December 2014	
United Kingdom	13.8	Panama (FOC)	19.1
United States	13.8	Liberia (FOC)	11.1
Liberia (FOC)	10.9	Marshall Islands (FOC)	9.4
Norway	9.8	Hong Kong (FOC)	8.3
Japan	7.5	Singapore (FOC)	6.7
USSR	8.2	Malta (FOC)	5.0
Greece	7.1	Bahamas (FOC)	4.5
Italy	5.7	China	3.8
W. Germany	5.3	Greece	3.8
France	5.2	Cyprus (FOC)	1.8

Source: Lloyd's Register of Shipping, *World Fleet Statistics, 1966*; UK Dept. of Transport, *World Fleet Statistics, 2015*.

Trade Deals: Tearing Down Borders

The more finance and manufacturing globalize the more the TCC demands a borderless world to serve the needs of capital. Through a series of global and regional trade treaties transnational corporations have gained tremendous power. Everything the TCC has ever dreamed and longed for has been projected into cross-border trade laws, an arena where negotiations can proceed without the messy interference of democratic input. The TCC corporate culture of hierarchy, secrecy, and technocratic bureaucracy has determined the political process by which these treaties are written and sealed: one world market, without national barriers, national regulations, national subsidies, national labor laws, or national environmental protections. This is the best of all worlds according to transnational elites.

Trade deals should be seen in the context of the overall

economic assault launched by the neoliberal policies of the TCC. Privatization, deregulation, austerity, attacks on unions, tax cuts for the rich, and trade treaties are all part of the same project. Consequently, the narrative about the resulting benefits of trade treaties is painted in glowing rhetoric: economic growth, more jobs, increased income, better stability, and greater freedom for all. But trade deals have a history, which once examined tell a different story. There are a good number of different trade regimes, and together they are the building blocks of the transnational economy. The General Agreement on Tariffs and Trade led to the founding of the WTO, the largest global trade institution. But there are also regional and bilateral agreements in every part of the world. The ones we will look at are NAFTA, the Trans-Pacific Partnership (TPP), The Trans-Atlantic Trade and Investment Partnership (TTIP), and trade courts known as Investor-State Dispute Settlement (ISDS). Additionally there are 3,271 international investment agreements and the trend continues. In 2014, more than 80 percent of investment policy measures were designed to further open borders to foreign capital.[59]

NAFTA was drafted during the George Bush administration, and passed under guidance of Bill Clinton. The purpose of the trade treaty was to established an integrated economy between Canada, the US, and Mexico. In a 12-year study of NAFTA the Economic Policy Institute summed up its effects in the following statement: "NAFTA rules protect the interests of large corporate investors while undercutting workers' rights, environmental protections, and democratic accountability. Hence, NAFTA should be seen not as a stand-alone treaty, but as part of a long-term campaign by the conservative business interests in all three countries to rip up their respective domestic social contracts."[60]

In the US about one million jobs were lost, 660,000 of those in manufacturing. This hit particularly hard the best paying jobs for workers with a high school degree. The report estimated that in 2004 alone US workers lost $7.6 billion in wages.[61]

In Mexico NAFTA resulted in the destruction of family

farms, an expansion of precarious employment, and sizeable profits for large corporations and the financial sector. Some 1.3 million agricultural jobs were lost as food commodities from transnational agro corporations flooded into the market. Wages of farm day laborers fell from 535 to 483 pesos per month, and the monthly earnings of self-employed peasants were decimated, declining from 1,959 pesos in 1991 to 228 pesos in 2003. Whereas agriculture employed the largest number of workers before NAFTA, today the largest sector is in retail trade. It's not surprising that the displacement of farm labor led to an increase in illegal migration as people desperately sought work. Pre-NAFTA flows are estimated at 260,000 people per year. From 2000-2004 yearly border crossing increased to about 485,000. In 2005 Mexicans sent home $15 billion to support their families. The maquiladora manufacturing zone along the US-Mexican border was set to be the great success story of NAFTA. But wages paid in the maquiladora factories are 40 percent lower than salaries in non-maquiladora manufacturing in Mexico's interior.[62]

Results in Canada were no better than in the US or Mexico. During the NAFTA years average income growth was at its lowest since World War II, and economic inequality increased for the first time since the 1920s. In trade-exposed manufacturing industries union membership experienced the biggest declines in Canada, falling from 45.5 percent to 32.6 percent. But for leading non-financial corporations, revenues climbed 105 percent while the labor force decreased by 15 percent. By 2002, corporate acquisitions comprised 98 percent of all foreign direct investment, as more than 10,000 Canadian firms were bought by foreign investors.[63] In summing up conditions in Canada, Bruce Campbell's description actually applies to all three countries,

> NAFTA is about much more than deregulating trade. It is about removing restrictions on the mobility of capital. It goes way behind the border to the heart of domestic policy making. It is an economic constitution, conferring enforceable

rights on investors, limiting the powers of
government, and making it extremely difficult for
future governments to change. At its core, NAFTA
is about shifting the power in the economy from
government to corporations, from workers to
corporations.[64]

As of this writing neither the Trans Pacific Partnership
(TPP) nor the Transatlantic Trade and Investment Partnership
(TTIP) have been approved by any government, and the text of
the agreements have been highly guarded secrets. Nevertheless,
there have been a number of major leaks on both treaties. Their
passage is questionable, since there is solid opposition at both
the political and grassroots levels. But an examination is still
worthwhile because these treaties reflect a consolidation of other
trade arrangements, and the economic projections of the TCC.
The TPP will establish investor-state dispute settlement tribunals
that will extend these trade courts to 9,000 foreign-owned firms
in the US and 18,000 US foreign subsidiaries. This arrangement
allows transnational corporations to sue governments and demand
taxpayer compensation for infringements on their right to profit.
Such infringements may include environmental or labor laws,
land-use restrictions, government regulations, or control over
foreign capital investments. Compensation can include what
corporations say they lost on "expected future profits." Under
US Free Trade Agreements and Bilateral Investment Treaties
$3.6 billion has already been paid out to corporations in Investor-
State Dispute Settlement (ISDS)-rendered decisions. Tribunals
are staffed by lawyers who rotate between advocacy and sitting
judges. Hourly compensation runs up to $700 an hour. The
tribunals also circumvent national courts, creating a global legal
structure above any nation. And while decisions can't be appealed
to domestic courts, if investors lose in a domestic court they can
appeal to the ISDS.

The TPP will also protect investors from citizens who
may elect a nationalist or leftwing government. If new policies

undermine corporate "expectations" they can claim damages. So if new environmental laws are passed, or a higher national minimum wage, or government-mandated health coverage, TNCs can claim they suffer from a reduced value of their investments. Any changes to the national regulatory structure that a corporation thinks is an infraction to the standards that existed when they made their investment can be challenged. According to past tribunal decisions, investor expectations must be honored. So if a government passes new legislation that ensures access to affordable medicines, it could be considered an "expropriation" of intellectual property rights. Moreover, TNCs can challenge government "performance standards" that support local job creation or the domestic purchase of materials.[65]

The TPP excludes China from the 12-country pact, and many see it as a move by the US to contain China. But a Communist Party newspaper stated China should join as the treaty's "broad aims were in line with the country's own economic reform agenda."[66] Moreover, China is negotiating a Regional Comprehensive Economic Partnership that includes seven of the TPP countries, plus India and South Korea. The two large regional trade pacts may represent some rivalry between the US and China, but the bottom line is the extension of global capitalism, and TCC political and economic power.

The TTIP between the US and Europe has all the essential elements of the TPP. A research report by John Hillary notes:

> The main goal of TTIP is, by their own admission, to remove regulatory 'barriers' which restrict the potential profits to be made by transnational corporations on both sides of the Atlantic. Yet the 'barriers' are in reality some of our most prized social and environmental regulations, such as labour rights, food safety rules…regulations on the use of toxic chemicals, digital privacy laws and even new banking safeguards…TTIP is therefore correctly understood not as a negotiation between

two competing trading partners, but as an attempt
by transnational corporations to pry open and
deregulate markets..."[67]

In preparing the TTIP the European Commission and
US officials held closed meetings with individual TNCs and
lobbyists on some 119 occasions. Access to documents that
cover negotiations will be closed to the public for 30 years, and
political representatives can only read draft copies in closed and
guarded rooms. However, information on government negotiating
positions can be shared between corporate advisors on both sides
of the Atlantic. Even with tight controls over information, enough
has leaked to do an analysis of the proposed treaty.

It's no surprise that governments want secrecy. The
European Commission has already admitted there would be
"prolonged and substantial" lay-offs and plant closures, because
corporations would migrate to US states where labor standards are
low and union membership virtually non-existent.[68]

One area of great concern to European citizens is food
safety regulations, which are stricter than those in the US.
European countries have largely rejected use of Genetically
Modified Organisms (GMOs), whereas in the US 70 percent of
processed foods contain genetically modified ingredients. Both the
European and US biotech industries are working closely together
to break down EU regulatory barriers. Other biotech corporate
attacks include: weakening restrictions on endocrine disruptors
that harm the human hormone system, already widely used in
US food products; allowing bovine growth hormones (rBGH)
that are used in US milk and beef production, and are linked to
cancers in humans; permitting turkeys and chicken carcasses to
be cleansed with chlorine; and spreading the use of pesticides by
downgrading the use of the "precautionary principle," a scientific
principle that insists products must be proven safe before sold to
the public. Corporations would turn this on its head, and demand
the public prove a product unsafe before its removal from the
market. Removing the precautionary principle would also open

Europe to a flood of toxic chemicals. In the US the Environmental Protection Agency has been only able to pass controls on six out of 84,000 chemicals in commercial use.[69] Lastly, trade tribunals would be established with the same powers described above in the TPP.

The transnational trade courts are one of the most controversial elements in all trade treaties, because they are a powerful institutional structure created outside of national state control. In effect, they establish a juridical system for global capitalism to function as part of the transnational state. By 2014 there had been 608 Investor-state dispute settlement cases, with their use on the rise every year. Concluded cases number 405. States won 36 percent, investors 27 percent, and the remainder either were settled or discontinued.[70] Investor victories have been on the rise; in 2012 they won 70 percent of the cases. Some 64 percent of all cases originate from TNCs located in the developed world and are directed at developing countries. Overall 95 states have been sued by investors. But those countries subjected to the most claims are Argentina with 52 cases, Venezuela with 34 and Ecuador with 23. Clearly the courts are used by the TCC as a battering ram against states attempting to chart an independent path of development. In comparison, 19 cases have been brought against Canada, and 15 against the US.[71]

It's instructive to examine some of the cases. First we can get an idea by looking at the investors and states involved, as in the following: *Chevron vs. Ecuador*; *Occidental Petroleum vs. Ecuador*, *Daimler vs. Argentina*; *Deutsche Bank vs. Sri Lanka*; *Bosch vs. Ukraine*; *Gazprom vs. Lithuania*; *Ping An Life Insurance vs. Belgium*; *Standard Chartered Bank vs. Tanzania*; and *Planet Mining vs. Indonesia*. Some of these cases reveal the complex transnational character of global capitalism. For example, the Standard Bank claim against Tanzania was initiated by an investor who owned substantial equity in a Hong Kong company that held Tanzanian debt acquired from Malaysian financial institutions.

An area of great concern is claims undercutting environmental protections. Examples include a Swedish investor demanding compensation for supposed losses suffered when Germany announced the closing of nuclear power plants, Lone Pine Resources suing Quebec for banning oil and gas activities in protected areas, Canada's national government being forced to pay $122 million over water and timber rights to Abitibi Bowater, and a Canadian company that used its US-affiliated office to sue its own government under NAFTA. In *SAUR vs. Argentina* the ISDS ruled sovereign power protecting people's right to water could not be exercised over the rights of an investor. The largest ISDS settlement, $1.77 billion, was awarded to Occidental Petroleum in a case against Ecuador. Another case being considered is by TransCanada against the US government over Obama's cancellation of the Keystone pipeline for the loss of expected profits of $15 billion. On the other hand, there are a number of pro-environmental cases. Italy, Spain, and the Czech Republic were notified of impeding suits against their withdrawal of solar energy subsidies because of the financial crisis.[72]

In the field of health, the tobacco company, Philip Morris, sued Argentina and Uruguay over packaging cigarettes with plain wrappers and health warnings. In Slovakia when a left-leaning government restricted insurance corporations profiteering from the privatization of health care, Achmea from the Netherlands sued and received 29.5 million Euros as compensation. Slovakia then attempted to establish public insurance that was to cover the entire country, but Achmea turned to ISDS a second time to successfully sue the government.

An overview of the above treaties and trade disputes plainly exposes just how the TCC sees and understands the world. Their vision for global capitalism is that markets should rule all economic interactions, and prevail over human rights and the environment. Moreover, the political process should structure, institutionalize, and protect their interests. The only democracy they understand is the rights of property. Or more clearly stated in class terms, their rights to own, control, and do as they wish, the world over.

Conclusion

Over the past 40 years national capitalism has reformed itself and entered a new era. This is nothing novel. Former crises and technological revolutions have propelled capitalism from mercantilism, to colonialism, national industrialism, and imperialism. The historic movement towards a more deeply integrated world system has been at work since the system's inception. The current era of global capitalism is characterized by transnational production and finance, the emergence of a transnational capitalist class and a remade working class to correspond to the new relations of production.

What may be truly different in this era is a historic reversal of human rights and democracy. The slow, erratic, but historically steady advance of democratic rights has characterized capitalism, creating hegemonic legitimacy for the system among mass segments of the world's population. Democracy, alongside growing economic well-being, have been the two pillars upholding political support for the belief that capitalism is the best of all possible worlds. But with spreading austerity, and the naked political power of the one percent on display, global capitalism is rapidly facing a worldwide crisis of delegitimization. Challenged from the left, the right, and by religious fundamentalism, can green capitalism offer a way out of the crisis? We'll explore this question in the next chapter.

Endnotes

1   Leslie Sklair, *Globalization: Capitalism & Its Alternatives* (Oxford University Press: Oxford, 2002); Leslie Sklair, *The transnational capitalist class* (Oxford: Blackwell, 2001); William I. Robinson, *Promoting Polyarchy: Globalization, US Intervention, and Hegemony* (Cambridge University Press: Cambridge, 1996); William I. Robinson, *A theory of global capitalism: production, class, and state in a transnational world* (The Johns Hopkins University Press: Baltimore and London, 2004); Jerry Harris, *The Dialectics of Globalization:*

economic and political conflict in a transnational world (Cambridge · Scholars Publishing: Newcastle upon Tyne, 2008).

2   Shawn Donnan, "Adapt trade policy to reflect globalisation, economic bodies warn," *Financial Times* (July 17, 2014).

3   William I. Robinson and Jerry Harris, "Towards A Global Ruling Class? Globalization and the Transnational Capitalist Class," *Science & Society*, Vol. 64, No. 1 (Spring 2000): 11–54.

4   Joseph Stiglitz, "Rewriting the Rules of the American Economy," *Roosevelt Institute* (2015): 23.

5   United Nations Conference on Trade and Development, *World Investment Report 2015 Overview* (UNCTD: New York, 2015).

6   United Nations Conference on Trade and Development, *World Investment Report 2015 Overview*, 13.

7   S.Vitali, J. B. Glattfelder, and S. Battiston, "The network of global corporate control," *PLoS ONE* 6(10) (2011): e25995. doi:10.1371/journal.pon.

8   McKinsey Global Institute, *Mapping global capital markets: fifth annual report* (McKinsey & Company, October 2008).

9   Costas Lapavitsas, "The era of financialization, an interview with Costas Lapavitsas: parts 1 and 2," *Dollars and Sense* (April 14, 2014).

10   Daniel Schafer, "Automation gets fillip from forex rigging allegations," *Financial Times* (April 6, 2014).

11   Daniel Schafer, "Asia set to overtake North America in wealth stakes," *Financial Times* (June 18, 2014).

12   Knight Frank, *The Wealth Report 2016* (Think: London, 2015).

13   Chrystia Freeland, Plutocrats: The rise of the new global super-rich and the fall of everyone else (Penguin: New York, 2012), 5.

14   Andy Coghlan and Deborah MacKenzie, Revealed-the capitalist network that runs the world, <http://www.newscientist.com/science-in-society> (2011).

15   S.Vitali, J. B. Glattfelder, and S. Battiston, "The network of global corporate control."

16   Stephen Foley, Kara Scannell, and Arash Massoudi, "Buffett's business wire ends feeds to high-speed traders," *Financial Times* (February 20, 2014).

17   Susanne Craig, "The Giant of Shareholders, Quietly Stirring," *The New York Times* (May 18, 2013).

18   BlackRock, *Annual Report* (BlackRock Variable Series Funds, Inc., December 31, 2012).

19   William Tabb, *The restructuring of capitalism in our time*. Columbia University Press: New York, 2012), 122.

20   Bain Reports, A world awash in capital, *Insights* (November 14, 2012).

21   Michael Lewis, Flash Boys (W.W. Norton & Company: New York/ London, 2014), 114.

22   Quentin Hardy, "A strange computer promises great speed," *The New York Times* (March 21, 2013).

23   Michael De La Merced & William Alden, "Scrutiny for Wall Street's warp speed," *Financial Times* (March 31, 2014).

24   Karl Marx, Grundrisse (Penguin: New York, 1993), 539.

25   Matt Phillips, "Blankfein Says He's Just Doing 'God's Work,'" *The New York Times* (November 9, 2009).

26   Wharton School of Business, "GE's Jeff Immelt on Leadership, Global Risk and Growth," <http://knowledge.wharton.upenn.edu/article. cfm?articleid=3241> (April 30, 2013).

27   Bureau of Economic Analysis, "Tracking Global Investment: Who Owns What-and Where," <http://blog.bea.gov/2013/02/12/tracking-global-investment/> (February 12, 2013).

28   Bureau of Economic Analysis, "U.S. Net International Investment Position: End of the First Quarter of 2015, Year 2014, and Annual Revisions," <http://www.bea.gov/newsreleases/international/ intinv/2015/ intinv115.htm#annualrevisions June 30> (June 30, 2015).

29   Bureau of Economic Analysis, "Tracking Global Investment: Who Owns What-and Where".

30   Bureau of Economic Analysis, "U.S. Net International Investment Position: End of the First Quarter of 2015, Year 2014, and Annual Revisions".

31   Shimshon Bichler and Jonathan Nitzan, "The asymptotes of power," *real-world economics review* No. 60 (June, 2012): 18–53.

32   Ian Urbina and Keith Bradsher, "Linking Factories to the Malls, Middleman Pushes Low Costs," *The New York Times* (August 7, 2013).

33   Li & Fung, <http://www.funggroup.com/eng/about/managers> (2013).

34   Wharton School of Business, "GE's Jeff Immelt on Leadership, Global Risk and Growth".

35   Finance online, "The iPhone Saga," <http://financesonline.com/ uploads/iPhone-infographic.jpg>.

36   Ibid.

37   Ibid.

38   Thomas Landon Jr and Eric Pfanner, "Even Before Apple Tax Breaks, Ireland's Policy Had Its Critics," *The New York Times* (May 21, 2013).

39   Nelson D. Schwartz, "Apple Avoided Billions in Taxes, Congressional Panel Says," *The New York Times* (May 20, 2013).

40   *Financial Times*, "Keeping it abroad," <http://www.ft.com/cms/s/0/ dd1e1a26-f223-11e3-ac7a-00144feabdc0.html#ixzz34WW3wqgP>

(June 6, 2014).

41 Micheline Maynard, "After Many Stumbles, Fall of an American Giant," *The New York Times* (June 1, 2009).

42 GM, <www.gm.com/company/aboutGM/our_company.html> (2014).

43 GM, <http://gmibm.avature.net/careers/SearchJobsAllJobs> (2014).

44 Nick Bunkley, "Ford tops GM in U.S. factory jobs," <http://www.autonews.com/article/20150215/OEM/302169970/ford-tops-gm-in-u.s.-factory-jobs> (2015)

45 GM, <http://careers.gm.com/worldwide-locations/asiamiddle-east/singapore.html> (2015).

46 Kelsey Mays, "American-Made Index: Which Automakers Affect the Most U.S. Workers?" <https://www.cars.com/articles/2012/07/american-made-index-which-automakers-affect-the-most-us-workers/> (2015).

47 GM, <http://opel.com/facts.html> (2015).

48 GM, "GM Brands Worldwide Locations," <http://www. Home / Worldwide Locations / Asia/Middle East / China> (2015).

49 GM, <http://careers.gm.com/worldwide-locations/asiamiddle-east/india.html> (2015).

50 GM, <http://careers.gm.com/worldwide-locations/asiamiddle-east/korea.html> (2015).

51 Francis Shor, "Auto De(con)struction: The Spatial Fixes and Racial Repercussions of Detroit's Deindustrialization," *Perspectives on Global Developments and Technology* Vol. 15, No. 1-2 (2016).

52 Dan Georgakas and Marvin Surkin, *Detroit: I Do Mind Dying* (South End Press: Cambridge, MA, 1998).

53 Jonathan Mahler, "General Motors, Detroit, and the Fall of the Black Middle Class," *The New York Times Magazine* (June 24, 2009).

54 Marek Hrubec, "Interview with Frank Hammer: The Deindustrialization of Detroit," *Perspectives on Global Developments and Technology* Vol. 15, No. 1-2 (2016).

55 Hrubec, "Interview with Frank Hammer: The Deindustrialization of Detroit".

56 Anthony van Fossen, "Flags of Convenience and Global Capitalism," Paper presented at the Third Bi-Annual Conference of the Network for the Critical Study of Global Capitalism. Academy of Social Sciences, Prague. September 27, 2015.

57 Ibid.

58 Ibid.

59 United Nations Conference on Trade and Development, *World Investment Report 2015 Overview*.

60 Robert Scott, Carlos Salas, and Bruce Campbell, Revisiting NAFTA:

Still not working for North America's workers. Economic Policy Institute, Briefing Paper #173, Washington DC (September 28, 2006).

61 Robert Scott, NAFTA's Legacy: Rising trade deficits lead to significant job displacement and declining job quality for the United States. Economic Policy Institute, Briefing Paper #173, Washington DC (September 28, 2006).

62 Carlos Salas, Between Unemployment and Insecurity in Mexico: NAFTA enters its second decade. Economic Policy Institute, Briefing Paper #173, Washington DC (September 28, 2006).

63 Bruce Perry, "TPP, Not Just Another NAFTA," *Winter 2015 Quarterly CPEG Notes*, Chicago Political Economy Group (2015).

64 Bruce Campbell, Backsliding: The Impact of NAFTA on Canadian Workers. Economic Policy Institute, Briefing Paper #173, Washington DC (September 28, 2006).

65 Lori Wallach and Ben Beachy, "Analysis of Leaked Trans-Pacific Partnership Investment Text," Public Citizen, (March 25, 2015); "China should join US-backed Trans-Pacific Partnership 'when time is right', says Communist Party newspaper," <http://www.scmp.com/news/china/policies-politics/article/1871975/china-should-join-us-backed-trans-pacific-partnership> (October 25, 2015).

66 South China Morning Post (2015).

67 John Hilary, *The Transatlantic Trade and Investment Partnership: A Charter for Deregulation, An Attack on Jobs, An End to Democracy* (Rosa Luxemburg Institute: Stiftung, Brussels, February 2014.

68 European Commission, "Impact Assessment Report on the future of U-US trade relations," Strasbourg, section 5.9.2. (March 12, 2013).

69 Hilary, *The Transatlantic Trade and Investment Partnership: A Charter for Deregulation, An Attack on Jobs, An End to Democracy.*

70 United Nations Conference on Trade and Development, *World Investment Report 2015 Overview.*

71 United Nations Conference on Trade and Development, "Recent Developments in Investor-State Dispute Settlement (ISDS)," *IIA Issues Note*, No. 1 (May 2013).

72 United Nations Conference on Trade and Development, "Recent Developments in Investor-State Dispute Settlement (ISDS).

Chapter Three

GREEN CAPITALISM AND SOCIAL JUSTICE

"Expansion is everything...
I would annex the planets if I could."
Cecil Rhodes

"From the standpoint of a higher economic formation,
the private property of particular individuals in the earth
will appear just as absurd as the private property of one
man in other men. Even an entire society, a nation, or all
simultaneously existing societies taken together, are not
the owners of the earth. They are simply its possessors,
its beneficiaries, and have to bequeath it in an improved
state to succeeding generations as boni patres familias."
Karl Marx

Can the transition to green capitalism create a more democratic and sustainable economic system? This is certainly the hope of many, whether rich or poor. But does saving the planet and curtailing global warming go hand-in-hand with social justice? Since any deepening of the ecological crisis affects human beings, and the harshest effects are visited upon the poor, it is impossible to separate green capitalism from a better future for the masses of people. It would bring environmental activists closer to political influence and government regulatory powers while involving government support for green technologies and companies, whether ownership was private or cooperative. So at first glance, it seems to solve questions over the balance of civil society, government, and the market raised in the introduction of this book.

But a more critical investigation reveals the deeper contradictions that undercut the ability of green capitalism to create a truly sustainable and just world. This includes both the growth and recessionary cycles inherent in the capitalist system, the transnational and competitive nature of green corporations, and the social relations between capital and labor.

Green Capitalism

Within the transnational capitalist class powerful voices have been raised advocating the need to convert the economy. Al Gore no longer stands out as a lone figure, the black sheep among the ruling elite. Robert Rubin, President Clinton's Treasury Secretary, co-chair of the Council on Foreign Relations, Goldman Sachs alumni, and Citicorp executive, wrote in the *Washington Post*, "We do not face a choice between protecting our environment or protecting our economy. We face a choice between protecting our economy by protecting our environment—or allowing environmental havoc to create economic havoc."[1] For Rubin, a former opponent of the Kyoto agreement on climate change, this is major about-face.

The main motivation pushing capitalists to confront climate change is the cost to business. An important wake-up call was the 2006 Stern Review, an economic analysis sponsored by the British government. Stern concluded that the cost of curbing climate change was affordable, and virtually insignificant compared with the impact on corporations if nothing was done. In the US an unusual alliance of conservative and liberal politicians and executives formed the Risky Business Project.[2] Founding members included Hank Paulson, ex-CEO of Goldman Sachs and Secretary of the Treasury under George W. Bush; former mayor of New York and billionaire political independent Michael Bloomberg; and former hedge fund billionaire and liberal Democrat, Tom Steyer. The project sponsored climate change research by the Rhodium Group. Their findings showed large losses to agriculture, large losses in property damage, and sharply rising insurance costs. Further Rhodium reports that focused on the Midwest and California indicated similar mounting future expenses.

All members of Risky Business agree that corporations must adapt or lose hundreds of billions of dollars. Yet among members are different political and economic strategies. Steyer has devoted $73 million in political campaigns to defeat Republican candidates who deny global warming. Paulson is a strong advocate for a carbon exchange market, although it has largely failed in Europe. Greg Page, executive chairman of the food conglomerate Cargill, opposes environmental regulations that impose restrictions on corporations. Some members support the building of the Keystone oil pipeline, and even reject the scientific fact that human activity is a major contributor to global warming. What unites them is essentially two points. The first is the fear of large-scale economic disruption due to climate change, whether man made or by natural causes. The second is that market-based solutions, whether imposed as new regulations that set competitive rules or through voluntary changes in business practice, are the only way forward. As Paulson stated, "The whole point of all of this is that it can be mitigated. The enemies of what we're trying to do are short-termism and a sense of hopelessness. But if we act soon we can avoid the worst outcomes and adapt."[3] In other words, the system can be saved if we begin to think in more strategic terms. The problem isn't the fundamental relationship between nature and capitalism, but simply the focus on short-term profits that drive business decisions.

Risky Business is a late entry into the field of advocates for green capitalism. Among these are a number of elite think tanks, lobby groups, and policy centers that function as a network within the TCC. The Club of Rome was the earliest, forming in 1972. Others include the following: Global Environmental Management Initiative (1990); Business Council for Sustainable Energy (1992); World Business Council for Sustainable Development (1996); International Emissions Trading Association (1999); United Nations Global Compact (2000); Global Climate Forum (2001); and the Copenhagen Climate Council (2007).

These corporate-supported groups function to link various networks that exist among the TCC across borders and across financial and industrial groups. Such ties abound within the capitalist class and are concerned with many different issues including defense, governance, foreign policy, ideology, and so on. Beyond promoting personal relationships and training class cadre, they develop projects, bring together class fractions, do research, engage in political and ideological debates, and create broader narratives for media and social consumption. On a sociological and political level it's one way elite class formation takes place.[4]

The above set of green capitalist organizations are an important form through which a new hegemonic bloc can emerge. Leading members of these groups sit on numerous corporate boards including Vodafone, Bank of America, Citigroup, Sony, Google, Intel, Unilever, Shell, and Total.[5] The end game would be a corporate-led transition insuring that capital accumulation would continue under a regime of green capitalism. Hegemonic blocs are more than elite formations, and need a diverse popular base of support. But leadership is key in setting the terms through which politics and economics function. As with Risky Business, all the above green groups promote neoliberalism, with only The Club of Rome supporting the Keynesian approach.

In a study of these groups, Jean Philippe Sapinski describes their dominant viewpoint,

> Business represents the main, and often only,
> force of change; governments at best play a minor
> support role to corporate actions, and at worst are
> a hindrance; NGOs, when present, can be junior

partners…human beings are non-existent in themselves, and appear only under the form of a population to be employed or managed; similarly, ecosystems are sources of wealth in the form of natural capital and thus objects to be managed as well.[6]

Even Bill Gates, who is investing $2 billion into green energy, doubts that corporate elites will do much without pressure from government action. Gates commented that, "There's no fortune to be made. Even if you have a new energy source that costs the same as today's and emits no CO2, it will be uncertain compared with what's tried-and-true and already operating at unbelievable scale and has gotten through all the regulatory problems. Without a substantial carbon tax, there's no incentive for innovators or plant buyers to switch."[7] To push innovation and governments Gates has created his own group of billionaires to invest in green research and development. Members include Jeff Bezos of Amazon, Jack Ma of Alibaba, Mark Zuckerberg of Facebook, Reid Hoffman of LinkedIn, Ratan Tata of the Tata industrial empire from India, and Saudi prince Alwaleed bin Talal.[8] But Gates may have trouble convincing other members of his class. A survey was conducted of 400 of the world's leading private bankers and wealth advisors who manage assets for about 45,000 individuals with a combined wealth of $500 billion dollars. Out of nine issues concerning "risk to wealth creation and preservation," environmental problems ranked the lowest, with just 14 percent registering concern.[9]

Stronger opposition to green capitalism comes from the fossil fuel industry, the American Farm Bureau Federation, the US Chamber of Commerce, and the National Association of Manufacturers, the best-funded and most powerful corporate lobbies in the country. Part of what drives such formidable foes is the unwillingness to spend their capital on adopting technologies and replacing assets, particularly if such changes won't produce profits in the short-term but will harm their stock price. But neoliberal ideology also plays a strong role. There is a deep suspicion that global warming science is a left-wing attempt to impose government regulations on the market. Consequently, when you combine ideology, profit, and greed the end product is an intense opposition to green capitalism. It is somewhat ironic then that green capitalism is not an enemy of neoliberalism. In particular, Paulson, Rubin, and Bloomberg are all architects of deregulation, financial speculation, and austerity. There is nothing in their strategic vision that questions low-wages, third world sweat-shops, the transnationalization of capital, and social austerity as the primary method to pay off financial debt. A green corporate strategy may seek to solve the contradiction between capitalism and nature, but makes no attempt to solve the contradiction between capital and labor.

There are other advocates of green capitalism that go further in their social vision. Environmentalists Paul Hawken and Amory and Hunter Lovins argue green capitalism can fully bloom within the confines of market competition and accumulation.[10] Human and natural resources must be properly valued, environmentally damaging technologies replaced, and poverty alleviation policies put in place. Green capitalism will be more competitive and profitable as it replaces fossil fuels and the improper use of resources. It's an attractive strategy and not hard to imagine. Al Gore and Thomas Friedman have worked hard to popularize a similar vision. Gore has argued that, properly financed, an entirely new national energy system could be built in a ten-year span.[11] In doing so, solar panels and wind turbines will create new markets that rapidly phase out the old energy system. Capitalist growth continues, but in a manner that reduces energy and resource consumption. Taken on a larger scale architecture, agriculture, transportation, and production all need to be converted, the end result being a redesigned sustainable society. This massive greening of civilization will lead to vast new markets, and profits for those corporations producing and deploying the proper technologies.

In an interesting turn of history the Rockefeller Fund,

built on oil profits, now devotes more than 40 percent of their grant dollars to fight global warming. According to their president, Stephen Heintz, "it is morally inconsistent to stay invested in the fossil fuel industry." Heintz hopes the Rockefeller Fund will "help to finish the oil age," and goes on to state, "It is time to move away from fossil fuels, and to move as quickly as possible to clean, renewable energy in order to save the planet. The oil age is now coming to its own end."[12] The Fund expects investors will remove more than $2.5 trillion dollars from the fossil fuel industry, and contends that 60 to 80 percent of known reserves need to stay under ground.

A global vision of green transformation was suggested by United Nations Secretary General Ban Ki Moon who called for a worldwide "Green New Deal" that would be a "wholesale reconfiguration of global industry."[13] As for Gore's plan to transform energy use in the US, a study published by *Scientific American* goes much further. Mark Jacobson and Mark Delucchi state that for a $100 trillion dollar program "100 percent of the world's energy, for all purposes, could be supplied by wind, water and solar resources by 2030."[14] That would be about ten percent of the world's GDP per year, necessitating a huge shift in spending and resources, virtually impossible without a political revolution.

A Green Hegemonic Bloc

But is that political revolution possible within the confines of capitalism, green, red, white or blue? Every year the environmental crisis becomes more damaging and widespread. The 2014 report from the United Nations Intergovernmental Panel on Climate Change forcefully warned of the danger that warming poses to the planet. Going beyond 3.6 degrees Fahrenheit could cause the collapse of ice sheets, a rapid rise in sea levels, food shortages, large scale destruction of forests, and mass extinctions of plant and animal life.[15] The tipping point is rapidly approaching.

For a large and growing number of transnational businessmen and elite politicians the reality can no longer be denied.

But can the TCC escape speculative financialization, and create a regime of green accumulation? And is a post neoliberal green hegemonic bloc possible under their leadership? Facing such a challenge the emerging green wing is developing a strategic vision that may solve three major problems facing the system: stagnation, legitimacy, and defense.

In terms of economic stagnation new investments in green technologies can set off a renewed cycle of accumulation, creating an expansion of new industries, jobs, and profits. New technologies have always played a key role for capitalist accumulation. The spinning jenny, blast furnaces, electricity, assembly lines, internal combustion engines, cars, and computers all have propelled economic reorganization and growth. Joseph Schumpeter referred to this as creative destruction, which he saw as an essential feature of innovation generating new business cycles.[16] For the green economy this would mean the destruction of fossil fuel industries, and the redirection of capital to new sustainable technologies. Furthermore, green capitalism would be based on new methods of production, rebuilding infrastructure, new physical assets, and new knowledge. This would constitute a decisive turn from an economy dominated by speculative finance.

Nonetheless, large transnational holders of capital remain unconvinced of the necessity or viability of green technology. In 2014 US corporations had accumulated nearly five trillion dollars in unused capital. At a global level Bain Capital reported that, "By 2010 global capital had swollen to some $600 trillion (creating) a world that is structurally awash in capital (yet) investors are straining to find a sufficient supply of attractive productive assets to absorb it all."[17] From their class viewpoint there is simply a lack of worthwhile investment opportunities in a depressed global economy. With the consumer market down because of weak spending due to low wages, putting money into expanding the real economy runs counter to capitalist logic. This is a classic contradiction. In the pursuit of higher profits offshoring, outsourcing, part-time work, temporary labor, and low wages were instituted as part of capitalist efficiency drives and globalization. With the real economy in a slump, money is thrown into speculative finance, driving up stocks, derivatives, futures, securitization, and all the other activities that eventually result in economic bubbles and a deeper crisis.

Yet a huge pool of new and existing green technologies cry out for investments. Such technologies not only address energy, but can transform transportation, housing, and agriculture, lower pollution, recycle waste, and reinvent the very process of production. The Risky Business project only points to the damage and economic downside of mounting environmental problems. But the Gore wing has seized upon the expansionary aspects of green technology producing a new era of accumulation, thus creating a strong strategic argument for a deeper conversion.

The second problem facing capitalism is that the economic crisis and deepening austerity has caused a decrease in political legitimacy, and rapidly disappearing trust in the ruling parties of government. In Gramscian terms the TCC is facing a crisis of ideological hegemony. A new elite narrative on their devotion to the planet, renewing the economy, creating jobs, and saving species can go a long way to reestablishing their hegemony. This would require the construction of a new social bloc entailing a popular base of political support led by the green sector of the TCC. Workers, engineers and scientists involved in designing and producing the new technologies would certainly be devoted backers. Even more importantly would be the inclusion of activists and supporters from the environmental movement. Leaders from civil society could be incorporated into advisory positions and political positions, what Gramsci termed a passive revolution. Aspects of this are already in play. For example, Bill McKibben, leader of the anti-Keystone pipeline movement, has been invited to private meetings with billionaire Steyer to help plot out ways to defeat Republican climate change deniers. Given that a large majority of the population understands global warming is a threat to society, building a new hegemonic bloc centered on the conversion to green capitalism seems a possibility well within the realm of political reality.

Yet here too serious roadblocks obstruct progress. For starters about 25 percent of the American population rejects climate science, and their political representatives appear to have a stranglehold on the Republican Party. A good section of the Democratic Party also takes large amounts of money from the fossil fuel industry. Consequently, a green bloc would need to achieve hegemony in the Democratic Party, and among Republicans, at minimum, the acceptance of a neoliberal understanding of green capitalism. Taking a global view, similar green hegemonic blocs would need to ascend to political power in China, India, and key fossil producing countries such as Russia, Saudi Arabia, and Iran. None of this is outside the realm of possibility. But the environmental window is rapidly closing. Planetary time is extremely long, but we are close to passing over the tipping point threshold within the next 50 to 100 years. Given the time, money, and effort needed for a substantial transformation, one significant enough to avoid major social disruptions, the time is short.

Lastly is the question of defense and stability. For the past decade the Pentagon and CIA have been warning of possible social and political chaos as the result of environmental problems. They have even predicted economic collapse in ecologically vulnerable countries such as Bangladesh. Such disasters would put into motion millions of environmental refugees. The cross-border flow of immigrants is one of the most contentious issues in the world. The flight of refugees from wars in the Middle East has already created political tensions throughout Europe. And Latin American immigrants seeking economic and physical safety in the US have fueled reactionary nationalism, with demagogues in the highest ranks of the Republican Party. Over the next one to two hundred years the rise in sea levels may swamp many of the world's largest cities, creating instability across the planet. For some in the defense establishment global warming is a greater strategic threat than terrorism.

But global warming is just one of the environmental problems stalking the corridors of the defense community. Upon request from the Department of State the Defense Intelligence Agency, alongside the CIA, Department of Energy and other security agencies produced the report, "Global Water Security." As the study states, "Our Bottom Line: During the next 10 years, many countries important to the United States will experience water problems—shortages, poor water quality, or floods—that will risk instability and state failure, increase regional tensions, and distract them from working with the United States on important US policy objectives."[18] As the report points out, this is directly related to climate change and deforestation. The future scenario includes the spread of arid regions in diverse areas such as Brazil, the Mediterranean Basin, and southern Africa. The resulting flood of migrants to cities will put greater demands on water consumption. When water shortages are combined with the problems of poverty, class tensions, and environmental degradation, state failure becomes a real possibility. The report sees social disruptions becoming particularly dangerous if people believe water shortages are the result of poor government, or the "control of water by elites." Therefore the water crisis has two aspects, one of too much water and the other of too little. Rising sea levels swamping coastal cities is matched by drought and shortages elsewhere, both resulting in a human crisis and new waves of refugees.

Agriculture is closely linked to shortages in water, accounting for about 95 percent of water use and producing 31 percent of greenhouse gases. People from ten countries including Viet-Nam, India, and Bangladesh depend on water provided by the Himalayan Mountain range, which is experiencing melting glaciers at ever more rapid rates. These 46,000 glaciers scattered over nearly two million square miles are crucial in sustaining 1.5 billion people,[19] hundreds of millions of whom are involved in farming. Bangladesh faces a double threat from global warming in the form of rising sea water flooding their delta croplands and the loss of fresh water from the mountains.

Subsequently, one focus of the report was on the high water content of food production and rising prices. The study states the Middle East and North Africa, through the import of food, purchase the equivalent of another Nile River in water content. Obviously food shortages and social instability are closely interconnected. But nowhere in the report do we find data on the water content of beef compared to grains and vegetables. One pound of beef consumes about 500 percent more water than one pound of chicken, and the water content of chicken is much higher than corn or wheat. Thus the report says nothing about Western food consumption patterns, and avoids the issue of inequalities inherent in the diets between poor and rich nations. Also missing is the role of speculative finance driving up the price of food. At the end we are simply left with solutions limited to technological fixes, such a drip-water irrigation.

With water becoming a more limited and precious resource transnational corporations have moved aggressively to privatize water rights. They contend the market is the best means to build a sustainable infrastructure for the delivery and use of water. Their explanations are always couched in terms of environmental rationality and concern for the poor. Yet the commercialization of water, so basic to human existence, is perhaps the ultimate expression of neoliberalism. The issue is pregnant with class and national tensions. In Bolivia, when Bechtel privatized water in Cochabamba, a mass rebellion erupted. Not only did prices skyrocket, Bechtel even claimed ownership of rainwater. The uprising was successful in kicking Bechtel out of the country, and helped create the conditions leading to the election of Evo Morelos and victory for the Movement to Socialism—just the type of social rebellion the defense establishment fears.

Such a radical response to the private ownership of water may have led the National Intelligence Agency to state, "Many economists advocate the privatization of water...however, properly run government water utilities can also provide excellent services." Furthermore, "Privatization...can threaten established use patterns by increasing the costs of water...also making water supply vulnerable to market forces which can conflict with societal expectations (and) can lead to instability as people become unable to afford water."[20] Their main concern here is not to advocate for or against market or government-owned utilities, but to pursue the best way to avoid disruptions that threaten global capitalism. It shouldn't be surprising, then, that a growing number of proponents in the security establishment support green policies. For them a sustainable environment sustains capitalism and US power. Therefore, significant sectors of the defense establishment would champion a green hegemonic bloc.

Social instability is certainly a condition the Pentagon wants to avoid. But could the environmental crisis lead to even more severe political ruptures? Slovak scholar Richard St'ahel argues that the capitalist growth imperative is in antagonistic contradiction to sustainability. He sees the problem as going beyond stability, particularly in the global South where the economic crisis is inseparably linked to ecology, land use, food supplies, and water resources. For St'ahel the contradiction cannot be resolved by global capitalism. As he states, "This antagonism creates a new category of revolutions and conflicts in states that reach the environmental and economic limits of growth. These conflicts result from food and water shortages and could...lead to the deep transformation of the global socio-political system."[21] Revolutions springing from environmental collapse is certainly an unappealing future for the capitalist class.

But some environmentalists take the opposite view from St'ahel, and are in perfect harmony with the viewpoint of the security apparatus. Hunter Lovins calls on the US to lead the world in green innovation because "they'll rule the world, economically, politically, and probably militarily."[22] Thomas Friedman wraps green technology in red, white, and blue, calling it the new currency of power. "It's all about national power...what could be more patriotic, capitalistic and geostrategic than that?"[23] Consequently, when it comes to maintaining military power and exploiting labor, promoters of green capitalism view it as in harmony with the system's basic DNA.

Green Capitalism vs. the Growth Imperative

Capitalism needs to continually grow. When it doesn't it

descends into recession or depression. A positive gross domestic product (GDP) is the system's fundamental indicator of a healthy economy. The entire history of capitalism has been one of expansion. More resources, more land, more production, and more markets. Our culture is built around consumerism, pushing us to construct our identity through the products we buy. We proudly seek out the best brands on our clothes. Our car informs others of our social class and economic standing. Success in life is based on accumulated wealth and material possessions. Powerful nations are wealthy nations. Jealousy, greed, desire, anxiety, and insecurity are all basic emotions often tied to what we or others possess. The promise of capitalism is unlimited growth and a middle-class lifestyle for all. But unlimited growth in a finite world is impossible. If everyone on the planet lived like middle-class Americans we would need 3.5 more worlds to supply the resources.

Marxist and anarchist ecologists link growth to the internal logic of capitalism, and argue that it undercuts any long-term reforms that green capitalism could bring forth.[24] Growth will always demand more and eventually deplete the planet's resources. As John Bellamy Foster has rediscovered in Marx, capitalism destroys a balanced metabolic relationship with nature. Only an ecologically orientated socialism can reestablish a sustainable use of earth's resources. Growth must be paced to what the planet produces, and replenished in a timely manner. Moreover, our concept of human progress does not have to be bound, tied, and gagged to unlimited growth. The concept of development needs to be delinked from growth. Better health, education, cultural access, peace, equality, social justice, and the flowering of human relationships are not outcomes often associated with competitive capitalism.

An examination of the oil industry's drive to exploit all of its assets is one way to explore the issue of growth. According to scientific estimates the atmosphere can hold 565 more gigatons of carbon dioxide and still avoid a temperature rise above 3.6 degrees Fahrenheit. Unfortunately, the amount of proven fossil fuel reserves contain 2,795 gigatons—500 percent greater than the limits to which 167 nations have agreed. As Bill McKibben explains, this fossil fuel has already been "figured into share prices, companies are borrowing money against it, (and) nations are basing their budgets on the presumed returns."[25] For transnational corporations these reserves are valued assets that mark their overall capitalization, producing the economic clout that translates into political power and influence. Buried underground waiting exploitation these assets have an estimated value of $27 trillion dollars.[26] But adhering to internationally agreed limits means abandoning 75 percent of all fossil fuel reserves. There is no corporation in the world willing to walk away from such assets.

A report issued by Exxon stated, "The scenario where governments restrict hydrocarbon production in a way to reduce GHG (greenhouse gas) emissions 80 percent during the outlook period is high unlikely...We are confident that none of our hydrocarbon reserves are now or will become 'stranded.'"[27] Clearly the oil industry intends to keep pumping fossil fuel into the atmosphere. It's impossible to know just how much, but it's a strong bet that it will be more than 565 gigatons. Over the past ten years emissions have risen at almost double the rate of the preceding decade. Even as political elites worry about global warming they keep feeding money to the fossil fuel industry. From 2007 to 2013 the gas, oil, and coal industry received $3.4 trillion in subsidies.[28] And it's no surprise. In Washington out of a total of 2,810 energy lobbyists, only 138 support renewables.[29]

Drawing attention to the problem, United Nations scientist Dr. Ottmar Edenhofer stated the world is "in the middle of a fossil fuel renaissance."[30] The real energy revolution is not renewables, but the rapid growth of fracking. In 2014 US petroleum production hit a 44-year high, and still maintains government subsidies six times greater than those received by alternative fuel. Fracking has had a huge impact on the energy market, cutting prices per barrel almost by half. For solar power this has resulted in investors fleeing the industry as oil and gas become less expensive. The cost of oil will certainly go up and down, and eventually solar power will again attract money. But market volatility is one reason why strategic planning to combat global warming is so difficult for capitalism to carry out.

The emerging economies of the South, particularly large countries like China and Brazil, are deeply imbedded in the capitalist growth cycle. Unfortunately this includes oil-dependent left governments such as Venezuela and Ecuador, where natural resources as a percent of GDP run 35 percent and 27.5 percent respectively. As Walden Bello points out there is "little willingness on the part of Southern elites to depart from the high-growth, high-consumption model inherited from the North..."[31] This is because Southern elites are part of the TCC, committed to all fundamental aspects of its ideology, and wedded to global finance and manufacturing. They are convinced that modernization cannot take place outside the capitalist world system and that their private fortunes, as well as social stability, are linked to such a model. They may have differences with their Northern partners, but these are over historic inequalities of power. What unites them is the drive to build an integrated transnational system, although they may diverge on particular questions and methods.[32]

These countries are caught in a fossil fuel mode of production, and in global circuits of accumulation. This is true even if they are committed to poverty reduction, have laws supporting sustainable development, and have leaders who speak of protecting the planet. No growth is not a political option under the weight of large inequalities. And catching up to Western living standards is characterized as a national dream, or as a mission to overcome historic colonialism. But these strategies take place within the confines of global capital, efficiency drives, land displacements, "good" governance, and other neoliberal limitations. Venezuela, Bolivia, and Ecuador may preserve some space for national projects outside of transnational pressures, but the TCC is more firmly in place in the BRICS[33] and most countries of the global South. In China serious commitments have been made to electric cars, solar panels, and wind turbines. The government has even set-up a $3.1 billion dollar fund called the

China South-South Climate Cooperation Fund to provide direct assistance to developing countries. And yet 20 to 30 percent of China's carbon emissions come from their export sector, a sector thoroughly integrated into global assembly lines and transnational finance.

China also struggles with its huge coal industry, which has strong regional and national political support. In 2015 another 210 coal-fired power plants were approved at a cost estimate of $100 billion. These plants have a capacity similar to 40 percent of US coal power, and would emit carbon dioxide equal to the annual amount in Brazil. Solar and wind companies are exempt from local taxes. So even though existing coal plants operate well below capacity, local officials push expansion because they can tax coal plants. Taxes provide an important source of funds, which helps the overall local economy, creates jobs, and boosts the careers of local party officials. Moreover, China's largest power distributor, the State Grid Corporation, is one of the largest owners of coal power plants and so is invested in continued production.

Coal production also impacts water shortages, which is a serious problem confronting China. China has 45 percent of the world's coal-fired power plants, which consume 7.4 billion cubic meters of water annually, enough to supply 406 million people, or about 30 percent of China's population. Moreover, the majority of new coal plants will be built in water-scarce regions. India and the US follow China as top countries with the highest water consumption by coal-fired plants in areas lacking water resources. Globally there are 8,359 coal power plants that consume enough fresh water for more than one billion people. Consequently, coal, which is a major contributor to global warming, impacts water shortages through both its production and environmental effects.[34]

In opposition to coal, renewable energy interests in China have been pushing the government to give priority to solar, wind, and hydropower. As Qin Haiyan, head of the Chinese Wind Energy Association, stated, "The conflict between coal and wind will become even more fierce in the next few years."[35] China's commitment to renewable energy is serious; in 2015 it spent $111 billion on alternative energy, one-third of all global investments and more than the US and Europe combined.[36] Given the size of the Chinese economy, their internal struggle over energy policy will have world impact.

Still, state leaders are caught up in the growth imperative typical of capitalist economies. Chinese transnational forces have initiated the New Silk Road, the largest infrastructure project in the world, the building of new transportation and commercial links stretching from its borders to the Middle East through Africa and on to Europe. Added to this effort is a proposed railroad, which will travel through the Amazon from the Atlantic coast in Brazil to the Pacific in Peru. These efforts will be covered in more detail in the chapter on China. The issue here is growth, and the consumption of more land, energy, trees, water, steel, cement, and all the resources needed in the path forward for China. The capitalist modernizers who run the Chinese state are using the profits of their government-owned enterprises to send their accumulated capital abroad. The result will be more integrated global markets, increasing the flow and speed of commodities, the production of more carbon emissions and a greater consumption of environmental resources.

The Greater Mekong Subregion includes China, Cambodia, Laos, Myanmar, Thailand, and Vietnam. It's an area where all the contradictions between growth, neoliberalism, and the environment are on display. Since 1992 under the guidance of the Asian Development Bank (ADB), there has been a program to develop the region's agriculture, energy, transportation, and communication systems, all while protecting the environment. Poverty reduction and sustainable development were to take place under ADB's leadership, guided by its neoliberal ideology that saw underdevelopment as a lack of connections to global markets. Disappearing from their analysis of underdevelopment was the history of British and French colonialism, and the wreck and failure of the US war that ravaged Cambodia, Laos, and Vietnam. While promising a "world-class, environmentally-friendly" regional infrastructure, the results were often "illegal logging, polluting mining operations, and environmentally destructive monoculture plantations such as rubber."[37]

To better integrate into the global economy, elite transnational investors were invited to take part. The outcome was a process that David Harvey defined as accumulation by dispossession.[38] In Kearrin Sims' study on Laos she reported that more than 25 percent of the country's total land was allocated to foreign investors. The end result was "habitat loss, species eradication, pollution, soil erosion, rising socio-economic inequality, loss of food sources and other natural resources, undermining of local economies, increased rates of communicable diseases such as HIV/AIDS, insufficient compensation payments for the displaced, and threat to the cultural value systems of resettled ethnic minority communities."[39] It was, in short, the exact opposite of poverty eradication and sustainable development, but typical of capitalist growth strategies.

Green Capitalism and Economic Recession

Most critics of green capitalism have focused on the imperative for growth as the most destructive aspect of the system. But capitalism has two fundamental cycles—growth and recession—and both undercut the ability for a fully sustainable transformation. At first glance recessions lower economic output may result in lower consumption of energy and resources, but they also cause bankruptcy. Green technologies that are competing with more powerfully entrenched fossil fuel corporations are in a vulnerable position. Their markets are smaller and often subsidies are key to their ability to survive and grow. As recessions grow in severity demand for green technologies such as wind turbines and solar panels rapidly shrinks. Additionally, there are political pressures to cut back subsidies as government budgets become constrained. Lastly, battles erupt over protectionism as national unemployment and business failures spread, putting new limitations on global markets.

The markets for solar and wind power are still quite small, consisting of only about two percent of the world's energy use. You would never get this impression by reading through alternative energy business literature, which boasts of large and rapid rates of growth. But expanding from one percent to two percent is a 100 percent rate of growth, so figures from green cheerleaders can often be misleading.

The economic crisis that began in 2008 opened up a unique opportunity for governments to promote jobs and growth through expanding subsidies to wind and solar power. China took this route before the recession began, going from almost no wind and solar manufacturing to leading the world in both areas within five years. This brought down costs significantly, expanded capacity, and made alternative energy competitive with fossil-fuel pricing.

A world functioning with a planned and sustainable energy market would have welcomed such a development, but financial and corporate elites saw the Chinese surge only as a competitive threat. As the recession reduced markets, prices shrank and so did profits. Stock prices then dropped, followed by bankruptcy. This led to lay-offs, closed factories, and a general crisis, particularly in the solar panel industry. When Evergreen, a US solar panel producer, saw its stock price fall from above $100 to just $3.03 they closed their facility in Massachusetts and moved to China. Other US green companies also saw their stock price plunge. Suntech went down 61.7 percent, First Solar sank 55.8 percent, and MEMC dropped 57.8 percent. When the recession hit the global production of panels could power 70 gigawatts of energy. But worldwide demand was for only 30 gigawatts. With supplies running ahead of the market by 130 percent the industry's crash was inevitable. Global overcapacity had become the problem.

In a world where global warming continues to worsen, and where people daily choke on air pollution caused by oil and coal, only capitalism could declare that there was an overcapacity in green manufacturing. In reality, the world needs every turbine and every panel that rolls off the assembly line. Not only is there not an overcapacity, but an actual under capacity exists. An environmental market that makes sustainability a priority would develop a global program using the full capacity of green manufacturing. Instead, competitive markets have resulted in undercutting the development and distribution of the very technology we need.

We can explore some industrial data to better understand the details of how the crisis affected the alternative energy market. With $67.7 billion in public and private funds in sustainable energy, China had the largest investments in the world and brought down the price of panels some 70 percent.[40] But China was hit hard by the recession. Speaking to the general condition of the industry Li Junfeng, president of the Chinese Renewable Energy Industries Association, said the "country's solar panel industry was like 'a patient on life support" that would have to undergo radical consolidation and cuts to emerge from the crisis of overcapacity...there is no way to solve this crisis (without) powerful market competition and cruel elimination."[41]

China was not the only country affected. *Forbes* reported on failures in both the US and Europe. As the magazine noted, "The solar manufacturing world began to crumble and, along the way, we saw the demise of high-profile US startups such as Solyndra and Abound Solar and the bankruptcies of long-time players such as Q-Cells in Germany. Dozens of companies in the US, Europe and Asia have gone under."[42] Additional shake-outs hit Siemens, which dumped their entire solar technology business, BP shut their solar division in 2009, and Shell gave-up on solar production in 2012. The Japanese company Sharp, one of the largest and strongest solar module makers, lost $66 million in 2011, and abandoned all manufacturing and distribution in the United States and Europe.

The New York Times offered telling insight on the recession's impact,

> Just a few years ago, Silicon Valley investors were pouring money into solar technologies and talking about how they would bring the same kind of innovation to green energy that they had to the computer chip. But few anticipated

that prices for silicon, the main component of traditional solar panels, would plummet or that Chinese manufacturers, backed by enormous subsidies from their government, would increase solar production capacity by a factor of 17 in just four years. The resulting plunge in solar panel prices wiped out the dream of a new Solar Valley. Despite making advances in the new technology, known as thin-film solar, the American companies just couldn't compete.... Last year, venture capital financing in the solar sector plummeted nearly 50 percent.[43]

All this hardly means the demise of the alternative energy industry. As the economy rebounds so will their markets. But the recession serves as a harsh lesson. Even venture capitalists and high-tech entrepreneurs, the very people market cheerleaders parade as the best innovators, must bow to the deformed logic of competition. Falling prices, increased capacity, and government subsidies, the exact elements needed to make green energy a widely adopted reality, instead caused its bankruptcy.

Protectionist lawsuits were another fall-out from the recession. These took place in both the US and Europe against Chinese producers. Although only one percent of the US energy market, solar power generates about $6 billion a year. When the economic crisis hit, Chinese solar panel companies held about 47 percent of the US market, while nationally based producers controlled 29 percent. A variety of other global manufactures held the rest. In 2012 the Commerce Department issued a 30 percent tariff rate on China following a complaint filed by seven solar panel companies. Ironically, the US-based German subsidiary, Solar World, initiated the action.

The US solar industry split over supporting higher tariffs. The Coalition for Affordable Solar Energy, representing installers that import Chinese panels, argued tariffs would destroy American jobs, as higher panel prices would shrink the market. A large part of the jobs based in the solar industry is generated by contractors and construction companies that put up panels on roofing. The trade group Solar Energy Industries Association also failed to agree on supporting legal action, because many of its members sell millions in equipment and raw materials to China.

The corporations fighting over solar markets are large transnationals, rather than companies with their feet planted in national production chains. Although rhetorical appeals vent concerns for jobs and the sanctity of the American or EU market, profits are their utmost concern. Much of US production is carried out by foreign subsidiaries. As for the biggest US companies, their assembly lines stretch to Asia and beyond. The battle has everything to do with individual corporations fighting over a shrinking world market. The end result of the recession-driven competition was to limit the spread of solar power by making panels more expensive. Higher tariffs meant bankruptcy for some, while increasing profits for others. Eventually the WTO, the ultimate protector and arbiter for global capitalism, said its rules were broken by the heavy tariffs imposed by the US.

Commenting on the actions taken by the Commerce Department, Shayle Kann, head of GTM Research, said "We're basically nowhere near having fixed the structural problem yet. There have been a few bankruptcies and a few plant closures and so on, but at this point it's just a drop in the bucket."[44] A sane and measured approach to global warming would make full use of the entire global capacity, but that would take a significant amount of government planning and ecosocialist rationality. The transnational character of the major alternative energy corporations ties them to logic of global capitalism and its competitive rules for survival. The effects are not only those discussed above, but also low-wage strategies, efficiency drives, outsourcing, and other common methods deemed necessary to flourish.

The Global Solar Industry

To fully understand the recessionary effects on the solar

industry we need to examine data that details its transnational character. Although wind power is more widely utilized, from 2010 to 2013 solar gained 52 percent of all renewable energy investments. Nonetheless, the economic crisis took a toll. There was a 23 percent overall decline in solar investments, as well as steep declines in other alternative energy technologies. The result is solar power still provides only about one percent of global electrical use.[45] The bright side is overall installation of photovoltaic (PV) cells has risen every year since 2005. Looking towards the future the International Energy Agency predicts solar will supply the principal segment of global electricity by 2040.[46]

First Solar is the largest US solar company. While a vertically integrated corporation, its work is mainly focused on building large projects throughout the world. Headquartered in Arizona it maintains offices in the following countries: Mexico, Brazil, Chile, Belgium, Germany, Turkey, United Arab Emirates, Morocco, South Africa, Australia, Japan, China, India, and Thailand. *Forbes* rated First Solar number one among the 25 fastest growing technology companies, and *Solar Power World Magazine* rated it number one among solar contractors. It has production facilities in Malaysia and Ohio, although those in Asia employ ten times the number in Ohio, and produce 83 percent of the company's solar panels. First Solar runs 24 production lines in Malaysia where wages are about $2 an hour for factory labor. The government also provides a ten-year exemption from taxes. When asked why First Solar was so heavily invested in Malaysia, executive vice president Maja Wessels stated, "That's easy, the 10 year tax holiday. When you look at solar manufacturing, and our manufacturing in particular, low labor costs contribute, but those taxes are critical."[47] Global subcontracting is another crucial element in First Solar's corporate strategy. Its website reports creating 40,000 jobs in its worldwide supply chain, but counts only 5,600 Solar First employees. Although the economic crisis caused the company to shut its factory in Germany and put off plans to open facilities in Vietnam, its profit margins have been excellent. In 2014 it reported gross profits in the second quarter of 17 percent, third-quarter profits rose to 21 percent, and fourth-quarter profits were higher still at 30.6 percent. Its reported effective tax rate in 2015 was two to five percent.[48]

An examination of its board of directors is revealing. Michael Ahearn was the first CEO. He was president of the equity investment firm, JWMA Partners, which he founded alongside John Walton. JWMA was formerly called True North Partners, the investment arm of the Walton family of Wal-Mart fame, and First Solar's majority shareholder. This would indicate a strong neoliberal corporate framework, given that Wal-Mart is infamous for harsh labor policies and the political history of the Walton family. Another director, Richard Chapman, was chief financial officer of Walton enterprises and oversaw "all aspects of the Walton family office in Arkansas." Director John Hughes spent ten years with Enron where he was president and chief operating officer of Enron Global Assets. After Enron's spectacular collapse Hughes became an investor in "North American distressed manufacturing assets." Director Paul Stebbins served as an important member of the Business Round Table, "an influential association of chief executive officers of leading US companies," known for its conservative lobbying efforts. He was also on the Leadership Council of the Fix the Debt Campaign. Founded by Erskine Bowles and Senator Alan Simpson the council recommended substantial austerity cuts in the federal budget. Other directors include William Post, deeply involved in both the mining and nuclear industries, and Michael Sweeny, former president of Starbucks.[49] Certainly a stellar cast of transnational capitalists and neoliberals.

The highly regarded Institute for Local Self-Reliance did a study on the Walton family, and found it funds close to two dozen anti-solar groups and continues to donate money to politicians who support the oil industry. Among those receiving money are the American Legislative Exchange Council (ALEC), the American Enterprise Institute, and Americans for Prosperity, all fighting to defeat clean energy policies.[50] Moreover, First Solar has launched a campaign against rooftop solar power in its effort to direct the industry towards large-scale centralized solar farms. Hughes wrote an op-ed for *The Arizona Republic*, arguing that because homeowners sell unused solar power to the utility company they should pay for grid infrastructure. A few months later First Solar went to the Arizona Corporation Commission protesting that subsidies given to homeowners were unfair to large scale solar corporations. Under pressure the Commission recommended raising rooftop solar installation fees from $5 to $21 per month.[51]

Total, the giant French oil and gas transnational, is the majority owner of Sun Power, the second largest US-headquartered solar company. Production is carried out in Malaysia, the Philippines, Mexico, and South Africa. Sun Power is also involved in several joint projects in China, including a partnership with Apple. The company has built large-scale solar farms worldwide. The scale of such projects is quite big. For example, a Sun Power solar farm outside Los Angeles has 1.7 million panels and covers 3,230 acres. The company's second largest shareholder is Wellington, which serves investors from more than 50 countries. Other major shareholders include BlackRock, Deutsche Assets, and Wealth Management, which caters to wealthy individuals, Allianz Global Investing from Germany, and Barclays from the UK.[52]

Globally there are 350 companies that produce solar cells. Ranked by production and shipment China dominates the top twenty with ten corporations, including the top four—Yingli, Trina, JA Solar, and JinkoSolar. Four of the remaining top 20 are from Taiwan, Sharp and Kyocera are headquartered in Japan, and First Solar and SunPower in the US. Canadian Solar ranks number five, but produces through six wholly owned subsidiaries in China. Lastly there is Renewable Energy, a joint concern involving business interests from Norway and Singapore.[53]

It's instructive to take a brief look at the transnational character of the above corporations. In 1999 China only produced one percent of the world's solar cells. The spectacular rise of Chinese production is a measure of the government's focus and support. For example, during the Beijing Olympics all seven major stadiums were run on PV systems. Even so bankruptcy hit Suntech, the previous industrial leader founded by the previous richest man in China. As Suntech fell, Yingli was ready to take first place. Yingli's original IPO was listed on the New York Stock Exchange, and its US subsidiary received $4.5 million in tax credits from the Treasury Department to help build manufacturing operations and headquarters in New York and San Francisco. Beyond the US, Yingli has offices in 30 other countries, and has sold more than 40 million panels to over 50 countries.

ReneSola is another Chinese corporation first established in 2005 and listed on the New York Stock Exchange in 2008. Although only number 20 on the top producers list, ReneSola has manufacturing capacity in China, Poland, India, Malaysia, Turkey, Japan, South Africa, and South Korea. It has 40 worldwide subsidiaries and some 5,600 employees.[54] Its ability to build such a global presence in so short a time is a good indication of just how volatile the industry is. ReneSola was able to take advantage of market openings when bankruptcy forced many others to shut their doors.

Hanwha is another top Chinese company, and carries out work in Germany, Malaysia, South Korea, and China. In 2012 Hanwha acquired Q-Cells, which had been not only the largest producer in Germany, but led the world as recently as 2008 with sales of $1.7 billion. Q-Cells had employed over 2,000 workers, and besides production lines in Germany and Malaysia it maintained joint ventures and subsidiaries in Switzerland, Norway, China, and the US. Germany still leads Europe in PV installations. And Europe has a small global lead in overall PV use. But global overproduction decimated its solar power industry. Among the top 20 PV manufacturers Hanwha is the only one that maintains production in Europe. The rapid decline of Europe's PV manufacturing base points to the chaotic impact of competition, and its negative effects on building a solid foundation for sustainable renewable energy.

In Japan PV production takes place through units in

much bigger transnational corporations. Kyocera manufactures solar panels in Japan, China, Mexico, and the Czech Republic. But Kyocera also holds 219 subsidiaries, employs over 59,000 workers, and earns the majority of its revenues outside Japan. Sharp first began to develop solar cells in 1959. It produces in Japan, but also has two joint ventures in Italy with ENEL Green Power and STMicroelectronics. Much of its manufacturing has moved to China and Taiwan.[55] Worldwide Sharp employs over 49,000 people, just over half outside of Japan.

In summary, we can see the solar industry, although relatively young, is thoroughly integrated into transnational patterns of accumulation and production. It is subject to the rules of competitive global capitalism, rules that demand low-wage production and world-spanning manufacturing networks. While being green, there is no commitment to social justice. That task is left to the progressive wing of the Green New Deal.

A Green New Deal?

As part of global capitalism the top executives, owners, and majority shareholders of alternative energy companies constitute a green sector within the TCC. By necessity a green hegemonic bloc would include them as a key component. Any step away from fossil fuel capitalism is welcomed and historically progressive. But environmental and left activists need be aware of the neoliberal character embedded in the outlook of the green TCC. Such an outlook is defined by global best business practices, working conditions are determined by cost-saving efficiency, low-wage structures constitute a do-or-die competitive edge, and survival is based on the failure of others. They may sincerely want to save the planet, it's just that workers will have to suffer for them to do so.

Green capitalism, as formulated and advanced by the green wing of the TCC, is already here. The 2015 climate conference in Paris raised hopes of a planetary deal to reduce carbon emissions, and was hailed as a turning point in world history by President

Obama and others. The accord was the first time that virtually every country on the planet recognized the threat of global warming and committed themselves to act. But critics note there are no enforcement mechanisms, and that markets, investors and corporations are the structure and method of change. Indeed the conference did attract the attention of major TNCs, with top executives from Bank of America, Citibank, Coca-Cola, DuPont, General Mills, HP, Unilever, BP, Shell, and Total all expressing support for conference goals. Markets also responded to the Paris agreement with the stocks of alternative energy companies gaining between one and 5 percent. Goldman Sachs added an upbeat report, stating the combined market for low-carbon technologies reached $600 billion in 2014. Nancy Pfund, managing partner of DBL Partners, expressed the hope of many concerned investors stating, "It's very hard to go backward from something like this. People are boarding this train, and it's time to hop on if you want to have a thriving, 21st-century economy."[56]

Environmental leaders took a more critical stance towards the accords than those in the corporate community. Renowned climate scientist James Hansen stated, "It's a fraud really, a fake...It's just bullshit... worthless words. There is no action, just promises."[57] Bill McKibben criticized the targets for failing to meet acceptable environmental standards. As McKibben notes, "So the world emerges, finally, with something like a climate accord, albeit unenforceable. If all parties kept their promises, the planet would warm by an estimated 6.3 degrees Fahrenheit...and that is way, way too much. We are set to pass the 1 degree Celsius mark this year, and that's already enough to melt ice caps and push the sea level threateningly higher."[58]

The accord targets a rise of 2 degrees Celsius (35.6 degrees Fahrenheit), and encourages countries to go further, hoping to limit warming to 1.5 Celsius. But research at Climate Central found that 280 million people could be driven from their homes by rising sea levels at 2 degrees Celsius, and 137 million at the lower target level of 1.5. This prompted *The New York Times* environmental journalist Justin Gillis to write, "Reaching either target will be exceedingly difficult...fossil fuel companies are spending hundreds of billions a year looking for new reserves that cannot be burned if either target is to be met...in less than two decades, the nations of the world would likely have to bring an end to gasoline cars, to coal- or gas-burning power plants in their current form, and to planes or ships powered by fossil fuels. Countries have offered no plans that would come remotely close to achieving either goal."[59]

As if to agree with the above critics, but from the opposite point-of-view, the business lobby US Chamber of Commerce stated, "None of the commitments made, including those by the US, are binding, and many aren't even complete. Moreover, Congress must appropriate any funds that the Obama administration has pledged."[60] Senate majority leader Mitch McConnell was quick to note that with a Republican president the Paris agreement would be "shredded in 13 months."[61] It's clear that moving to a green economy will be a fight that splits the capitalist class.

Whether or not the green TCC fraction can build the social base to consolidate a new hegemonic bloc is an open question. And chained to its economic dogma, capitalism may be unable to fully respond within the limits of ecological time. All this raises an important question. How should the left relate to the green wing of the capitalist class? Long time radical activist Tom Hayden poses this question in strategic terms.

> As more finance capitalists go green, the trend will be problematic for those with an anticapitalist or socialist agenda. They blame capitalism for the unfettered exploitation of the Earth's resources and life-supporting ecosystem. History shows that fundamental critique to be on the mark, though it can be dogmatic in its assumptions. To demand that the environmental movement turn socialist —or anarchist—as a precondition of progress, however, is a hopeless venture. Socialists and progressives of all stripes need to recall the lessons

from history where capitalists surprised their detractors by incorporating substantial reforms, partly in order to save capitalism itself. The New Deal was such a model. We are entering another historic moment of potential market adjustment born out of necessity. Progressives can play a vital role in the unpredictable transition ahead. They can help broker a Green New Deal.[62]

Hayden's assessment is right on target. A Green New Deal carries the progressive implications of the New Deal era of the 1930s. The critical support the left gave Roosevelt's New Deal helped produce major reforms that benefited the working class. Roosevelt put together a Keynesian hegemonic bloc that included labor and radical social movements. It didn't lead to a revolution, nor will a Green New Deal. But in advocating a broad front of all those working towards a post fossil fuel society the left will begin to seriously engage in transitional thinking, not just protest and mobilizations. It will be forced to articulate concretely how to develop economic and social strategies and to contend for power. It's important that the left have its own Green New Deal narrative to create a broad base for radical social consciousness and action—one that demands greater democratic content than elite reformism. This means fighting to expand labor rights, and racial and gender justice within the new economy. A left Green New Deal would also include expanding the role of civil society through social movements; creating worker owned cooperatives in the field of green technology; and doing electoral work so that federal, state, and local governments give economic and legislative support for an environmentally sane society.

Green New Deal rhetoric and strategies are already being developed, each with some similarities, but also with their own vision and program. There is the United Nations Environment Programme's Global Green New Deal; the Green New Deal for Europe promoted by the Green European Foundation with backing by the EU parliament's Green Party section; the British

New Deal Group; and the Green Recovery Programme from the Center for American Progress. All have excellent and important components of a progressive sustainable strategy. A summary of their programs is provided by Birgit Mahnkopt in Table 3.1.[63]

For all the thought and insight that has gone into these programs they largely ignore, or give little role, to social equality. But we need a political approach that ties the economic crisis and environmental collapse together, with capitalism as their root cause. It's a new tale of two cities, not London and Paris, but Detroit and New Orleans. The United Nations makes the strongest connection between environmental destruction and its devastating effects on the poor. Yet it advocates the "privatization of ecological commons and the financialization of nature," the exact economic foundation that is causing the problem.[64] All of the above programs are trapped by the reigning hegemonic market ideology. As Kathleen Mcafee noted, "In this world view private initiatives, monetary pricing and market exchange are inherently more efficient than collective action, public planning, and regulation, and all resources and services are potentially tradable commodities."[65] Birgit Mahnkopt adds another factor most often overlooked. The green economy creates jobs in male-dominated industries such as manufacturing and construction. Mahnkopt argues that human services must be seen as part of a sustainable economy, one that creates gender equality as part of its articulated strategy.

Decentralized solar panel technology can play an important role in a left Green New Deal because it's adoptable by individual homeowners, farmers, and businesses. Moreover, the widespread application of residential solar systems has already been proven in Germany, Japan, and a number of other countries, even as far north as Canada's Hudson Bay. In fact, Germany is a leader in solar energy and wind power. The transition from nuclear power and fossil fuels created 400,000 jobs and 900 new energy co-ops. Overall solar accounts for seven percent of Germany's energy needs. The spread of rooftop solar panels was encouraged with government subsidies, and above market rates for excess energy

Organization	Seize (Billions)	Measures	Job creation
WORLD			
United Nations Environment Programme	US$750	Retrofitting buildings; More energy efficient and less polluting modes of transport; Smart grids and renewable infrastructures; Sustainable agriculture and freshwater systems	ILO: 15-60 million
EUROPEAN UNION			
Green European Foundation	€300	Sustainable transport policy; Sustainable energy policy; Sustainable resource policy	6 million
UNITED STATES			
Center for American Progress	US$100	Retrofitting buildings; Mass transit and freight transport; Electrical grid transmission systems; Wind power; Solar power; Next-generation bio fuels	2 million
SOUTH KOREA			
Government	US$38	Low carbon vehicles; Mass transport; Water and waste management	960,000
SOUTH AFRICA			
Government	N/A	Waste management; Water management; Green buildings; Sustainable transport; Clean energy and energy efficiency; Agriculture and forestry	300,000 (in renewable energy)

Table 3.1 Green New Deals

Source: Birgit Mahnkopt, "Green new Deal, Green Economy and Green Jobs: Consequences for Environmental and Social Justice," <http://www.global-labour-university.org/fileadmin/GLU_conference_2014/papers/Hermann_Christoph.pdf>.

sold back to the utility grid. In Japan 95 percent of all solar energy is produced by rooftop units. In the US, Hawaii is leading the nation with 12 percent of homes using solar panels. Additionally, in 2015 the White House announced an effort to triple the capacity of solar and other renewable energy systems it installs in federally subsidized housing.

But such an approach to energy is under attack, and not only by the Waltons and First Solar. In the UK rooftop panels experienced a boom under a government subsidy program. In a five-year period Britain went from having virtually no homes powered by solar energy to nearly 750,000. But with the Conservative Party holding a majority in Parliament subsidies were cut by 87 percent, effectively shutting down the industry. Similar attacks have taken place in Spain where the conservative-led government imposed a retroactive cut in subsidy payments. Conservatives also initiated plans to charge fees against independent rooftop panel owners who generate their own energy. As many as 60,000 small and large producers will be affected, many facing insolvency. In another small but telling example, Ohio's Republican dominated public utilities board stopped a solar farm from being built on strip-mined land. As *The New York Times* reported, "Many utilities are trying desperately to stem the rise of solar, either by reducing incentives, adding steep fees or effectively pushing home solar companies out of the market."[66]

Besides the Waltons, attacks on US home-owned solar power comes from a person many consider a progressive capitalist, Warren Buffett. Nevada has been called the poster child of rooftop installations with the highest per capita solar employment in the nation. But NV Energy, owned by Buffett's Berkshire Hathaway, lobbied hard to get the Public Utilities Commission of Nevada to slash credits and raise fees by 40 percent. The result was bankruptcy, lay-offs, and higher bills in a once thriving new industry. NV Energy has a government-guaranteed 10.5 percent return on equity. But when solar rooftop owners sell excess energy to NV there is no profit. As Buffett once stated, "Owning utilities isn't a way to get rich, it's a way to stay rich."[67] That is, unless a system of citizen-owned alternative energy upsets your revenue stream.

A decentralized system of solar power can have a profound social impact in helping to create a people-centered sustainable energy network. This would undermine not only the fossil fuel industry, but also the big utility corporations that control the flow of energy. Utility lines and national networks would still be needed, but they would hold less political clout and economic power. While an array of energy technologies, producers, and providers will be required in the future, decentralized solar technology can be the key component in a world built around sustainable energy models. If solar panels existed on the roofs of millions of homes, schools, and businesses, people would have a largely independent supply of energy. A decentralized system would also prevent the rise of new green energy monopolies that employ neoliberal policies to labor costs and market pricing. Consequently, the transnational character of the industry today stands in sharp contrast to the ecosocialist future we need to build.

Another key reason to fight for a decentralized system of energy is the possibility of creating thousands of worker-owned installation cooperatives in communities across the country. Such cooperatives in low-income and minority neighborhoods could be built around local hiring and training. Once constructed large centralized wind and solar farms employ only a handful of workers. But the installation and maintenance of rooftop panels would provide a large and long lasting job base. The connection between a decentralized system of solar power, worker-owned cooperatives, and racial justice is of particular importance. It ties job creation to worker empowerment, combats racism rooted in economic discrimination, begins to address youth unemployment, and strengthens communities through stakeholder involvement. It offers a strategy that can untie the economic exploitation of capitalism to racism, by presenting a concrete strategy for oppositional institutional development. Van Jones and his organization, Green for All, have been promoting a strategy along these lines for a number of years.[68] Moreover, the Evergreen Corporation in Cleveland is a living example of the strategy in motion. Evergreen has already brought together the issues of minority employment and sustainability, developing worker-owned hydroponic urban agriculture, solar panel installations, and green industrial laundry services. Such efforts should become an important part of a left Gramscian outlook, building working class institutional power that promotes a practical understanding of how to run a sustainable economy, rather than just demanding one.

Marx pointed out that revolutions often occur when the relations of production prevent society from initiating the necessary introduction of new groundbreaking methods of production, and the full application of the most advanced technologies.

Industrialization could not be fully developed within the political restraints of feudal society and the power of the aristocracy, whose fortunes were tied to the land and the social relations between landlord and peasant. A society built upon institutions that guarded such relationships could not institute the changes demanded by the new forces of production that included steel mills, textile factories, and a large urban working class. One of the great historic innovations of capitalism is its ability to constantly revolutionize technology. Developing green technology is not the problem. Creating the social conditions for its full use and implementation is.

Today's social relations are trapped in the absolute need to extract profits from labor under the whip of competition. This internal logic continues to drive the system and creates all the problems discussed above. Green capitalism may have the ability to develop the appropriate technology, but not the means to fully realize its social organization. The fast approaching tipping point for planetary warming may also be the tipping point for capitalism. Unfortunately green capitalism will offer too little too late. But perhaps a Green New Deal can construct a transition to building a democratic ecosocialism where the full flowering of sustainability can be achieved for both the planet and for people.

Endnotes

1   Robert Ruben, "Robert Rubin: How ignoring climate change could sink the U.S. economy." *Washington Post* (July 24, 2014).

2   Burt Helmjan, "Climate Change's Bottom Line," *The New York Times* (January 31, 2015).

3   Ibid.

4   William K. Carroll, *The Making of a Transnational Capitalist Class: Corporate Power in the 21st Century* (Zed Books: London and New York, 2010).

5   Jean Philippe Sapinski, <https://www.researchgate.net/publication/280080550_Climate_capitalism_and_the_global_corporate_elite_network>, (2015).

6   Ibid, 5.

7   Tom Cahill, "Bill Gates: Only Socialism Can Save the Climate, 'The Private Sector is Inept'," <http://usuncut.com/climate/bill-gates-only-socialism-can-save-us-from-climate-change/> (October 26, 2015).

8   Coral Davenport, and Nick Wingfield, "Bill Gates Takes on Climate Change With Nudges and a Powerful Rolodex," *The New York Times* (December 8, 2015).

9   Knight Frank, *The Wealth Report 2016*, (London: Knight Frank, 2016).

10   Paul Hawken, Amory Lovins and Hunter Lovins, *Natural Capitalism: Creating the Next Industrial Revolution* (New York: Little, Brown and Company, 1999); Paul Hawken, *The Ecology of Commerce* (New York: Harper, 1993); Amory Lovins, and Hunter Lovins, *Factor Four. Doubling Wealth—Halving Resource Use* (London: Earthscan Publications Ltd, 1997).

11   D. Shapley, "Al Gore's 10-Year Plan to Solve the Climate Crisis," thedailygreen, <http://www.thedailygreen.com/environmental-news/latest/gore-speech-47071701> (2008).

12   Irene Hell, "Rockefeller Fund: 'The oil age is coming to an end,'" <http://www.dw.com/en/rockefeller-fund-the-oil-age-is-coming-to-an-end/a-18854028> (2015).

13   Ban Ki-moon, "We need a big green jobs machine," <http://sfgate.com/cgi-bin/article.gci?f=/c/a/2008/11/26/EDHN14BDV9.DTL> (November 26, 2008).

14   Mark Jacobson, and Mark Delucchi, "A Path to Sustainable Energy," *Scientific America* (November 2009).

15   Justin Gillis, "U.N. Climate Panel Warns Speedier Action needed to Avert Disaster," *The New York Times* (April 13, 2014).

16   Joseph A Schumpeter, *Capitalism, Socialism and Democracy* (London: Routledge, 1942).

17   Bain Report, "A world awash in money," *Insights* (November 14, 2012).

18   Intelligence Community Assessment, Global Water Security, Intelligence Community, Washington DC (2012), iii.

19   Edward Wong, "Chinese Glacier's Retreat Signals Trouble for Asian Water Supply," *The New York Times* (December 8, 2015).

20   Ibid, 10.

21   Richard St'ahel, "Environmental Crisis and Political Revolutions," Paper delivered at Third bi-annual conference of the Network for the Critical Studies of Global Capitalism, Prague, Czech Republic (September 26, 2015).

22   Randy Paynter, "The US Carbon Footprint and Good Business: the Rest of the World Gets It, Why Don't We?" <www.care2.com/causes/global-warming/blog> (2010).

23   Thomas Friedman, *Hot, Flat, and Crowded* (Farrar, Straus and Giroux: New York, 2008), 172-73.

24   Murray Bookchin, *Remaking Society* (Boston: South End Press, 1990); John Bellamy Foster, *Marx's Ecology: Materialism and Nature* (Monthly Review Press: New York, 2000).

25   Bill McKibben, "Global Warming's Terrifying New Math," *Rolling Stone*, (August 2, 2012).

26   Ibid.

27   Ed Crooks, "Exxon warns global warming targets 'unlikely' to be met," *Financial Times* (March 21, 2014).

28   Arnulf Jager-Waldau, PV Status Report 2014. European Commission, DG Joint Research Centre, Institute for Energy and Transport, Renewable Energy Unity, (November 2014).

29   Jeff Goodell, "As the world burns," *Rolling Stone*, (January 6, 2010).

30   Justin Gillis, "U.N. Climate Panel Warns Speedier Action Is Needed to Avert Disaster," *Financial Times*, (April 13, 2014).

31   Walden Bello, "Will Capitalism Survive Climate Crisis? Global Labour Institute," <http://www.globallabour.info/en/2008/04/will_capitalism_survive_climat_1.html> (April 30, 2008).

32   Jerry Harris, "Emerging Third World Powers: China, India and Brazil," *Race and Class,* Vol. 46, no. 3 (2005); Jerry Harris, "Statist Globalization in China, Russia and the Gulf States," *Science & Society,* 73, no. 1 (2009); Jerry Harris, "Desert dreams in the Gulf: transnational crossroads for the global elite," *Race and Class,* Vol. 54, no. 4 (2013); Jerry Harris, "Outward bound: transnational capitalism in China," in *Financial Elites and Transnational Business: Who Rules the World?*, Editors Georgina Murray and John Scott (Edgar Elgar Publishing: UK, 2012).

33   William I. Robinson, "The transnational state and the BRICS: a global capitalism perspective," *Third World Quarterly,* Vol. 36, no. 1: 1-21 (2015).

34   Edward Wong, "Report Ties Coal Plants to Water Shortages in Northern China," *The New York Times,* (March 22, 2016).

35   Edward Wong, "A Glut of Coal-Fired Plants Raises Doubts About China's Energy Priorities," *The New York Times,* (November 11, 2015).

36   Tom Randall, "Solar and Wind Just Did the Unthinkable," <http://www.bloomberg.com/news/articles/2016-01-14/solar-and-wind-just-did-the-unthinkable> (January 14, 2016).

37   Kearrin Sims, "The Asian Development Bank and the production of poverty: Neoliberalism, technocratic modernization and land dispossession in the Greater Mekong Subregion," *Singapore Journal*

of Tropical Geography (2015).

38   David Harvey, *A Brief History of Neoliberalism* (Oxford University Press: Oxford, 2005).

39   Sims, The Asian Development Bank and the production of poverty.

40   Pilita Clark, "China Retakes Renewables Investment Lead," *Financial Times*, (January 14, 2013).

41   Ibid.

42   Ucilia Wang, "Growth Pace Slows for the Global Solar Market." *Forbes*, <http://www.forbes.com/sites/uciliawang/2013/02/21/the-slowing-pace-of-growth-for-the-global-solar-market/> (2012).

43   Diane Cardwell, and Keith. Bradsher, "Chinese Firm Buys US Solar Start-Up," *The New York Times*, (January 9, 2013).

44   Diane Cardwell, "Solar Tariffs Upheld, but May Not Help in US," *The New York Times*, (November 7, 2012).

45   Gardner Harris, "U.S. Unveils Measures to Encourage Solar Power Use," *The New York Times*, (August 24, 2015).

46   Jager-Waldau, PV Status Report 2014.

47   Keith Bradsher, "Solar Rises in Malaysia During Trade Wars Over Panels," *The New York Times*, (December 11, 2014).

48   First Solar, <http://www.firstsolar.com/About-Us/Locations.aspx> (2015).

49   First Solar, <http://www.firstsolar.com/en/About-Us/leadership#bod> (2015).

50   Institute for Local Self-Reliance, <http://www.ilsr.org/walton-report/> (2013).

51   "ACC judge kicks APS proposed solar fee hike down the road into rate case," <http://www.bizjournals.com/phoenix/blog/energy-inc/2015/08/acc-judge-kicks-aps-proposed-solar-fee-hike-down.html> (August 4, 2015).

52   Sun Power, <http://investors.sunpower.com/annuals.cfm> (2015).

53   Jager-Waldau, PV Status Report 2014.

54   Ibid; <http://www.renesola.com/article/aboutus.html> (2015).

55   Jager-Waldau, PV Status Report 2014.

56   Clifford Krauss, and Keith Bradsher, "A Signal to Industry to Go Green in an Era of Carbon Reduction," *The New York Times*, (December 13, 2015).

57   Daniel Marans, "Legendary Climate Scientist Is Not Impressed With The Paris Talks," <http://www.huffingtonpost.com/entry/james-hansen-paris-talks_566c48dce4b011b83a6b7acc?rne6zuxr> (December 12, 2015).

58   Bill McKibben, "Falling Short on Climate in Paris," *The New York Times*, (December 13, 2015).

59   Justin Gillis, "Climate Accord Is a Healing Step, if Not a Cure," *The New York Times*, (December 12, 2015).

60   Justin Gillis, "To Achieve Paris Climate Goals, U.S. Will Need New Laws," *The New York Times*, (December 19, 2015).

61   Ibid.

62   Tom Hayden, "Environmentalists, Capitalists Should Broker Green New Deal," *San Francisco Chronicle*, (July 8, 2014).

63   Birgit Mahnkopt, "Green new Deal, Green Economy and Green Jobs: Consequences for Environmental and Social Justice," <http://www.global-labour-university.org/fileadmin/GLU_conference_2014/papers/Hermann_Christoph.pdf> (2014).

64   Ibid.

65   Kathleen Mcafee, "Nature in the market-World: Ecosystem Services and Inequality," *Development*, Vol. 55, No. 1 (2012), 25-33.

66   Diane Cardwell, "Solar Power Battle Puts Hawaii at Forefront of Worldwide Changes," *The New York Times*, (April 18, 2015).

67   Alexis Bonogofsky, "Nevada Residents Fight Energy Monopoly's Attempts to Control Solar Power," *Truthout*, (February 24, 2016).

68   Van Jones, *The Green Collar Economy* (Harper One: New York, 2008).

Chapter Four

THE CONFLICT IN UKRAINE: BETWEEN TWO WORLDS

"Nothing is more precious than independence and self-determination."
Ho Chi Minh

The Ukrainian conflict has been a complex battle between numerous national and transnational political and economic interests. Unfortunately it is commonly portrayed solely through the framework of old Cold War rivalries, the US and NATO versus Russia, borders and territorial control, a choice between joining the democratic West, or continuing under the heel of authoritarian Russia. The struggle goes to the very concept of what constitutes the Ukrainian nation, with different nationalisms at odds within the country. All of these tensions are present and powerful, but transnational economic ties play a significant role in how the political battles have twisted and turned. These crosscurrents of interests are a major barrier to settling the crisis.

The Ukraine has become an unfortunate example of both old and new contradictions, a mixture of both national and transnational conflicts, and illustrates how they push and pull the upheaval. The Ukraine is caught in a transformative historic period. When the modern nation-centric system was established in

Europe in 1648 with the Treaty of Westphalia, national sovereignty became a principle of co-existence. Non-interference in domestic affairs alongside a balance of power was the basis for maintaining peace. Eventually the principle of sovereignty became central to international law, although constantly violated over the years particularly with the advent of colonialism. Sovereignty also came to mean control of the national economy by each individual nation-state and its local capitalist class. But globalization has unleashed cross-border flows of trillions of dollars, established transnational production chains and is in the process of creating world governance bodies. Consequently, the tension between national political legitimacy and transnational capital has become a central contradiction that characterizes the current transformation period of capitalism.

The National/Transnational Conflict

Critics of transnational capitalist class theory often describe it as one-sided. They wrongly assert TCC theory ignores the nation-state by arguing the world system is ruled by a unified transnational capitalist class whose hegemonic project is complete. Examples are offered of nationalist ideology and nation-state military power to prove that national interests are still primary and politically dominant. This analysis is evident in mainstream as well as left interpretations. But TCC theory has always positioned history as a dialectic, a moving process of continuous change, impelled by ever-present contradictions. Therefore, the world system is defined by uneven and combined development, and a struggle between old and new forces. This offers a deeper understanding of transformation, not a march of stages lined-up in some historic queue, demanding we see the world as only nation-centric states, or a fully arrived transnational system.

Rather the current dialectic is seen in national relationships and social structures that are in constant struggle with emerging transnational forces. All the old forms of power, habits, identities, and privileges fight to maintain their full existence. As a result class contradictions erupt between the working class and capitalist class, between different strata of the same class, and social forces embedded in old and new forms of production. This includes both progressive and reactionary tendencies from the industrial era that battle for position and influence as global capitalism seeks hegemony within nations and across borders. Additionally, there are religious fundamentalists who fight against the advances of cosmopolitanism. Neither the nation-centric nor transnational relationships exist in isolation from the other. They continually define and determine each other within a changing balance of forces. This unity of opposites in tension and conflict is what produces the historic transformation towards global capitalism. No outcome is predetermined, but produced by the dynamic itself. Consequently, what aspects of nation-centric relationships survive depends on the agency of political struggle. Although transnationalization is on the ascent, and the nation-centric system on the decline, national forms can still become the dominant element in particular contradictions. The historic dialectic is much like the birth of a child. Each new being has the DNA of its parents, and as it grows it's conditioned by the habits, culture, and lessons that surround its development. Yet each new being is totally unique and much more than a reflection of its DNA and upbringing. The past exists in the present and the future. So too with social systems. One can always point to the old and argue it's the totality of the present, but only at the risk of political folly, mistaking the parent for the child.

An additional consideration is that each country assimilates into global circuits of accumulation in its own unique manner and pace. Uneven and combined development is a principle of the historic process. Diverse elements make up the character of a country and determine its transformation—important elements such as natural resources, the strength of the financial system, the level of economic development, technological knowledge, the quality of the educational system, history of class struggle, character of political democracy, role of the state, and a country's place in the world system, politically and geographically. As former national champions turn into global corporations the capitalist class reshapes the domestic economy and social relations. In response the state must restructure its institutions and rules to house the new modes of accumulation. Not only the relationships with private sector workers change, but those working for government also come under neoliberal coercion. Major trade arrangements must be ratified, banks bailed out, corporate taxes cut, and workers fired. This mixture of national and transnational conditions creates a powerful vortex of pressure. Class conflicts are the responsibility of the nation-state, since political and social compliance are the tasks of local governments concerned with their own legitimacy. Therefore, national conditions are key to understanding how globalization is reshaping the world.

The dialectic between nation-centric beliefs and structures, and the powerful and rapid thrust of global capitalism is fully on display in the Ukraine, a prism of current contradictions. Perhaps the only possible peaceful resolution was a state-sanctioned and internationally overseen vote on self-determination in both Crimea and eastern Ukraine. A referendum could have offered choices between a federated union, autonomy, independence, or annexation to Russia. This would have created a sovereign political process, limited outside interference, and offered a democratic solution. Shortly after the Maidan protest overthrew Victor Yanukovych, groups in Donbass called for just such a referendum, but Kiev ignored their demands. Holding such elections was not farfetched. Similar elections on independence have been held in Scotland and Quebec, and in both elections the majority voted to continue their union with the national state. In Spain, Catalan and Basque have been demanding similar votes. Therefore, such a path to political resolution is well established in contemporary Western nations.

The Bolsheviks were the first modern political party to establish the right to self-determination, and they carried out the policy by recognizing the independence of Finland. After Napoleon's disastrous eastern campaign, Finland had come under Russian rule in 1812 in an agreement between Russia and France. A century later, with the overthrow of the Czar in 1917, Finland called for its independence. But the Cadet Party, which headed the government and represented the capitalist class, refused to recognize Finland's right to self-determination. Lenin reaffirmed the Bolshevik program stood "for the *right* of Finland, as of all the other underprivileged nations, to *secede from* Russia...If we are really against annexations, we should say: give Finland the *right of* secession!" (emphasis in the original)[1] On December 6, 1917 Finland declared independence. Shortly afterwards the Communists ratified Finland's freedom. The highest Soviet body, the All-Russian Central Executive Committee, stated, "The people of Finland have by this step taken their fate in their own hands; a step both justified and demanded by present conditions. The people of Finland feel deeply that they cannot fulfill their national and international duty without complete sovereignty. The century-old desire for freedom awaits fulfillment now; Finland's people step forward as a free nation among the other nations in the world."[2]

The situation in the Ukraine isn't fully similar to the historic position of Finland, which was an oppressed nation. Eastern and western Ukraine are competing regions with different national aspirations. But the problem does closely resemble Scotland, Quebec, and the nationalist demands in Catalan. Therefore, a referendum on self-determination could be reasonably held within the current system of western sovereignty, and Finland remains a relevant historic experience.

Things Fall Apart

As with many modern states, Ukraine had a long historic development. Important parts of modern day Ukraine were incorporated into Russia as early as 1654. The southern and eastern sections were added in 1920. The far western region integrated in the 1940s after 200 years under Austrian-Hungarian rule. Finally Crimea was added in 1954. Until 1991 Ukraine never existed as a state. Consequently, regional divisions of history, language, identity, culture, and religion have been present for many years.

These differences have been manipulated by an economic and political ruling class that drove the country to ruin even while they became fabulously wealthy.

After independence the economy revolved around the export of raw materials, such as agricultural goods, iron ore, and coal. Although the eastern economy was industrialized it had been closely integrated with Russia. Now its aged technology makes it uncompetitive in the global market. For example, a ton of steel required 52.8 hours of work in the Ukraine, compared to only 16.8 hours of labor in Germany. The western region, with the national capital Kiev, was largely agrarian and after independence looked increasingly towards Europe. The dominant sector of the ruling class was the owner of these industries, coming to power through the privatization of state-owned corporations. This oligarchy did little to develop the internal market, instead exporting $165 billion to offshore tax havens, mostly to banks in Cyprus. When the global economic crisis hit the bottom fell out of the export economy, with GDP falling 15 percent in 2009. The rise in foreign debt gives a clear picture of the economic collapse. In 2004 gross foreign debt stood at $23.8 billion, by 2013 it had grown to $126 billion. Millions left to find work in Russia and the EU causing a 13 percent drop in the population. By 2012 workers abroad sent home $7.5 billion dollars, more than the $6 billion in foreign direct investment.[3]

It was the internal economic crisis and corruption of the ruling class that brought on the Ukrainian crisis. Although outside interference by Europe and US played an important role, the roots of the rebellion were to be found in domestic conditions. But widespread anger lacked progressive political direction, with no influential left party or social movement that could offer leadership on the scale of Syriza or Podemos. Instead nationalists inflamed regional identities on both sides, through which foreign interests took advantage.

Victor Shapinov, leader of the left-wing Ukrainian political organization Borotba, offers an insightful analysis of the transnational elites in the Ukraine. Shapinov argues the new billionaires had accumulated enough capital to buy into financial and industrial assets in the West, and abandon crisis ridden Ukraine.

> This shift was so-called 'Eurointegration', through which the Ukrainian billionaires, in exchange for ending protection of the internal market and effectively surrendering it to international monopolies, received recognition from Europe. The fact that the price would be the destruction of various sectors of industry and a new spiral of deindustrialization, with an inevitable growth of unemployment and other social ills, did not trouble this peak ruling-class group in the least.[4]

But the Eurointegration strategy lacked hegemony. It was questioned by national capitalists still attached to the internal economy, and lacked enough capital to join the transnational elite. This contradiction laid the groundwork for the explosion known as the Maidan movement, Maidan being Kiev's central plaza where the protest erupted. The initial crisis revolved around both the West and Russia offering Ukraine desperately needed loans to meet their debt obligations. President Victor Yanukovych vacillated between transnational and national interests, and the pull of the West and Russia. The Russian package of $15 billion lacked the neoliberal reforms demanded by the IMF, which threatened important interests of the national bourgeoisie. Moreover, Yanukovych's political base was in pro-Russia eastern Ukraine, where he had received overwhelming electoral support. Finally Yanukovych backed out of signing the IMF agreement, setting off the protests in Kiev. For western Ukrainians, who looked to Europe as both a democratic and economic alternative to Russia, turning down the Western offer was a political choice they could not tolerate. This began the Maidan protests that the government moved to repress.

These actions only radicalized the movement, in which reactionary nationalists now gained influence. Within western Ukraine a virulent anti-Russian narrative had been kept alive by right-wing groups, many of whom celebrated the pro-Nazi activities of Ukrainian fascists in World War II. With an ideological, cohesive and motivated membership they were able to play a leadership role in the demonstrations, even though the majority were liberal pro-Western activists.

When Yanukovych was driven from office and fled to Russia, many people in the east felt that the national elections had been violated. Others had never fully accepted the split from Russia. Now an eastern movement began to advocate for autonomy or independence. Kiev launched armed attacks against the east, declaring an "anti-terrorist" offensive. Yet protests in the east were at that time no different from those that took place in the west. With growing armed conflicts, nationalists on both sides essentialized and emphasized regional differences. Eastern Ukrainians were characterized as vulgar, ignorant, and less educated. In return the government in Kiev was painted as a fascist junta, and a threat to Russian language and cultural rights. Both regional nationalisms fed off of each other, the result being greater violence and civil war.

The Neo-Fascist Threat

When the new government formed in Kiev six members from the Svoboda party received cabinet positions, including national security, military, prosecutorial, and educational affairs. Svoboda claims the tradition of the pro-Nazi Ukrainian Insurgent Army, which participated in the mass killing of 70,000 Jewish and Polish citizens in World War II. Various reactionary nationalist parties hold about 20 percent of the seats in Parliament. Moreover, with a weak national army the oligarchical government turned to neo-Nazi and right-wing militias to launch attacks on the protest movement in the east. There are about 30 such militias engaging in battle. One of the most important is the Azov battalion, which carries the Wolfsangel flag, formerly used by Hitler's SS divisions. In an interview their commander, Andriy Biletsky, stated, "The historic mission of our nation in this critical moment is to lead the

White Races of the world in a final crusade for their survival. A crusade against the Semite-led Untermenschen (sub-humans)."[5]

The Azov battalion eventually joined the official command structure of the Ukrainian army, but another powerful militia, the Right Sector, still operates independently. In a convoluted anti-Russian alliance, three battalions of Islamic Chechen nationalists crossed the Russian border and joined the battle under the leadership of the Right Sector. But fighting in eastern Ukraine is only part of the group's agenda. In 2015 the Right Sector engaged in a shoot-out with west Ukrainian police and rival groups over the control of the cigarette market, a market that was also a point of violent conflict between criminal gangs during Russia's rush to privatization. When Right Sector leaders threatened to hold armed protests in Kiev, *The New York Times* reported that officials were worried over a "possible second wave of the revolution in Ukraine, led by this extreme right wing of the country's politics, particularly as the economy unravels."[6] Rival neo-Nazi leader Belitsky stated, "This is a gravely dangerous situation for our country. With the economy falling, social instability rising and a war in the east, the last thing we need is a second front."[7] Right Sector leader Dmitro Yarosh received 127,000 votes in the 2014 election, but the party itself only won 1.6 percent of the total vote.

Reining in various independent militias has been an ongoing problem for the Poroshenko regime, but control of the government is clearly in the hands of a neoliberal pro-Western elite. The parties of President Petro O. Poroshenko and Prime Minister Arseniy P. Yatsenyuk won the largest number of seats in Parliament, with 21.4 and 21.7 percent respectively.

Whether or not a right-wing putsch occurs, proto fascist forces are an important part of the governing alliance. The situation is reminiscent of how the German bourgeoisie allied with the Nazis, only to lose control over their fascist friends. But Viktor Shapinov, who along with members of Borotba fled to Crimea, offers a different analysis. As he argues, "This situation does not exactly resemble classical German or Italian fascism. It's more like the pro-fascist paramilitary movements of the 1970s and 1980s in

Latin America. The oligarchs create paramilitary groups and use them to spread terror."[8] No matter the exact state of fascism in the Ukraine, the West has largely ignored and covered up their role. The alliance between neoliberal transnational capitalists and extreme right-wing nationalists may seem strange, but such politics are also present in the Republican Party with its Tea Party wing, in India in the BJP, with the ruling Justice and Development Party in Turkey, and the governing Liberal Democratic Party in Japan. It's an unstable alliance based in the transition of conservative politics between nation-centric and transnational capitalist eras, new and old forms of right-wing hegemony, the nationalist variety being the most reactionary because it is linked to disappearing nation-centric structures, national modes of accumulation, racial myths, and patriotic symbols, aspects of which transnational capitalists find politically useful, but a strategic dead-end to their global aspirations. In the Ukraine the civil war is the cement that holds the coalition together, yet continuing internal struggles are sure to unfold.

Outside Interference

Ukrainian nationalism and pro-Western elites provided the spark to reignite big power nationalism and competition over territorial alliances. Cold War rivalries were buried in a shallow grave, easy to revive in a battle over energy, raw materials, agricultural goods, and border security. Russian control over Eastern Europe was an accepted arrangement in the balance of power among international realists who ruled foreign policy circles before the fall of the Berlin Wall. Since 1989 Russia has been eager to reassert influence over its former territorial regions, and viewed Western meddling in Georgia and the Ukraine as a threat to its border security. Powerful nations regard surrounding countries as their natural sphere of influence and their personal geostrategic buffer zone. The desire of their neighbors to chart their own independent paths is of little importance. In this regard Russian chauvinism is no different from Western imperialism. Russia's most provocative act was their seizure of Crimea. Crimea had been a base for the Russian Black Sea fleet since 1783, and the seizure was popular among Crimea's Russian-speaking population.

Nevertheless, it was a violation of national sovereignty, and increased Ukrainian nationalism and Western influence. As left scholar and activist Alexander Buzgalin has pointed out, Russia has a "blatantly contradictory position ...on the right of peoples to self-determination. If the peoples of Crimea or Novorossiya want to secede from Ukraine, the Russian government maintains, they have a legitimate democratic right to do so. But if a particular national grouping *within* Russian aims to secede...then that is a criminal offence."[9] In the long-term Russia's strategy seems to focus on keeping Ukraine out of NATO, protecting Russian language and cultural rights, and maintaining strong ties with the Ukrainian economy.

Russian political elites and private transnational capitalists have their own unique relationship. It centers on balancing a historically strong state and a private capitalist class that became rich by looting state property. After the fire sale held by the Yeltsin regime, Putin reasserted central power by sending a number of oligarchs to jail, making energy a state-dominated industry, and promoting certain financial institutions. Oligarchs who proved themselves politically loyal, or at least not disruptive, became part of the ruling hegemonic bloc. Both state-owned industries and banks, as well as private industries, became closely integrated with global capital. The result was a state-led process of transnationalization.[10]

This presented a profound contradiction for the Russian political and economic elite. As Russian Marxist Boris Kagarlitsky has pointed out, "The situation confronting our elites in this respect is more or less straightforward, they cannot enter actively into confrontation with the West without dealing crushing blows to their own interests, to their own capital holdings and to their own networks, methods of rule and way of life."[11] According to Credit Suisse Russia's 110 billionaires control 35 percent of the nation's wealth. There is no doubt that the economic boycott has hurt. FDI inflows fell from $69 billion in 2013 to $21 billion in 2014. This dropped Russia from the fifth place to number 16 in attracting global FDI. But oligarchy investments abroad still continued to occupy an important part of the Russian economy. In 2013 FDI outflows of $87 billion put the Russia TCC in fourth place among global investors. In 2014 the outflow was reduced to $56 billion, but the oligarchy still occupied sixth place as the world's most important foreign investors.[12]

In the west Gideon Rachman, the political editor for the *Financial Times,* made similar observations. As he stated, "The deep connections between politics and business in modern Russia mean that the country's most powerful people often have a direct personal stake in the continued prosperity of Western Europe. They have business relationships to maintain, investments to protect, houses in the south of France, children at school in Britain…people with international business interests tend not be nationalists. They cannot afford to be."[13] But this also held true for western transnational capitalists; the ties are a two-way street crossing borders and nationalist politics. Hurting Russian economic interests hurt Western interests as well.

Even so, the ghosts of superpower nationalism remains influential among those in top Kremlin positions, 58 percent of whom are former members of the security, police, and military apparatus, as is Putin himself. Collectively this group is known as the 'siloviki,' many of whom head major state-owned industries and banks. While the siloviki represent great power nationalism within the state, their economic position ties them to transnational capital. The duality of their interests, as well as the global ties of the private sector oligarchs, is the contradiction at the heart of Russian politics. Nationalism still rears its head, particularly over issues that touch upon regions of the old Soviet Union. And no region has greater political and economic significance than the Ukraine. If Russia is to regain status as a core country in the world system, it needs the ecological and industrial resources available just across its border. Taking all these factors into account, a shifting balance between nationalism and transnationalism is a central dialectic within Russia itself, as it is between Russia and the EU and US.

Besides geostrategic concerns the Ukraine is a major consumer of Russian exports, including energy. It also has acted as a major transshipment point for Russian energy to Western Europe, which receives 40 percent of its oil and gas from Russia. Additionally, the Ukraine has large shale gas and oil reserves, the majority located close to the Russian border in Crimea, and along Crimea's Black Sea coastline. As part of its annexation Russia claimed a new maritime zone of 36,000 square miles, more than three times the size of the Crimean landmass. Western Ukraine has long been considered a breadbasket for Europe, being the world's third largest corn exporter and fifth largest exporter of wheat. In recent years foreign agro transnationals have purchased 1.6 million hectares of land. Lastly the Ukraine is a source of cheap labor, in 2014 the average net wage being 150 Euros, compared to the average EU wage of 1489 Euros.[14] Given all these elements there is a lot at stake, and the unique divide politically and economically between western and eastern Ukraine plays to the old divisions between West and East.

Under attack and labeled as "terrorists," the people in eastern Ukraine organized armed self-defense militias to combat the western military offensive. But the battle did not remain an internal dispute. Russian arms and volunteers quickly crossed the border to join the fight. Participation of the Russian army has never been definitively proven, but many of the volunteers are clearly reactionary nationalists. Alexander Borodai, who became prime minister of the Donetsk People's Republic, came from a group of Pan-Slavic nationalists who published the far-right newspaper Zavtra. His rebel commander, Igor Strelkov, is known as a religious fundamentalist zealot. His militia of Russian volunteers carried the Middle Age banner of 'Holy Rus,' and look to the Russian Orthodox Church for inspiration and support. The head of the church, Patriarch Kirill I, characterized the conflict as a religious war with the breakaway Ukrainian Orthodox Church, which became a target for Strelkov's militia. Russian Cossacks have also joined the battle with a religious nationalist identity, calling themselves the Cossack Orthodox Army. At one point they claimed to control 80 percent of the Luhansk region, including major towns, strategic roads, and border crossings into Russia.

The Kremlin's relationship to these ultra-nationalists is similar to that of Kiev to the neo-fascists. Neither government exerts full control. Rather these are alliances of convenience. The strategies of Kiev and Moscow and the reactionary nationalists aligned only so far. Putin was willing to back off supporting the Russian volunteers as a ceasefire came within reach. And the neo-fascists continue to fight Kiev's transnational capitalists over money, contracts, and power. It's also important to note that the often repeated story of massive amounts of Russian arms flowing to the rebels is false. A careful study by Armament Research Services found the majority of weapons used by eastern militias did not come from Russia, but stockpiles of Ukrainian weapons.[15]

As for the West, US, and EU political interference openly and unsparingly encouraged Ukrainians to pursue an exclusive pro-Western direction. After the Maidan coup Western powers deepened their involvement by openly supporting the military offensive into the east while ignoring the influence of neo-fascist militias, and the sway of reactionary nationalists in the new government. The Western economic boycott against Russia revived cold war politics, and some Pentagon leaders labeled Russia as the main global threat to the US.

Inside the Ukraine, American neo-conservative Victoria Nuland and US ambassador Geoff Pyatt played important roles in financing and promoting pro-Western activists and organizations. Meddling directly into Ukrainian politics a phone call by Nuland to Pyatt was caught on tape as they discussed getting rid of Yanukovych's government. Nuland and Pyatt also helped to channel funds from The National Endowment for Democracy (NED) and the Agency for International Development (USAID) to pro-Western media groups and NGOs. This first came as a $48,533 grant to Hromadske TV. This was soon followed by $19,183 from the George Soros International Renaissance Foundation (IRF), and $95,168 from the Embassy of the Netherlands. Pro-western media became an important tool in promoting and mobilizing anti-government protests, and creating a narrative that played to US and European audiences. For its part, Western media has in large part failed to cover Kiev's repeated artillery and air attacks that struck residential buildings, shopping malls, parks, schools, kindergartens, and hospitals. Conditions became so horrific that over 200,000 Ukrainians fled to Russia seeking shelter, jobs, and in many cases, residency.

Other important groups receiving financial support included the private non-profit contractor, Pact Inc., and a Ukrainian coalition of 150 NGOs called New Citizen. New Citizen acted as a hub for anti-government groups portraying itself as promoting civil society, democracy, and good governance. Pact received over $7 million from USAID, while the Swiss and British embassies, the Swedish International Development Cooperation Agency, the Canadian International Development Agency, NED, and IRF gave funds to Pact, New Citizen, and associated organizations.[16] Although the West provided money and political support, military support has been limited. Germany and France have even opposed sending defensive military systems, arguing that it would only result in a Russian escalation. And while the US provided military training for the National Guard, it refused to train and supply the neo-fascist militias.

On the international economic front there have been some interesting deals. One that saw little attention in the western press concerned Burisma, the Ukraine's largest independent gas producer. The company is controlled by Nikolai Zlochevsky, who served as secretary of Ukraine's National Security and Defense Council under the previous Yanukovych government. Zlochevsky is an example of how easy it is for the Ukrainian elite to move back and forth between Western and Eastern economic interests. Zlochevsky made Alan Apter, a US investment banker, chairman of the Burisma board. Apter then recruited Hunter Biden, Vice-President Joe Biden's youngest son, as a board member. Also joining the board was Devon Archer, a close family friend of

Secretary of State John Kerry and a trustee of the Heinz Family Office that oversees the family business. Biden and Archer worked for the investment firm, Rosemont Seneca Partners, a subsidiary of the private-equity firm Archer founded alongside his college roommate Christopher Heinz, heir to the Heinz Company family fortune.[17]

Transnational Bonds and Influence

Russian and European economic ties are strong. This is less true for the US/Russian relationship, although ties with Western oil majors, including those headquartered in the US, are important. The bonds between transnational capitalists created problems for the full implementation of the anti-Russian sanctions, most forcefully pushed by the US, but most deeply affecting Europe. In 2014 Russia's imports from the US were just 3 percent of its totals, while imports from Germany, France, and Italy totaled 22 percent. At the same time Russian exports to the US were 3.6 percent of their national total, while exports to the Netherlands, Germany, and Italy were 22.4 percent. Petroleum, comprising 64 percent of exports, is overwhelmingly the most important Russian commodity. But imports and exports, more typical of older economic relations, are just part of the story of integration. At the *Financial Times* Gideon Rachman noted, "The defining difference with the crises of the cold war is that nowadays a confrontation with Russia, and potentially one day with China, involves economic relationships that did not exist when the world was divided into rival political and economic blocs."[18]

A key aspect of the new relationships is cross border financial flows. Shortly before the Ukrainian crisis huge amounts of money flooded Russia as global investors rushed into emerging markets. Between 2005 and 2008 transnational capitalists sank $325 billion into Russian corporations, with large amounts going to state-owned entities like Sberbank and the energy giant Gazprom. Among the biggest investors were the financial giants JP Morgan, BlackRock, and Pimco.[19] Loans were also being made, reaching $400 billion from some of the biggest global banks including, Citigroup, HSBC, BNP Paribas, and Deutsche Bank. Consequently, both debt and profits from Russian state-owned companies meant profits for US and transnational investors the world over. More than 75 percent of foreign executives reported the operating environment was as good as or better than China, India, or Brazil, and 90 percent were planning to expand before the crisis erupted. Russian transnationals have also been active raising capital abroad, particularly on the London Stock Exchange. In one of the most important IPOs Russian state bank VTB raised $8.2 billion and appointed James Wolfensohn, former head of the World Bank, as board adviser.

Germany is the country most deeply tied to Russia, with about $30 billion in foreign direct investments and another $30 billion in exports. There are some 7,000 German companies active in Russia, from the biggest to numerous mid-size enterprises. Adidas, BASF, Siemens, Volkswagen, Opel (owned by GM), and Daimler all have major facilities, and all rank among the largest transnationals in the world. On the financial front all major German commercial banks are active in Russia with Deutsche Bank having the strongest market position. In terms of oil and gas, Germany's biggest energy group Eon is the largest foreign shareholder in Gazprom. Moreover, Eon and BASF joined with Gazprom in building a $6.6 billion Baltic Sea pipeline. The Germans hold 20 percent of the joint venture known as Nord Stream with former chancellor Gerhard Schroder as chairman and Matthias Warnig of Dresdner Bank its chief executive. Germany relies on Russia for 35 percent of its oil and 50 percent of its gas. So it's no surprise that the business community has strongly opposed sanctions. Even after the seizure of Crimea, Siemens CEO Joe Kaeser met personally with Putin to confirm their long-term commitment to sell trains, energy infrastructure, medical technology and manufacturing automation to Russia. Important cross-border deals continued as well, with German energy firm RWE selling its oil and gas subsidiary to Russia's LetterOne for over $7.5 billion. But sanctions have hurt. German trade with

Russia dropped by 35 percent in early 2015, affecting the 300,000 jobs in Germany dependent on such economic activity.

In negotiations over the Ukraine German Chancellor Angela Merkel was willing to take NATO membership for the Ukraine off the table, a major concession to Russian concerns. Germany's deputy chancellor, Sigma Gabriel, further explained his country's negotiating position. According to Gabriel, "The goal was never to push Russia politically and economically into chaos. Whoever wants that will provoke a much more dangerous situation for all of us in Europe. We want to help solve the conflict in Ukraine, not to force Russia to its knees."[20] French President Francois Hollande took an even softer stand, suggesting the possibility of lifting sanctions, and opposing their further tightening, a position supported by Italy, Austria, Finland, Spain, Slovakia, Hungary, Bulgaria, Greece, and Cyprus. Heavy corporate lobbying was effective, particularly the warning that Russia could retaliate with sanctions against European business interests. The European Commission itself was sharply divided. Antonio Tajani, the industry commissioner, spoke for many when he stated, "We are not the US, we don't have shale gas as they do, so any move to sanction them [Russia] would hurt our companies a lot. At a time when Europe is getting back on its feet after the worst crisis in decades we need to be very careful and use our judgment before shutting down important investment and trade relations such as the ones we have with Russia."[21]

As the sanctions battle heated up the Italian government took a leading oppositional role. Italy is the second largest trading partner with Russia within the EU, its relationship worth over $30 billion per year. UniCredit, Italy's largest bank by assets, is also the second largest foreign-owned bank in Russia. Investments moving from Russia to Italy are also important, Rosneft is the largest shareholder in Pirelli, a major Italian tire manufacturer. The energy sector is particularly well integrated between the two countries. Italian state-owned energy company Eni is a major investor in the Russian pipeline project South Stream. Eni also buys energy from Gazprom and they share projects in both Russia and Africa. Eni and Enel, Italy's second major energy transnational, together hold a 20 percent stake in Gazpromneft, Gazprom's oil arm. Enel also became the first foreign company to join Russia's power sector, paying $1.5 billion for shares in OGK-5, and a 49 percent stake in the electricity distributor, Rusenergysbyt.

The UK has its own unique relationship to the Russian TCC because London is home to many of the oligarchs. In 2012 the number of Russian children in British schools rose by 25 percent, and the average cost of a London home bought by a Russian was $6.7 million. Some 50 Russian-based corporations are listed on the London Stock Exchange, where they have raised more than $82 billion. Russian transnational capitalists have always looked abroad for safe offshore banks and property.[22] New York has recently become another favorite site for property acquisitions and homes.

In implementing sanctions the US believed Russia would view its global business ties as too valuable to lose, and so economic pressure would force their retreat from eastern Ukraine. But from the other side of the mirror Putin believed global business's ties to Russia were too valuable and would undercut Western sanctions. In important ways both were right. When the first sanctions hit they only affected a handful of Russian oligarchs close to Putin. But as the US continued to up the ante to "category three," which included Russian banks and energy companies, the Obama administration faced stiff resistance not only across Europe, but in the US as well. In opposition the two biggest business associations in the US, the National Association of Manufacturers and the US Chamber of Commerce, began lobby efforts and took out critical ads in national newspapers. Also elite opposition insisted that sanctions should not hurt financial institutions that held significant Russian debt. As US Treasury Secretary Jacob Lew said, "Obviously, there's two sides to every transaction. The goal is to have the maximum impact in Russia and to have as little damage done to the global economy."[23]

A fascinating area of conflict was over US ties to the Russian space program. Since 2000 the Department of Defense has been buying Russian rocket engines to launch military and intelligence satellites. These satellites include some of the most important and secret defense and intelligence technology held by the Pentagon. But after the annexation of Crimea, Congress banned the purchase of Russian engines, with sales worth about $300 million to the Kremlin. Soon the Pentagon began a campaign to get Congress to back off. America's two biggest defense contractors, Boeing and Lockheed Martin, added their considerable influence to ease the restrictions. Secretary of Defense Ashton Carton and the Director of National Intelligence, James Clapper Jr., became directly involved, sending a letter to senior congressmen to change the legislation. The pressure worked, and soon the Pentagon once again was able to purchase rockets made by the Russian company Energomash. As pointed out by Representative Duncan Hunter, Republican of California and member of the House Armed Services Committee, "Some of our biggest defense companies are lobbying on behalf of the Russians. That's a strange position for the defense industry to have."[24]

Another important area was Russia's energy industry. Companies weren't banned from conducting business with Russian state-owned gas giants Gazprom and Rosneft, although banks were sanctioned from making them loans. This arrangement allowed Exxon to keep a $3.2 billion Arctic offshore drilling contract, and in the deal Rosneft obtained minority stakes in the US Gulf of Mexico and oil fields in Texas. Tim Ash, an official at Standard Bank Group LTD wisely observed, "The U.S. government's very, very eager that companies with traded assets are excluded" from the sanctions. The hands-off Rosneft policy was also important to protect their many transnational institutional investors. But the US did move to sanction Rosneft's president, Igor Sechin. This prompted Jack Mack to resign from the Rosneft board. Mack was former chief executive of Morgan Stanley, which had sold its global oil trading business to Rosneft. But US law didn't prohibit US citizens from sitting on the board, and so Donald Humphreys, former chief financial officer of Exxon Mobil and BP chief executive Bob Dudley, continued to serve. BP owns 20 percent of Rosneft. Furthermore, Rex Tillerson, chief executive of Exxon Mobile, received the Order of Friendship award from Putin in gratitude for Exxon's commitment to Russia.

The energy industry is the 900-pound gorilla of the Russian economy. For many years it worked with other oil majors and so deserves a more detailed analysis. Rosneft emerged as Russia's largest oil producer when Putin dismantled Yukos, and sold its $90 billion assets for just $2 billion. Western banks then rushed in to loan Rosneft $22 billion as it upgraded to Russia's dominant energy company. Financial backing came from ABN Amro, Barclays, BNP Paribas, Citigroup, Goldman Sachs, JP Morgan, and Morgan Stanley. Rosneft moved onto the transnational stage, raising $10.7 billion in a huge IPO on the London Stock Exchange. Strategic investors were British Petroleum, Petronas (Malaysia), and CNPC (China). Russian oligarchs joined in, with Roman Abramovich, Vladimir Lisin and Oleg Deripaska each investing $1 billion. As Joerg Rudloff, chairman of Barclays and board member of Rosneft noted, Russia was "on the track of international economic integration."[25] In 2006 Rosneft turned east, joining with China's Sinopec in a $13.7 billion buyout of TNK-BP's Udmurtneft oil. In a key deal after the Crimea sanctions were imposed Rosneft signed a 30-year contract with the state-owned China National Petroleum Corporation worth about $400 billion. Rosneft is an excellent example of statist transnational capitalism. As a state-owned corporation it has led transnational capitalist class integration, bringing together Russian private and state capitalists, alongside their European and Asian private and state counterparts.

Nevertheless, as Western sanctions tightened they did cause difficult problems for Rosneft, denying it important global resources. But at the same time, Rosneft turned to other transnationals to work around the sanctions. Rosneft had joint venture contracts to help exploit its vast Arctic holdings, but sanctions forced Eni, Exxon, and Statoil to withdraw from a $20 billion exploration deal. To replace the loss of advance drilling technology Rosneft took a 30-percent stake in North Atlantic

Drilling, a subsidiary of Seadrill, the world's largest offshore driller controlled by Norway's richest man, John Fredriksen. In turn Fredriksen bought a "significant portion" of Rosneft's land drilling operation. Rosneft also faced problems when sanctions cut access to foreign capital markets. To counteract the sanctions it arranged a series of prepayment deals with some of the largest western oil traders including Glencore, Trafigura, and BP. Also Rosneft bought Morgan Stanley's global oil merchant unit. This gave Rosneft an international network of oil tank storage contracts, supply agreements and freight shipping contracts as well as a 49 percent stake in Heidmar, a manager of oil tankers. The acquisition put Rosneft in competition with Glencore and Vitol and other oil traders, opening new avenues to sell their energy on global oil markets. Obviously there is a constant push and pull between national sanctions and transnational economic networks. This tension continues to play out as the central dynamic in the Ukrainian crisis.

A brief look at Gazprom, the second state-owned Russian energy giant, furthers our understanding of the depth of major transnational joint projects. In developing Shtokman, one of the world's largest gas fields, Gazprom partnered with Total from France and StatoilHydro of Norway. Total has a close relationship with the Russians. The French oil major has investments in two other Russian oil fields, and a 16-percent stake in Novatek, the country's largest gas producer after Gazprom. In turn Gazprom is the number two gas supplier to France. The largest foreign investment project in Russia, the Sakhalin-2 oil field, involved the British and Japanese. Although Gazprom retains majority ownership, Shell holds 27.5 percent, Mitsui 15 percent, and Mitsubishi 10 percent. Overall European countries have continued to rely on Russian gas, with 20 to 50 percent use for Germany, France, Poland, and Italy to 80 percent reliance for Finland, Hungary, and the Czech Republic.[26]

The South Stream project, which was building a pipeline for Gazprom through Bulgaria, Serbia, Hungary, and into Austria and Italy had eleven groups bidding for contracts in the face of

US opposition. This included corporations from Austria, Belgium, Germany, India, Italy, Japan, and Sweden. The geopolitical conflict in the Ukraine and disagreements over Gazprom's monopoly resulted in Putin cancelling the project. But as pointed out by Marco Siddi from the London School of Economics, "It is more difficult to tell whether Russia and the European Union will gain or lose from the cancellation of South Stream...Gazprom has lost an opportunity to further strengthen its position in the EU energy market. However, from an economic viewpoint, the construction of South Stream made little sense at a time when European gas demand is dwindling and gas prices are low."[27] Instead Russia has furthered its global energy connections by turning to China, India, and Turkey.

One way to judge the success of the economic boycott is to see who attended the St. Petersburg International Economic Forum. In 2014 some 560 foreign executives and government officials came, down from 700 the year before. The French were well represented with the chief executive of Total, as well as leaders of Alstom, Danone, Suez GDF, and Societe Generale. Besides Total other oil heavyweights included Shell, ExxonMobil, Statoil, and BP. Rosneft signed more than a dozen contracts including a big multiyear deal with Venezuela's state-owned oil group. US financial heavy weights JP Morgan Chase and TPG also attended. In total 70 US corporations were present, but a number of important US executives stayed away, including Lloyd Blankfein of Goldman Sachs and Indra Nooyi of PepsiCo.

o Worlds

e can be no doubt that sanctions have hurt the Russian ting its exports, stock market, and global financial cting the profits of transnationals operating inside y 2015 capital flight soared to over $100 billion, of the ruble fell by a third. Additional economic aps even more important, was the deep drop in world oil prices. Western sanctions also caused the cancellation of an important military deal with France for \$1.6 billion, over the grudging but yielding opposition of the French government. This was the biggest arms sale ever by a NATO country to Russia. But French/Russian military ties were renewed and strengthened with the terrorist attacks in Paris, and their mutual involvement against ISIS in the Syrian conflict.

Putin's nationalism gained an 80 percent approval rating among Russians, while the press promotes stories about the "neo-fascist junta" in the Ukraine. Moreover, Russia began its own sanctions against importing a range of food and agricultural goods from Europe and the US. The boycotts from both sides resulted in some Russian companies, from farms to banks, growing their internal markets. Yet overall growth is down and prices are up, creating stagflation.

The relationship between Russia's private transnational capitalists and statist capitalist class continues to be a balancing act. Over the years Putin has swung from promoting cross-border economic integration, to criticizing private capitalists for investing too much abroad. On the one hand the Russian state spent billions to make the Sochi Winter Olympics a showcase for an international audience, and on the other is the current blast of nationalist rhetoric. In both cases it's the statist fraction of the TCC that's in charge, and a reminder that the state leads the pace of transnationalization according to its political needs. But Russia needs its transnational partners, whether from the West or from China. And perhaps these economic ties have been the key blockade to an all-out Russian military annexation of eastern Ukraine.

But the same dilemma confronts the West. Transnational capitalism is not about domination, but integration. And so the pace and extent of economic sanctions has been cautious and opposed at every step by the Western TCC. This has also slowed military provocations by the US and Europe. The flow of new arms to western Ukraine has been limited and its membership in NATO put off. Both Russia and the West prefer to fight through their reactionary proxies. But it's highly doubtful that ultra-nationalists will win political power in either western or eastern Ukraine.

Taking all the political and economic factors into consideration we can see the complex interplay between local nationalism, old Cold War geopolitical rivalries, and the powerful interests of transnational capitalism counteracting these forces. This is the current state of global capitalism. A period of transition in which the dialectic between nationalism and transnationalism is fully on display. Each opposition defines and limits the other. While the historic movement is towards a world system of global capitalism, nationalism and geopolitics can still play an important role, and in some cases become the dominant political element. In such a period the Ukraine is an important and useful example of how the contradictions unfold.

Endnotes

1   V.I. Lenin, *Lenin Collected Works* (Progress Publishers: Moscow, 1964), Volume 24: 335-338.

2   Finnish Declaration of Independence, <https://en.wikipedia.org/wiki/Finnish_Declaration_of_Independence>.

3   Viktor Shapinov, "A Class Analysis of the Ukrainian Crisis," *Links, International Journal of Socialist Renewal*, (June 13, 2014).

4   Ibid.

5   Robert Parry, "Ignoring Ukraine's Neo-Nazi Storm Troopers," *Consortium News*, (August 14, 2015).

6   Andrew E. Kramer, "Police in Western Ukraine Clash With Paramilitary Group; 7 Are Hurt," *The New York Times*, (July 12, 2015).

7   Ibid.

8   Viktor Shapinov, "The Ukraine junta's fascist foot soldiers," <http://www.workers.org/articles/2014/10/31/ukraine-juntas-fascist-foot-soldiers/> (2014).

9   Alexander Buzgalin, "Ukraine: Anatomy of a Civil War," *International Critical Thought*, Vol. 5, No. 3, (2015).

10   Jerry Harris, "Statist Globalization in China, Russia and the Gulf States," *Science & Society*, Vol. 73, No. 1 (January 2009).

11   Boris Kagarlitsky, "Crimea annexes Russia," *Links International Journal of Socialist Renewal*, (April 9, 2015).

12   United Nations Conference on Trade and Development, *World*

Investment Report 2015 Overview (UNCTD, New York, 2015).

13   Gideon Rachman, "Medvedev will not declare cold war," *Financial Times*, (March 4, 2008).

14   Leonardo Figueroa Helland, Tim Lindgren, and Tori Pfaeffle, "Civilization On a Crash Course? Imperialism, Subimperialism and the Political-Ecological Breaking Point of the Modern/Colonial World System," Paper given at the 14th Annual Global Studies Association Conference, Toledo University, July 13, 2015.

15   John Ismay, "Tracking the Weapons Used to Fight Ukraine's War," *The New York Times*, (February 2, 2015).

16   Steve Weissman, "Meet the Americans Who Put Together the Coup in Kiev," <http://readersupportednews.org/opinion2/277-75/22758-meet-the-americans-who-put-together-the-coup-in-kieve?> (March 25, 2015).

17   Paul Sonne, and James V. Grimaldi, "Joe Biden's Son Appointed to Board of Largest Gas Company In Ukraine," <http://www.popularresistance.org/joe-bidens-son-appointed-to-board-of-largest-gas-company-in-ukraine> (May 18, 2014).

18   Gideon Rachman, "If the Chinese leadership were ever to 'do a Putin', how could the US and allies react?" *Financial Times*, (March 10, 2014).

19   Landon Thomas Jr., "Foreign Investors in Russia Vital to Sanctions Debate," *The New York Times*, (March 17, 2014).

20   Euractiv.com, <http://www.euractiv.com/sections/europes-east/france-germany-concerned-about-russia-sanctions-policy-311046> (June 1, 2015).

21   Christian Oliver, James Fontanella-Khan, George Parker, and Stefan Wagstyl, "EU sanctions push on Russia falters amid big business lobbying," *Financial Times*, (April 16, 2014).

22   Daniel Schafer, "City jobs ads importance of rich Russians to wealth sector," *Financial Times*, (March 19, 2014).

23   Natasha Doff, "Fitch Says U.S. Limiting Putin Sanctions to Help Bondholders," *Bloomberg*, (April 30, 2014).

24   Steven Lee Myers, "Pentagon Seeks Easing of Ban on Russian Rockets for U.S. Space Missions," *The New York Times*, (June 3, 2015).

25   Stefan Wagstyl, "Russian boom will end in pain, says banker," *Financial Times*, (April 24, 2007), 5.

26   Chi-Kong Chyong and Vessela Tcherneva, "Europe's vulnerability on Russian gas." <http://www.ecfr.eu/article/commentary_europes_vulnerability_on_russian_gas> (March 17, 2015).

27   Marco Siddi, "Who are the winners and losers from the cancellation of the South Stream pipeline?" <http://blogs.lse.ac.uk/

europpblog/2014/12/18/who-are-the-winners-and-losers-from-the-cancellation-of-the-south-stream-pipe> (December 12, 2014).

Chapter Five

CHINA: THE STATE
AND GLOBAL
CAPITALISM

"It's glorious to get rich!"
Deng Xiaoping

"China now has 596 billionaires,
surpassing the U.S. tally for the first time."
Hurun Report, *Shanghai Luxury Magazine*

No examination of the world would be complete without an analysis of China. The convergence of state power and the global market is the driving force of the Chinese economy and its accelerated development. While bloggers, protesting farmers, angry workers, and environmental activists have pushed open the door to civil society, the state maintains a heavy hand in allowing these social actors only limited room. The transnational capitalist class has two fractions—the dominant statist sector and those capitalists in the private market place—but they are closely aligned through thousands of networks that run through state financing, political power, corruption, and a mutual commitment to realize the Chinese dream.

The ruling class of each country has engineered its own particular insertion into the global economy. Smaller countries with a weaker capitalist class and state do so under the guidance of the IMF, World Bank, and transnational financers. This reflects the historic world system of imperialist domination. But the transnational elites of each country, small or large, have integrated their fortunes into global circuits of accumulation. Led by a statist transnational capitalist class, no country has been more successful than China. Other countries have taken similar state-directed paths, including the Gulf States, Singapore, and Russia.[1] But China has emerged as the second largest economy in the world, and now sits at the center of a rapidly developing new world order.

When thinking about the Chinese TCC it is important not to think of the statist fraction as national capitalists and private capitalists as transnationalists. In many ways the statist TCC has deeper global ties than private capitalists, many of whom are small and midsize producers. In fact, a large number of private enterprises are more dependent on the internal market, and their owners are members of the national bourgeoisie. Although private technology companies like Alibaba and Tencent have emerged as major global players, a larger sector of private entrepreneurs tied to global production are subcontractors.

Statist leaders do have their own national vision of Chinese globalization, and it's not one defined by traditional Western powers. Rather they want to help rewrite the rules and determine a new global economic/political infrastructure. In great part this derives from China's history as the "middle kingdom," its humiliation by imperialism, and revolutionary Maoism. China's path is its own. But its goals of modernization and a moderately wealthy country are circumscribed by global integration. The project of building a transnational system of global capitalism is similar in east and west, but the struggle over how this unfolds is ongoing. Once again we see the dialectic between a nation-centric past and the emergence of a new era of capitalism. The tensions between the Chinese TCC and their counterparts in the US, Europe, and Japan are often seen as a clash of national powers. At times the contradictions may assume such forms, but the content is transnational as the Chinese TCC fights to insert itself into the golden circle of global accumulation on its own terms.

State Transformation and Remaking the Working Class

To transform China into a market economy the Communist Party used the state to re-engineer society. The first steps taken under Deng Xiaoping privatized the rural collectives into family and individual holdings. This change affected some 800 million people, and produced class divisions in the countryside. Even after land redistribution ownership still resided in the hands of the local government, a power which allowed Party officials to profit by selling property to private developers. Changes in the countryside pushed some 60 million peasants into the cities looking for work. As the state opened China to transnational corporations the former peasants supplied the cheap sweatshop labor so necessary to attract foreign direct investments into manufacturing. This new urban proletariat also lacked official state support in housing, education, and health care, creating the lowest rung of the working class.

Kevin Lin, from the China Research Centre in Australia, provides an excellent description of the above process,

> The transnationalization of capitalist production
> has been instrumental in transforming the
> working class, and one of the most significant
> consequences is the proletarianization of rural
> labour on a massive scale in the Global South and
> their integration into the circuits of global capital.
> In recent decades, this is most starkly witnessed
> in China, where hundreds of millions of rural
> population, drawn by employment in foreign
> invested companies, have joined the ranks of the
> working class, making the Chinese working class
> the largest in the world.[2]

Deng Xiaoping famously said, "It's glorious to get rich!" And there are many gloriously rich people in China today. The connection between this new wealth and Party corruption are links in an iron chain. When the government divided land in the countryside there were those who got the most fertile land, the best equipment, and easy access to water. Many others were not so lucky. When an enterprise needed land to build a facility it was the government that expropriated peasant and village holdings, and sold it to private interests. Such expropriations include many millions of acres for which hundreds of billions of dollars were paid. Of course as the Party is the state, those Party members in positions of power and influence benefited and profited the most. This vast privatization was carried out at the same time that neoliberalism was on the ascent in the West with Ronald Reagan and Margaret Thatcher.

The project to privatize and reshape labor relations that shook the countryside was also launched in the cities. From 1997 to 2002 tens of thousands of state-owned enterprises (SOEs) were privatized or shut, and 30 million laid off. In 1978 over 99 percent of urban workers were employed by state companies, by 2011 it was only 11 percent.[3] In effect, large sections of the socialist industrial working class were pushed into the capitalist market place. Still employment in the SOE sector is the best, with average wages 40 percent above pay for migrant workers.

Beyond privatization Deng's China had other similarities with Western neoliberalism, including sweatshop labor, deep cuts to the social contract known as the iron rice-bowl, and the elimination of the right to strike from the constitution in 1982. During the Mao era workers and their families were provided with housing, health care, education, and pensions. Now they mainly must provide these for themselves. Alongside privatization was the growth of 10.8 million private enterprises employing over 100 million workers. As mentioned above, migrant workers became a key sector of the urban working class, particularly in the construction industry where many of China's billionaires made their fortunes. In the great industrial city of Shenzhen with a population of 18 million, 80 percent are migrants without permanent residency permits. But the second generation of migrant workers have grown more militant, and aware of new labor laws that often form the basis for their growing protests.

Another important new sector are temporary workers used by both state and private firms. Their numbers are expected to soon reach 60 million, or 20 percent of the workforce. These large numbers of temporary workers constitute a Chinese precariat, alongside the many college graduates unable to find suitable work. In terms of pay, migrant and temporary workers help make labor less than 10 percent of operating costs. The advantage of offshoring operations to China is obvious. In developed countries labor costs often run about 50 percent. Having millions of super-exploited workers makes China one of the most unequal societies in the world, with a Gini coefficient reaching 0.73 in 2012.[4] Another new sector of labor are those who go abroad laboring for Chinese corporations throughout the world. In 2008 the Chinese Ministry of Commerce stated 740,000 Chinese were officially employed overseas.[5]

The establishment of vast zones for the operation of foreign corporations and their network of subcontractors fits both Robinson and Struna's analysis of transnational labor relations cited in chapter one. Additionally, the export of laborers to overseas Chinese projects is an example of what Struna explained as labor travelling to transnational work. In this case it's neither professional workers nor migrants, but workers occupying a middle position between high and low sectors of labor, sent abroad attached to state-owned transnational corporations.

One last sector to consider are those who benefited from the remade class structure, the new middle class, which numbers about 150 million. This includes entrepreneurs, managerial and technical staff employed by foreign enterprises, state enterprises, financial and technology firms, professionals, and self-employed persons.[6] A good number of these are party cadre who number 85 million members. This class alongside the very wealthy constitutes the 120 million Chinese tourists whose foreign spending accounted for 46 percent of global luxury sales. All told Chinese travelling abroad spent $183 billion comprising 12 percent of global consumption.[7]

Alongside the new working class and new private

capitalists there emerged a statist capitalist class. Every contract that was signed, every regulation that needed to be followed and approved, every building constructed, all had to go through Party officials from the smallest local to the highest level. There could be obstacles, or smooth and quick results. Deal making became the new ideology. Many officials became rich, as well as their families, not by creating wealth, but through their control of state-owned assets and their control of the market. Bao Tong, former advisor to Party General Secretary, and Prime Minister Zhao Ziyang criticized the new policies as being "in direct contradiction to the Party's founding aim... The upshot of Deng's revolution was that those with significant power got significantly rich, those with modest power got modestly rich, and those with no power remained in poverty."[8] But whether corrupt or honest, Party elites were united in using the state apparatus to free the market and insert China into global capitalism. The result was the emergence of a Chinese transnational capitalist class in both the state and private sector.

The Chinese TCC has also made innovations to the labor process itself, termed "high tempo cost out"[9] by Edward Steinfeld of the Brookings Institute. Steinfeld compares this to the Japanese innovations when production was reorganized into lean manufacturing. The process starts with taking a hi-tech product, assigning a large body of engineers to break down the commodity, and redesign it for lower costs while making it easier to manufacture. It's then sped into production creating a simplified lower cost version of a popular global product. This is sold to customers locked out of the higher end market, creating a middle market that previously didn't exist. The Chinese sales force interacts with the customers to debug the product and find new types of desired functions. These are quickly redesigned into the product, knocked out on the factory floor and put back into the market. Therefore, the Chinese competitive advantage is not just that workers are paid little and worked hard, but that managerial organization has cut design costs, created a more rapid turnover of capital accumulation by speeding the cycle of production, and created new markets.

The State and Transnational Integration

By the end of 2001 China was ready to join the WTO, and begin full integration into the global economy. A key process began in the 1980s with the establishment of special economic zones. These were areas in which the state could experiment with expanding foreign manufacturing and investments. This led to the opening of China, making it the world's factory and second largest economy. Today virtually every major transnational corporation operates in China, creating hundreds of thousands of ties involving joint ventures, subcontractors, foreign direct investments, Greenfield projects, and the employment of hundreds of millions of workers. Much of this production takes place in special economic zones (SEZs) that employ about 40 million workers. That's about two-thirds of the global workforce laboring in special export zones.

To make foreign investment easier the current government eliminated the law that required approval on a case-by-case basis and a review of each joint venture. This means most foreign projects will no longer need government approval, and ensures "national treatment" for foreign companies. This aligns China more closely to WTO rules and transnational practices, and puts foreign investors on the same legal footing as domestic companies.[10]

Further use of special SEZs is now focused on financial liberalization. New zones have been established in Shanghai, Guangdong, Fujian, and Tianjin. Helen Wong, chief executive of HSBC Greater China, enthusiastically noted the zones reflect "significant progress in accelerating financial sector liberalization ... (and) will also have a major catalyzing impact on cross-border trade and investment flows."[11] Shanghai will remove certain financial and currency restraints holding back foreign investors, as well as promote more offshore borrowing for the region's companies. Guangdong is expected to play a role in the liberalization of the Yuan, and expand business relations with foreign traders and banks. Overall the project continues the state's use of regulatory power to further align China with transnational capitalism, and it has proven to be very successful. In the first eleven months of 2015 nearly 24,000 foreign-funded TNCs rushed into the new special economic zones.[12]

When the global economic crisis of 2008 hit China some 20 million workers lost their jobs. The Party responded with a massive stimulus program of huge infrastructure projects and investments. As a result the biggest SOEs became even more powerful as they received an infusion of cash and contracts. But because growth translates into a successful career for every Party official, economic expansion often nurtured corruption. Banks catering to rich families established private wealth management units whose holdings swelled to nearly $2 trillion in funds by 2014.[13] With the income gap growing to one of the largest in the world, cynicism about the Party also swelled. Party leader Hu Jintao expanded health care and passed important labor laws that increased the wages of most urban workers. But compared to the millions and billions being made by the capitalist class and their business partners in the Party, Hu's reforms had limited impact. Marx once observed that the culture of the ruling class becomes the culture of the people. This clearly is the case in China, where material wealth, consumerism, and individualism became widespread.

With new leadership taking office in 2013 decisive measures were taken to change direction. The anti-corruption campaign of current leader Xi Jinping is driven by the crucial need to maintain the political legitimacy of the Chinese Communist Party (CCP). Xi has used the campaign to strike out at some political rivals, but the campaign is more expansive than that. As of 2015 over 270,000 low and high officials have been arrested or disciplined. The Party has been particularly sensitive over exposures of the immense family wealth of state leaders. Four members of the Standing Committee before Xi each owned or controlled assets of more than $150 million. When *The New York Times* ran extensive research on the family riches of Prime Minister Wen Jiabao the paper was blocked from Internet access in China.

Wen was known for speaking out on income inequality, but his family had amassed about $300 million in wealth. A large part of this was through Ping An, a financial services and insurance corporation worth $65 billion, and bigger than A.I.G., Prudential, or MetLife. Wen's family bought large stakes through Taihong, one of their investment companies, well below market rates. Taihong's $65 million investment was acquired from Chinese state-owned entities, and eventually peaked at about $2.2 billion for shareholders. Goldman Sachs and Morgan Stanley also profited nicely from their 15 percent ownership of Ping An, selling their stake to HSBC for about $1 billion, or a 1,300 percent increase.[14] By the time HSBC sold those shares to a billionaire from Thailand they made an after-tax profit of $2.6. billion. There were no accusations that any of these deals were illegal, but it certainly speaks to power and influence, and the exclusive networks that exist between state, private, and transnational wealth. Xi's own sister and family are worth about $300 million, although he has demanded that they divest some of their fortune.[15] Given China's equalitarian past such stories have a strong impact on ordinary citizens. Walking through the halls of Tsinghua University with a faculty member we came upon a picture of Wen. The professor turned to me in anger and stated, "I hate him, he and his family are corrupt millionaires!" Such statements are certainly not what CCP leaders want to hear.

Xi's anti-corruption campaign and personal power has led some to compare him to Mao Zedong. But Xi's reforms are the opposite of those of China's socialist period. Instead there is greater room for the market, and deeper integration with transnational capital. Xi's main concerns are financial reform, promoting Chinese TCC interests abroad, and seeking political stability through his anti-corruption campaign. There is a fundamental commitment to ensure inward bound capital continues to flow, and outward bound capital continues to expand. Reforms under Xi make mixed ownership between private and state interests the basic form of the socialist economic system. Foreign companies can even obtain controlling shares in some SOEs.

While policy debates go on, among the statist leadership there is general consensus that the economy must turn to greater internal consumption to grow. The CPP's mainstream ideology can be defined as Confucian neo-Keynesianism. The state should be ruled by an efficient and honest bureaucracy, benevolent to its people, with clearly established rules to live by. Those rules mean you don't challenge the Party's control of the state, which is responsible for the well-being of the nation. The existence of both political and economic elites is accepted as natural and necessary for China's modernization and its historic level of development. So, as in any good Keynesian state, the government should play an active role when necessary to stimulate the economy. But the main interest of the billion-plus ordinary citizens should be their own material wealth, they should have no political interests outside their immediate field of vision, and most importantly they should be loyal supporters of the Party. There is some room for civil society, and indeed protests take place widely throughout China. But these are not allowed to coalesce into national social movements; unions are kept under Party leadership, and the state sets the pace and structure of the market. All this takes place within the context of global capitalism, and China's expanding role in transnational accumulation as well as its more pronounced part in writing the global rules.

There are other voices to the left and right. One of the most influential is the finance minister, Lou Jiwei, who previously headed China's $600 billion sovereign wealth fund. Lou is a strong proponent of globalization and has fought against rising wage levels. Fearing enterprise-level bargaining could result in industry-wide wage scales, he warned strong unions would hurt China and blamed workers for destroying the auto industry in Detroit. Lou stated, "On the industrial relations front, we cannot become like the US and Europe, where workers get together from the same region or company and bargain aggressively with their employers. We must increase flexibility in the labour market and let employers and individual workers decide on their employment arrangements."[16] Of course this means individual workers are at the mercy of corporations, a policy which transnational capitalists strongly approve.

One of Lou's targets was the Labour Contract Law, which he criticized for reducing "mobility" and "flexibility" in the labor market—code words for reshaping labor to the needs of business. The opposite of mobility and flexibility is job security and higher wages, something no good neoliberal can abide by. The finance minister's strategy is to maintain China's competitive low-wage advantage over other poor countries. Again we can turn to his own words, "In 2014, our GDP per capita was US$7,500, lower than Malaysia but higher than Thailand. However, a report from the Chinese Academy of Social Sciences says that wages in Shanghai are 1.16 times higher than in Kuala Lumpur and 1.8 times higher than in Bangkok. Our wages are no longer competitive, and the Labour Contract has further reduced flexibility in the labour market."[17] Clearly the finance minister wants to continue the path of sweatshop wages, rather than creating a better paid labor force to drive the economy. In order to supply more cheap labor for industry Lou is advocating exposing farmers to transnational agro competition. This would drive more peasants off the land and into the cities where Lou would allow them to register as official urban residents. It's a progressive reform, but one that Lou believes is essential to maintain a mobile labor force for TNCs. In line with other neoliberal economists, Lou has argued that rising productivity must stay ahead of wages, although the western middle class came about when incomes rose alongside gains in productivity. His ultimate solution for increased wages is less workers and more robots. Already half the world's total work on China's assembly lines.

Among economic experts there are many fans of Ronald Reagan and Margaret Thatcher. Jia Kang in the Ministry of Finance is a well-known and outspoken advocate of market reforms. As Jia has stated, "Thatcher and Reagan are highly regarded because it was proven that they made the right choices under heavy pressure, their spirit was one of boldly taking on challenges and innovating, and that's certainly worth Chinese people emulating."[18] Those bold challenges were breaking national strikes by miners and air traffic controllers and innovating neoliberal reforms. It seems Mao and Chou En-Lai have been replaced by Reagan and Thatcher as models for Chinese development.

Lou and Jia are not so far out of step with Xi and Prime Minister Li Keqiang. In 2013 as the new leadership took over the politburo they quickly indicated their intent to expand market reforms that favor globalization. The National Development and Reform Commission issued its new policy directive stating the government will "promote the effective entry of private capital into finance, energy, railways, telecommunications and other spheres."[19] This included room for foreign investments and private Chinese capital in key areas that were SOE monopolies.

By 2014 private equity deals by Chinese firms surged, hitting a record $73.2 billion and included large investments into SOEs. Overall there are 280,000 SOEs that employ only about one percent of the entire workforce, when considering both urban and rural labor. But just 113 SOEs run by the central government account for 53 percent of total state-owned assets. Overall SOEs generate $7 trillion for the Chinese economy, and the top three generate more revenue and profits than the combined totals of the largest 500 private firms. There are 88 SOEs on Fortune's Global 500, the annual list of the largest corporations by revenue. SOEs dominate most of the key economic sectors, including automobiles, information technology, petrochemicals, aviation, insurance, energy, banking, railways, media, shipping, construction, metals, telecommunications, and industrial chemicals.[20]

Now a growing number of these SOEs will be targeted for mixed ownership, judged by shareholder value, and subject to less political control. The eventual goal is to integrate state and private capital and have them act as partners in the big SOEs. Dependence on the private sector as the driver of reform is in keeping with Prime Minister Li's economic perceptions. As Li has stated, "The market is the creator of social wealth…"[21] Marx had a very different view, which focused on the working class as he famously wrote, "labor creates all wealth." The word "market" sounds technical, neutral, and absent of class content, but corporations run the market, and capitalists run corporations. In the case of China's market socialism, state managers with a capitalist orientation run corporations.

Market-driven reforms also strike out at the corrupt institutional structure embedded in many SOEs. As mentioned above, senior corporate officials use their power to make and influence appointments, which are key steps to advance the careers of party cadre. In turn this creates a power base and network of influence for those in top positions. These networks are lubricated by illegal financial deals often resulting in corrupt fortunes. The best known case is that of Zhou Yongkang who used his control of the energy sector to create a vast patronage network.

Zhou was one of the most powerful men in China and a member of the elite Standing Committee. His arrest, and the arrest of top managers of China National Petroleum Corporation, must be seen not only in the context of reforming the SOEs but also as a warning to those forces opposing change.

In sum, the anti-corruption campaign, new efforts to apply the "rule of law," and using the market to guide business decisions are all aspects of the same policy. Xi and the current leadership are using the power of the state to re-engineer how the economy works. By increasing the power of finance and the market the Chinese economy becomes more closely aligned with mainstream transnational capital class practices. The leadership is so committed to global capitalism as the road for development that other strategies for reform aren't considered. Consequently, a socialist approach to organizing and unleashing powerful social movements to attack corruption is to be avoided at all costs. Conceding autonomy to civil society and the unions is seen as the most dangerous disruption the Party could face. One can refer to Mao in speeches, but mass struggle is a ghost that haunts the CCP.

Another important reform jointly pushed by the World Bank and State Council to undercut SOE power networks is the establishment of capital investment companies, using Singapore's Temasek state holding company as a model. Singapore has long been admired ever since Deng stated China should learn from its experience. Thousands of SOE senior executives have traveled to the city-state to study, with 30,000 officials sent in 2011 alone.[22] Singapore is respected as one of the best-run capitalist states in the world, authoritarian, stable and with a strong state sector. Temasek manages state-held assets, but gives management operational autonomy. This separates ownership from management. But the state, as an important investor, influences corporate decisions by withdrawing or investing capital according to stockholder interests.

In China the plan is to transfer state equity to state-owned institutional investors such as insurance and private equity funds. These will invest in SOEs, but only focus on maximizing shareholder value. He Fan, Senior Research Fellow at the Chinese Academy of Social Sciences points out, "This will bring a sea change to the Chinese economy. The government can free itself from the awkward situation of meddling with the daily operation of SOEs and concentrate on the task of maintaining fair market competition and property rights protection. It will also try to stimulate competition among the SOEs. If the enterprises are not performing well, the state-owned capital investment companies can reduce their investments or sell their shares. This will force SOEs to behave more like other market entities and increase efficiency."[23] In effect, this will bring China's state more closely into alignment with Western institutions, where the TCC has achieved hegemony and established best practices, now to be emulated in China.

On the other hand, there are neo-Keynesian aspects to the reforms, one of which will direct more profits to the central government for social services. Also some 200 top executives of key SOEs will have their income cut as much as 70 percent, and their salaries made public. The general rule is executive salaries should be no larger than six to 12 times that of the average worker—significantly different from US standards where CEOs and top executives make about 300 times their average employee's wages. China's SOE executives are appointed and dismissed by the CCP's central organizational department, and hold a position equivalent to cabinet ministers. The balance between the CCP's direct influence and that of capital investment firms remains to be worked out. Questions that touch on how much control the state will retain, and corporate governance practices that oversee management reflect key political battles taking place inside the ranks of China's leadership.

Other reforms focus on bringing China into line with transnational finance. One important opening was to link the Shanghai stock exchange to Hong Kong. As more than a billion dollars a day floods into Hong Kong, Charles Li, the chief executive of the exchange was in a celebratory mood. As Li stated, "We are in the midst of a profound structural change: the gradual but accelerating opening of mainland China's financial markets... The party has begun, and you can feel the excitement today. It's hard to say when the music will stop."[24]

The surge of money comes in part from pension funds and insurance companies that can now invest up to 30 percent of their assets in equity funds, bonds, the money market, securities, and futures. Money also flows more rapidly into China because the Hong Kong link means Western fund managers can invest in the 2,500 listed companies on the Shanghai exchange. Hong Kong is home to some of the most globally integrated TNCs in the world. The United Nations Conference on Trade and Development (UNCTAD) creates a "transnationality index" based on the ratio of foreign held assets, employment, and sales compared to similar national figures. Hong Kong TNCs occupy ten of the top 15 positions for corporations in the Global South,[25] acting as a key gateway for capital to flow in and out of China.

One of the most important financial reforms taking place is making the Yuan a global currency. The state has carefully guarded the Yuan, putting limits on its convertibility, blocking speculative runs, and allowing only small amounts to circulate outside China. But financial liberalization is changing many of these regulations. One of the most important changes is letting global markets set the exchange rate for the Yuan, something the

IMF and US have been demanding for a good number of years. China was rewarded by the IMF, which included the Yuan in its global basket of currencies. This is an important step in making the Yuan a broadly traded international currency as is the dollar, the euro, and the yen. The first evidence of this was in August 2015 when there was a sudden devaluation that marked a weakening of the Chinese economy. As with all currency fluctuations there were winners and losers, and for China it gave a boost to their export sector, a sector which is still key, with or without all the talk about a stronger consumer economy.

Since the end of the Cultural Revolution, China has been on a steady march to expand the market as the key element in the national economy. The process is driven by the Party itself, and continues with each succeeding leadership change. Through unquestioned political hegemony Party elites have used state power to reshape the relations of production between capital and labor, inserted the economy into global capitalism, enriched themselves and their families, and created a private and statist TCC.

Their success has been nothing short of amazing. When I see China today and compare it to the China of my first visit in 1982 the growth is staggering. And while inequality and hardship is the daily reality of hundreds of millions, there are millions in the middle class. Opportunity for good and bad abound. China is the success story of twenty-first century capitalism.

Inward Bound Capital

Family networks and the ties between politics and business are key to many fortunes, and to the formation of the TCC in China. But there has also been room for entrepreneurs. The story of some, like Jack Ma, rival the biography of Steve Jobs. Inbound foreign capital is a key link in the emergence of the Chinese TCC. The links between global capital and local capital is what transformed the Chinese economy into its transnational form. Cheap labor and the internal market have been the two magnets pulling billions of dollars to China year after year. When Deng stated "some will get rich first!" He failed to add, "on low wage labor."

We can look at FDI inflows to China and the country's cumulative FDI stocks in Table 5.1.[26,27]

Table 5.1 China FDI Inflows and FDI Stocks (US$ Billions)						
	2008	2009	2010	2012	2013	2014
Inflows	171.5	131.1	243.7	280.0	253.4	239.0[25]
Stocks	915.5	1,314.8	1,569.6	1,906.9	2,159.6	2,550

Source: OECD, "FDI in Figures: International investment struggles," <http://www.oecd.org/daf/inv/FDI-in-Figures-Dec-2014.pdf> (February 2014).

Even though the global financial crisis began in 2008 we see by 2010 FDI was again surging into China, with total FDI stocks going over two trillion in 2013. In terms of US FDI the figure is $50 billion, just two percent of the total. In return, China's investments into the US is $36 billion. Hardly a case for US economic domination. Comparing China's 2013 FDI of $252 billion to Brazil and India, we see Brazil attracted $62 billion and India just $24 billion. The centrality of China to the transnational economy is obvious. Looking at 2014 in more detail, service sector FDI grew to 55 percent. Meanwhile, capital-intensive industries dropped to 33 percent, the slowdown marking rising labor costs in manufacturing. Inbound cross-border mergers and acquisitions, a key marker of globalization, hit a record high in value reaching nearly $25 billion, with banking and finance attracting the lion's share.

Key to transforming the financial sector was bringing the four major state-owned banks into acceptable global business practices. This meant cleaning up bad debt, overhauling management systems, imposing strict corporate governance standards, and then selling stakes to global investors. This was accomplished by establishing a foreign advisory council that included: Sir Edward George, former governor of the Bank of England; Gerry Corrigan, former president of the New York Federal Reserve; Andrew Crockett, former general manager of the

Bank of International Settlements; David Carse, former deputy chief executive of the Hong Kong Monetary Authority; and Sir Howard Davies, former head of the UK's Financial Services Authority. Working with TCC supervision the Chinese banks were now deemed ready to attract global capital through stock offerings. Morgan Stanley did the initial public offering (IPO) for the China Construction Bank, and Goldman Sachs and UBS the IPO for Bank of China. Credit Suisse First Boston helped list the Industrial and Commercial Bank of China, which at the time set an IPO record by attracting $21.9 billion. The Agricultural Bank of China, with 24,000 branches and 350 million customers, was the last to list in 2010. By 2012 the four banks had assets about the size of the British, French and German economies combined.

Financial investments in the Chinese SOEs are a vote of confidence by global capitalists in their Chinese statist partners. In Table 5.2 we find a merging of interests between the most important transnational financial institutions and the most important SOEs. The government and Chinese investment firms owned between 56 to 81 percent of the total stock in the listed SOEs. But foreign TCC interests don't need to control SOEs. Rather they are focused on making profits from their investments, and trust the statist TCC in China to manage these giant corporations according to capitalist best business practices. Global capitalists share in the

Table 5.2 Financial Investments in Chinese SOEs

SOE	BlackRock	Fidelity	HSBC	JP Morgan	Invesco	Vanguard	UBS
Bank of China	✓	✓	✓	✓	✓	✓	✓
China Communications Construction Corporation	✓	✓	✓	✓	✓	✓	
China Construction Bank	✓	✓	✓	✓	✓	✓	✓
China Rail Engineering General Corporation	✓	✓	✓	✓	✓	✓	
China Railway Construction Corporation	✓		✓	✓	✓	✓	✓
China Telecommunications	✓	✓	✓	✓	✓	✓	✓
Industrial and Commercial Bank of China	✓	✓	✓	✓	✓	✓	✓
SINOPEC	✓	✓	✓	✓	✓	✓	✓
PetroChina	✓	✓	✓	✓	✓	✓	

Source: David Peetz, and Georgina Murray, "Global 2009 shareholding unit database," Osiris database, Bureau van Dyk, Amsterdam, 2010.

188 | GLOBAL CAPITALISM AND THE CRISIS OF DEMOCRACY

profits and losses of these "national" champions, more properly labeled transnational monopolies due to the character of their financial structure.[28]

Other important stockholders include Barclays, Capital Group, Deutsch Bank, Franklin Resources, Hong Kong's HKSCC Nominees Limited, Massachusetts Mutual Life Insurance, Schrodders, State Street Corporation, Waddell and Reed Financial, and the French banks Axa and BNP Paribas. These transnational financial institutions invest for global capitalists the world over. The networks are deep and broad, and represent far more than just investors from the country where the firms happen to be headquartered. This is the financial process that helps to integrate the TCC, with Western money facilitating the global expansion of Chinese SOEs while sharing in the profits. Transnational capitalists aren't concerned about the national origin of money, or whether it comes from state or private sources. For global capitalists money has no national identity.

The largest equity firms are also in the game. TPG Capital and Kohlberg Kravis Roberts jointly acquired Morgan Stanley's 34-percent stake in China International Capital Corporation (CICC), the leading investment bank in China. Both Henry Kravis of KKR and TPG's David Bonderman sit on the board. CICC controls 14 firms listed in Hong Kong and China, investing in real estate, finance, manufacturing, and mining. Holding another 20 percent in CICC through a joint venture are Itochu of Japan and the Charoen Pokphand Group (CP Group) of Thailand. This brings together three Asian giants. Itochu has interests in multiple areas, and CP Group is another conglomerate controlled by Thai billionaire Dhanin Chearavanont. Speaking to the transnational character of CICC its former chairman Chang Zhenming stated, "Not only have we brought in private investors, but they are attractive global conglomerates who will extend our reach and complement our infrastructure and knowledge. This investment is a continuation of our reform and globalization."[29] The current chairman, Ding Xuedong, is also chairman and chief executive of China's sovereign wealth fund.[30] Additionally, Jin Liqun, who holds a 43-percent ownership in CICC, will head one of the government's most important institutions, the Asian Infrastructure Investment Bank.[31] Overall, CICC is an excellent example of the close relationship between state, private, and transnational financial interests.

US financial institutions are active with other important companies. Both TPG and Blackstone have multi-billion dollar investment funds in partnership with the city government of Shanghai. And TPG holds equity stakes in Lenovo, the Shenzhen Development Bank, and China Grand Auto. Another investment sector is buying bad debt and non-performing loans on the cheap, something in which transnational finance has expertise. An opportunity arose when Huarong Asset Management, with assets of $66 billion, sought investors. Buying into Huarong were Goldman Sachs, Morgan Stanley, Deutsche Bank, private equity firms Warburg Pincus and Fosun Group, Malaysian state investor Khazanah Nasional Bhd, China state-backed COFCO Corp, and Citic.

The Private Tech Sector

Jack Ma's Alibaba is the most recognized internet company in China's most dynamic private sector. Ma, and the manner in which he funded Alibaba, is a good example of transnational capitalism. Alibaba's fabulous IPO on the New York Stock Exchange made the company worth $231 billion, more than Amazon and eBay combined. Ma went to financial centers around the world to pitch the IPO to TCC investors, and urged them to see Alibaba as a global tech company that just "happens to be in China." When IPO trading was over, a previous one-percent stake would now be worth over $1 billion. Alibaba is more than an e-commerce corporation operating inside China, its money market fund Yu'ebao has $100 billion in assets and 200 million users. It's one of the largest money market funds in the world. Alibaba has also invested aggressively in Silicon Valley, buying stakes in six companies. The investments are strategic, providing insights into cutting-edge technologies and making global alliances.

Yahoo and Softbank from Japan were both early investors in Alibaba. Softbank owned 34 percent and Yahoo held 23 percent. Although foreign corporations aren't allowed to hold stakes in China's internet enterprises, using a complex investment vehicle known as the variable interest entity (VIE), foreign investors are able to channel money through offshore business shells. Alibaba is headquartered in China and listed in New York and Hong Kong, but its governance structure and profits are held in the Cayman Islands. These are channeled through VIE Shares, which are held by Athena China Limited in the British Virgin Islands, which is controlled by Prosperous Wintersweet BVI, which in turn is owned by Boyu Capital Fund I in the Cayman Islands.[32]

State regulators have turned a blind eye to the VIE practice used by many of the new and most profitable private Chinese companies. The government's major concern is that the main offshore portion of ownership is Chinese rather than foreign. About 108 of the 225 Chinese companies listed on NASDAQ and the New York Stock Exchange use the VIE structure.[33] State officials have good cause to allow such transnational financial strategies to continue. Major Chinese investment firms with close ties to top leaders often hold stakes in tech companies.

Again Alibaba is a good example. Four financial firms with Alibaba stock had executives that are sons or grandsons of two dozen elite Standing Committee members since 2002. Corporations with princeling executives include the private equity firm New Horizon Capital; the holding company Boyu; CDB Capital, the private investment arm of state-owned China Development Bank; and the state's sovereign wealth fund CIC. The network of "princelings" is thick, and family ties extend into the most important state ministries.[34] Consequently, we uncover the ties between the statist TCC, new private capitalists like Ma, capitalist princelings like Winston Wen and Alvin Jiang, and transnational corporations and global financial investors. In an internal program titled "sons and daughters," J.P. Morgan facilitated these networks by hiring family and friends of executives from 75 percent of the Chinese firms they helped take public.[35] The circulation of global capital flows through every country, from state banks in Beijing, shell companies in the Cayman Islands, to the suites of New York and London financial firms.

Xiaomi, China's smartphone firm, has also turned to transnational investors to expand its capital base. Lei Jun, CEO of the $45 billion company, sought ties with Mark Zuckerberg of Facebook. Zuckerberg has been looking for ways into China's market, but the social networking company is banned by the government. Evidently the independent networking capabilities of Facebook are too socially dangerous for the CCP. The political danger made Lei walk away from any deal with Zuckerberg. Instead Lei turned to the Hong Kong-based fund All Stars Investment; DST Global, the private equity firm of Russian billionaire Yuri Milner; Singapore sovereign wealth fund GIC; Chinese private equity group Hopu Management; and Ma's Yunfeng Capital.

Xiaomi has also contracted with Foxconn to produce its phones in Brazil for the local South American market. The Taiwanese transnational Foxconn is the largest employer in China, churning out electronic products for the world's biggest tech companies. Foxconn makes Apple's iPhone, putting to work more than 200,000 people in the city of Zhengzhou, and one million throughout China. Foxconn has often been criticized for its sweatshop conditions and barracks-like living quarters. The corporation also assembles iPhone and iPads at its Sao Paulo plant in Brazil, where Xiaomi will be added to the production line.

Other important deals by IT companies relatively unknown in the West have also taken place. Tsinghua Unigroup bought a 51-percent stake in Hewlett-Packard's China-based data-networking business, H3C Technologies, for $2 billion. And in another Tsinghua deal the company received a $1.5 billion investment from Intel. Of further note, Huaxin bought an 85-percent stake in Alcatel-Lucent's computing business.[36] American citizens may be unfamiliar with these Chinese companies, but leading US tech corporations are busy integrating their operations.

China's tech sector is gaining a global reputation with such giants as Lenovo, Huawei, Xiaomi, Tencent, Weibo, and Baidu.

These companies have attracted top executive and research talent, and are getting elite Western managers, scientists, and engineers to jump ship and join the Chinese surge. John Suffolk, the top information officer of the British government joined Huawei, and former BP chief executive Lord Browne was recruited to become its chairman; Hugo Barra, Google's vice president for Android, went to Xiaomi; Baidu grabbed Zhang Yaqing, a top executive from Microsoft, along with top software architects Wei Xu from Facebook, Andrew Ng from Google, and Ren Wu from AMD; Alibaba made former Goldman Sachs vice chairman Michael Evans its president and James Wilkinson, who served as a top official to Condoleezza Rice and Hank Paulson, was put in charge of its international corporate affairs. Another indication of the rise of the Chinese tech sector was seen in KPMG's annual survey. The survey asks about 800 global tech and business executives to rank the top 25 cities that lead as technology innovation centers. Shanghai ranked number one, Beijing number three, Hong Kong placed ninth, and Shenzhen placed at number 14.[37]

As the tech sector grows it becomes more integrated into the transnational economy through the use of IPOs. From 2010 to 2014 more than 50 percent of global tech listings came from China. In fact, China led the world in overall categories with 195 IPOs, while all other countries listed just 218. Moreover, Chinese companies made greater use of cross-border listings, more than the totals from the rest of the world.[38] Venture capitalists took notice and poured $15.5 billion into deals in 2014.

Early investors in technology companies hit it big with IPO listings. Baidu pre-IPO equity holders included US venture capital firm Draper Fisher Jurvetson, which held 28 percent; Integrity Partners with 11 percent; Peninsula Capital with 10 percent; and IDG at five percent. A South African media company, Naspers, had 38 percent of Tencent, which after its IPO was worth $120 billion. Other investors who made millions to billions in tech IPOs have been hedge fund Tiger Global; software firm DST; Prince Alwaleed bin Talal of Saudi Arabia; and Silicon Valley venture firms Sequoia Capital and GGV Capital.[39]

Stocks are a key area for the circulation of global capital, allowing the TCC to scan the world for investments through financial firms such as BlackRock, Vanguard, or JP Morgan. Whether it is new tech companies selling equity, or SOEs listing corporate bonds, the economic results are greater global integration. In 2014 total foreign direct investment in China hit $2.55 trillion.[40] Additionally, cross-border borrowing by Chinese corporations is another source of funds, although also a source of debt. The Bank for International Settlements recorded $880 billion in foreign currency loans to China in early 2013.

It is evident from this brief survey that transnational capital plays an important role in China's economy, and that in turn the Chinese economy is integral to global capitalism. This is true in every sector, from the giant SOEs to the dynamic and growing private sector, financial institutions, state banks, and global export factories that supply manufactured goods to the world. Such institutional ties and economic structures build the foundations where the TCC sinks deep roots. But this is only part of the picture. We now can turn our attention to the export of capital and Chinese corporate expansion abroad.

Outward Bound Capital

The Mercator Institute for China Studies and the Rhodium Group state that, "Today, we are on the verge of a massive growth in China's cross-border capital flows, which will result in major shifts in the global financial landscape."[41] They estimate that by 2020 China's global assets may rise from the current $6.8 trillion to almost $20 trillion. China is already the third top exporter of overseas direct investments (ODI), with funds shifting from natural resources to IT equipment, autos, and consumer commodities. ODI in financial institutions is at $664.8 billion. In Table 5.3 we see the continual rise in China's total FDI stock in spite of the global economic crisis. FDI has a somewhat different definition (see below) from ODI, which is a firm extending operations to a foreign country via Greenfield investments, merger/acquisitions, or expansion of an existing foreign facility.[42]

Table 5.3 China's Outward FDI* Stock, 2009-2014 (US Billions)					
2009	2010	2011	2012	2013	2014
245,755.40	317,210.60	424,780.70	512,584.70	613,584.70	729,584.70

* FDI defined as investments that lead to significant (> 10%) and long-term interest in a foreign business by setting up a subsidiary in the foreign country, acquiring shares of an overseas company, or through a merger or joint venture.

Source: United Nations Conference on Trade and Development, "FDI Outward Stock, by region and economy, 1990-2014."
<http://unctad.org/en/Pages/DIAE/World%20Investment%20Report/Annex-Tables.aspx>
(2015).

China's outbound capital is growing by leaps and bounds. In the first quarter of 2015 it invested in 2,884 overseas-based corporations in 146 countries.[43] By the end of the year China's global investments and cross-border acquisitions had reached a record high of $123 billion.[44] SOEs dominate this activity with almost 90 percent of the investments. In early 2016 Chinese acquisitions abroad accounted for 47 percent of all cross-border activity, and four of the top six deals.[45] Just 110 world-class corporations owned by the central government have $4.3 trillion in assets abroad.

A historic turning point came in 2015 when China exported more capital than it received by inward investments. Zeng Peiyan, former vice-premier and top economic policy expert spoke to how China could now help determine the structure of global capitalism, "The large going-out of Chinese capital means the country is able to participate in the restructuring of global industrial, supply and value chains, which are the keys to foster new competitive advantages."[46] The Chinese TCC is now an integral part of the world system. Transnational capitalists from all continents depend on China's internal economy, and its outbound capital for growth and stability of the world system. Just as the Chinese TCC depends on their global relationships for their own power and stability.

In examining China's assimilation into global capitalism a look at some of its main financial institutions is instructive. China's sovereign wealth fund, CIC, holds $650 billion in total assets. It's best known for its large holding of US Treasury debt and investments in private equity funds with Blackstone and Morgan Stanley. But with $220 billion in overseas assets CIC has diversified into long-term investments, expanding its global portfolio. In the United States CIC has shares in AIG, Apple, Bank of America, Citigroup, Coca-Cola, Johnson & Johnson, Motorola, News Corp., and Visa. By 2010 CIC had $9.63 billion in equity stakes in more than 60 US corporations and added Morgan Stanley's CEO to its advisory council. In Canada it has positions in Research in Motion, the maker of BlackBerry mobile phones, and a $3.5 billion stake in the mining company Tech Resources.[47] Additionally CIC invested $1 billion in Oaktree Capital Management, $1 billion in JSX KazMunaiGas in Kazakhstan, $956 million with UK's private equity firm Apax, and $850 million for a 15-percent stake in Hong Kong's conglomerate Noble Group. CIC has also bought up European debt, purchasing government bonds in Greece, Portugal, and Spain. Other holdings in Europe include 10 percent in London's Heathrow Airport, 9 percent in Thames Water, and 7 percent in Eutelsat Communications in France.[48]

China Development Bank is larger than the World Bank and already the biggest funder of global infrastructure projects. "It is responsible for thousands of kilometers of roads and rail in Africa, its projects keep the lights on in Pakistan and Indonesia, the trains running in Venezuela and Argentina and it has probably done more to address climate change by building renewables projects in developing countries than any other bank."[49] From 2013 to 2014 China's development banks extended almost $700 billion in export financing. That's greater than the US total for the last 80 years.

China's banks are among the most significant in the world. In keeping with the policy of outbound capital, foreign lending by the four biggest banks hit $378 billion by the beginning of 2014. The Industrial and Commercial Bank of China (ICBC), is the world's third-most profitable transnational corporation, and the largest bank by market capitalization. In the biggest foreign acquisition by a Chinese bank, ICBC bought 20 percent of South

Africa's Standard Bank for $5.56 billion. After the purchase in Africa ICBC proceeded to buy 80 percent of Standard's subsidiary in Argentina, where they had previously taken 75 percent of the Bank of Boston. ICBC has also entered Brazil, Mexico, Peru, and Thailand. The bank's international strategy is focused on establishing a presence in countries where Chinese corporations do business. In Argentina over 90 percent of Chinese companies have taken loans from ICBC. The bank is also using its relationship with Standard to buy its London-based commodity trading business. This will give ICBC a hold in the global trading of crude oil, copper, and other raw materials, an area where China has minimum presence despite its need for vast amounts of such commodities.

Although large and profitable, ICBC is still a state-owned bank with significantly lower executive compensation. In 2013 ICBC chairman Jiang Jianqing took home about $326,000 in salary, bonuses, and benefits, compared to the $12 million compensation package of Jamie Dimon at JP Morgan. Jiang has never been charged with any unlawful act, but as some Chinese managers look with jealousy at their Western counterparts, lower wage scales become one element leading to corruption.

Perhaps the most important story regarding China's financial foray into the world of global capitalism is the establishment of the Asian Infrastructure Investment Bank (AIIB). It is estimated that developing countries will need $8 trillion to finance its infrastructure needs, beyond existing funds in such institutions as the World Bank and the Asia Development Bank. Constructing large infrastructure projects plays to China's experience and strength. Moreover, traditionally Western-dominated institutions, such as the World Bank and IMF, have not recognized China as the world's second largest economy. At the IMF, even after an adjustment giving China six percent of the vote, the US maintains a much larger influence with 18 percent. After years of asking for greater voting rights, China has decided to write new rules for global capitalism. The US has viewed China as a challenge to its political leadership in constructing and maintaining the world system. Neither China nor the US are against the transnationalization of capital, but their different visions of how the project should be built and run are points of conflict. The US tried to contain China's influence by pushing the Trans Pacific Trade Pact without Chinese participation, and launching an intensive lobbying effort to keep countries from joining the AIIB. But even within elite US foreign policy circles there was criticism of Obama's position from stalwarts like former National Security Advisor Zbigniew Brezinski and World Bank president Robert Zoellick. As former head of Goldman Sachs and Secretary of the Treasury Hank Paulson stated, "China is not going to try and throw out... the global financial infrastructure. They are going to want to participate in it; we need to make room for them; they are going to want to have some initiatives themselves and we need to participate with them."[50]

The attempted boycott of the AIIB turned into an embarrassing rout when Great Britain decided to join. This was quickly followed by Germany, France, Italy, and Norway. In Asia, US allies joined the stampede including South Korea, New Zealand, and Australia. This left Japan as the only significant Asian power on the outside looking in. By the time Xi hosted the bank's founding member nations, fifty-seven were present including Brazil, India, Russia, Iran, Saudi Arabia, and Israel. Praise rolled in from the Asian Development Bank, the European Bank for Reconstruction, the World Bank, and the IMF. Christine Lagarde, Director of the IMF, said the fund would be "delighted" to work with the AIIB. China will have 26 percent of the vote, much better than its six percent in the IMF.

The rush to join the AIIB indicates how deeply global capitalists are committed to a transnational system of economic governance. In fact, the European Investment Bank quietly advised China on governance standards and best practice in setting up the bank. Shortly after the establishment of AIIB, China was invited to join the European Bank for Reconstruction and Development. The bank's governor noted their activities complimented China's Silk Road strategy, and indicated that he looked forward to

198 | GLOBAL CAPITALISM AND THE CRISIS OF DEMOCRACY

working closely with AIIB. Writing for *EuropeanCEO*, Elizabeth Matsangou stated, "In stepping in to play a pivotal role in the development of various countries, its voice on the world stage grows stronger with each such move that it makes. China's formation of the AIIB thus forms a central pillar to this strategy, particularly as it is Asia's only development bank that has little control from the West, and essentially, is independent from the US."[51]

Plans for US hegemony have been dead from the start, an emperor without clothes. If money is to be made, the TCC will not be held back. In response to the US boycott of AIIB Kevin Rafferty, former managing director of the World Bank, stated, "The United States has lost its way and is rapidly forfeiting claims to global financial, economic, political and moral leadership."[52]

Although some in Washington see the new bank as a move to replace US economic influence, Jin Liqun, who is president of the AIIB, has sought US participation. He hired two American veterans of the World Bank as staff members and stated, "We have a standing invitation" for the US to join the bank.[53] This approach is similar to China's willingness to possibly join the Trans Pacific Partnership trade pact. It seems their main interest is in expanding global capitalism, rather than playing containment politics with the US.The AIIB must be seen as part of a new generation of financial and political institutions being constructed by developing countries. This reflects a TCC no longer simply centered in the West, but a more broadly based global capitalism. The old comprador bourgeoisie of the Third World have been replaced by a new Southern fraction of the TCC, more wealthy and independent.

Among the most important initiatives is the One Belt and One Road infrastructure project, often referred to as the Silk Road Economic Belt and the Maritime Silk Road. This vast project envisions expanding and building sea ports, airports, railways, and highways from China to Europe, encompassing 60 countries. This includes eliminating trade barriers; greater exploration and extraction of natural resources, oil and gas pipelines; fiber optic and communication cables; and stronger financial ties. Free trade areas will be established throughout participating countries opening up services in education, culture, and health care, while also encouraging investments in child and elderly care, architectural design, accounting and auditing, logistics, and e-commerce.[54] The Economic Belt hopes to link China, Central Asia, Russia, and Europe, while the Maritime Road will go from China to Europe through the South China Sea, the Indian Ocean, and South Pacific. It's a major reason countries rushed to join the AIIB.

Already being planned is a connection with Russia's Euro-Asia Railway, a logistics terminal jointly built by China and Kazakhstan, and the development of the Bangladesh-China-India-Myanmar Economic Corridor. In China's largest single foreign deal, Pakistan received a $45 billion loan for the China-Pakistan Economic Corridor. When completed the infrastructure project will give China direct access to the Indian Ocean.

One of the important components in the funding plans for the Silk Road is the BRICS bank with $100 billion in capital. Headquartered in China it will act as a development institution for Brazil, Russia, India, South Africa, and China. Its main focus will be on making loans for infrastructure projects, which fits perfectly into the Silk Road.

The Silk Road constitutes the most extensive infrastructure undertaking in the world, but two ocean-to-ocean schemes in South America rank in the number two and three positions. Still in the planning stage, China is working with Brazil and Peru to build a $60 billion transcontinental railway cutting through the Amazon forest. Latin American expert Kevin Gallagher noted, the railway is "really a test case for the China-Latin America relationship. If it's done right, a high-speed railway with high-level engineering, a minimal amount of environmental damage and engagement with local communities is going to be a win-win all around. But it could also be the complete opposite."[55]

The second venture is the Nicaragua Canal, running from the Caribbean coast to the Pacific. This project is not a state-backed endeavor, but headed by billionaire Wang Jing. The $40

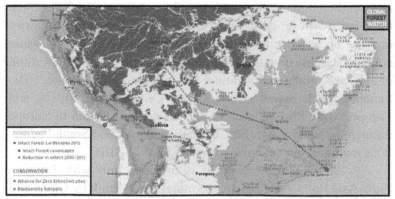

Figure 5.1 Transcontinental Railway Route from Brazil to Peru

billion canal project has run into mass protests because, as an environmental study states, "there is no route through Nicaragua that can avoid the areas with the most high-biodiversity... Furthermore, the entire country lies within the Mesoamerican Biodiversity Hotspot, meaning that its conservation is a matter of global importance."[56]

Whether done with sensitivity towards the environment and indigenous peoples, all three mega projects mean a greater consumption of energy and natural resources, deforestation, disruption to animal migration patterns, and roads that bring settlers into previously uninhabited areas. China is embedded in the growth imperative that affects all capitalist economies. Expansion is necessary to keep the system running and profits growing; expansion makes the global machine operate. With these projects the vision of the Chinese TCC, both state and private, are central to the global developmental plans of the world capitalist system. It's no longer a question of China's internal growth and export zones, but also its outbound capital and strategic leadership.

When it comes to Latin America the extraction of natural resources dominates China's interests. Following the US, China has become the second major export destination for Latin American goods. But only five commodities made up 71 percent of those exports: iron ore at 20 percent; soybeans and oilseeds at 18 percent; copper at 14 percent; copper ores at 10 percent; and crude petroleum at 9 percent. In terms of mergers and acquisitions, 70 percent have taken place in the oil and gas sector. Complementing the focus on resources, loans between 2007 and 2014 totaling $118 billion were almost exclusively for infrastructure, dams, oil and gas, and mining projects. In the decade to come Xi has promised another $250 billion in new investments.[57]

The relationship with China has provided important economic space for Latin America countries to distance themselves from the US and exert greater political independence. This is particularly true for Venezuela, Bolivia, Ecuador, Brazil, and Argentina. But there has been an environmental price. Because of the emphasis on primary commodities, exports to China emit about 12 percent more global warming gases, and use about twice as much water as other exports.[58] When it comes to growth there is always an environmental price. As for labor and environmental laws Chinese state and private corporations perform similarly to domestic or other international firms. In some projects they outperform competitors, in other instances they do worse. What is key is that the Chinese/Latin American relationship is one of the foundation stones of global capitalism, not only in terms of trade and investments, but also because the commodities sent to China help fuel the factories owned by the global TCC, and are essential in the transnational circulation of goods and capital.

The EU and the US

The European Union (EU) is the most important area of the developed world for Chinese investments. As a study by Thilo Hanemann and Mikko Huotari suggests, "China's changing global OFDI footprint presents a once in a lifetime opportunity for attracting capital to Europe and helping to re-start investment and economic growth...China is so unique and important because it is already a major global investor and it has the potential to become the single most important driver of global FDI growth over the next decade."[59]

China has more than 1,000 Greenfield projects and

acquisitions throughout the EU worth about $50 billion. The major investment areas have been in energy at 28 percent; auto, 13 percent; agriculture and food, 12 percent; real estate, 11 percent; industrial equipment, nine percent; and IT at six percent. Additionally China has large agriculture holdings in the Ukraine. About 78 percent of investments come from state-owned corporations. Germany, France and the UK have attracted the most investments, with Germany leading. About 82 percent of Chinese FDI involves acquisitions, denoting deep integration into local economies.[60] But as large as FDI figures run the data may undercount the actual flow, because investments routed through Hong Kong are counted separately.

As part of the Chinese surge, private firms are rapidly increasing their investments in the EU. Contrary to the common perception that Chinese companies are low tech and labor intensive, their R&D and innovation are leading the way in Europe. Huawei has an R&D headquarters in Munich and more than 30 research and development facilities throughout the EU, including centers in Belgium, Finland, France, Germany, Ireland, Italy, Sweden, and the UK. In auto and transportation, Shanghai Automotive has a design center in the UK, Chang'an Automobile Group does testing in Italy, and CSR carries out R&D in Dresden. In the field of industrial machinery Sany and Xuzhou Construction run R&D facilities in Germany. In the biotech and pharmaceutical industries Beijing Genomics does work in Prague. Another manner in which Chinese transnationals are active in technology is through acquisitions. In Table 5.4 are some of the most important cross-border deals.

As the state opens the spigot and capital flows from China, the hunger of global capitalists can hardly be contained. Currently China's OFDI stock to GDP ratio stands at only seven percent. But for advanced economies it is much larger, 47 percent for Germany, 38 percent for the US, and 20 percent for Japan. Consequently, in the near future the movement of Chinese capital is expected to significantly expand. Besides private corporations having more freedom to invest abroad, new institutional investors

Table 5.4 Chinese Acquisitions Targeting European Technology Companies in Europe

EU Company	Chinese Investor	Location	Industry
Schwing	Xuzhou Construction Machinery Group	Herne, Germany	Industrial Machinery and Tools
WISCO Tailored Blanks	Wuhan Iron & Steel	Duisburg, Germany	Automotive Equipment and Components
Thielert Aircraft Engines	AVIC International	St. Egidien, Germany	Aerospace Equipment and Components
Medion	Lenovo	Essen, Germany	IT Equipment
Alcatel-Lucent Enterprise in Colombes, France	China Huaxin Post & Telecommunication Economy Development Center	Boulogne-Billancourt, France	IT Equipment
PSA Peugeot Citroen	Dongfeng Motor Group	Paris, France	Automotive Equipment and Components
Compagnia Italiana Forme Acciaio	Zoomlion Heavy Industry Science & Technology Development	Milan, Italy	Industrial Machinery and Tools

Source: Rhodium Group

include China's sovereign wealth fund, social security funds, pension funds, insurance firms, asset management companies, private equity funds, and other large financial institutions.

Recognizing the importance of China, European leaders invited its financial institutions to join the EU's new $356 billion infrastructure fund. The fund will build synergy with the AIIB for Silk Road projects. In his 2015 trip to Europe, Premier Li pledged a multi-billion dollar investment. The fund's financing is mainly derived from private firms and development banks. Interest was high among Chinese institutions attracting the five leading banks and telecommunication TNCs, such as Huawei and ZTE. Alessandro Carano, an advisor to the European Commission on the fund, stated, "The purpose is to mobilize the liquidity in the market. We don't differentiate among the owners of the funds. China is a big investor already. We don't want any prejudice."[61] Again we see the transnational orientation of global capitalists, who remain unconcerned with the national origins of capital. Moreover, given the close transnational ties between the EU and China, it becomes clear why so many European countries rushed to join the AIIB over US objections. Although not always true, economic relationships tend to override political concerns. It's the reason why global capitalism is emerging as the hegemonic system, while big power politics slowly fades in the rear-view mirror.

For the US the transition to a multicentric political reality, and an even deeper economic transnationalization, is full of contradictory pressures. The belief that globalization is and must be a US-led project is still strong among many political and military elites, and for some this means China is the next great competitor.[62] As Obama noted, "When more than 95 percent of our potential customers live outside our borders, we can't let countries like China write the rules of the global economy...We should write those rules...."[63] But as vice-finance minister Zhu Guangyao stated, "The two largest economies in the world, China and the US, are inseparable."[64] Underwriting this relationship is the $1.28 trillion in US treasuries held by the Chinese state. Nonetheless, while efforts to build global capitalism remains a unifying project, there exist an array of visions among the competitive complexity of groups, countries, and transnational monopolies.

Although Chinese investments into the US have been more limited than into other areas of the world, they are growing significantly. By early 2015 investments had hit $59 billion and involved some 1,500 enterprises. One of the key factors in recent investments, different from the rest of Chinese global activity, is that more than 80 percent come from private corporate interests. Some of these include the large insurance transnationals Ping An and Anbang, and China's largest private financial investment firm, Fosun. Other factors consolidating US/China ties are the $600 billion in annual bilateral trade, the 275,000 Chinese studying in America, and the 25,000 Americans studying in China.

One of the largest US investments by a Chinese corporation was Shuanghui's $4.7 billion acquisition of Smithfield Foods, America's number one pork producer. While seen as a Chinese takeover, in fact this was a typical transnational action. Majority stakes in Shuanghui are held at 36 percent by its Chinese investors. But CDH, a US private equity firm, is the next largest stakeholder with 34 percent. Goldman Sachs holds five percent, with another five percent in the hands of New Horizon Capital, a private equity firm co-founded by the son of ex-premier Wen Jiabao. The last major stock holder is Singapore's sovereign wealth fund Temasek at about three percent. To complete the acquisition Shuanghui set up an offshore entity based in the Cayman Islands with help from Morgan Stanley, the company's banker in the deal.[65] The deal may appear Chinese in form, but in reality it is transnational in content.

Although minor in the overall scheme of global investments, Keer Group's location of a $218 million yarn mill in South Carolina is of special interest since textile jobs were among the first to go abroad, seeking low-wage labor in China and other emerging economies. But today the Carolinas host some 20 Chinese manufacturers, including China's Volvo auto plant. Even though US wages are higher, the gap has been narrowed with pay hikes in China. Additionally, higher US wages are offset by subsidies, cheaper cotton, and lower energy costs. Keer received about $20 million in subsidies that covered infrastructure grants, tax credits, and revenue bonds. Spinning yarn is more capital intensive than textile mills; even so Keer employs about 500 workers under favorable corporate conditions. As *The New York Times* pointed out, "Keer has found residents desperate for work, even at depressed wages, as well as access to cheap and abundant land and energy and heavily subsidized cotton."[66] It seems globalization has turned the tables, from the US to China and back again.

China's Dream: Socialism or Capitalism?

This survey of China's transnational relationships is far from complete. Nevertheless, evidence indicates the central importance of inward and outbound capital for the Chinese economy. Since the 1980s China has proceeded down the road of global integration, each step cautious, but the direction has been clear. The entire process has been led by the Communist Party using its control of the state apparatus. In doing so vast opportunities have become available to Party cadre, from the very top down to the local level—opportunities both legal and corrupt. No matter which path private wealth has taken, the capitalist market has been its foundation, a market intricately tied to global capitalism. Thus we have the formation of a Chinese statist transnational capitalist class fraction, unique to the country's history and culture, locked arm-in-arm with the statist TCC, through networks of family, business and politics, to private capitalists who through their own dealings further extend links to the world-wide transnational class.

Capitalism in China is based in two overwhelming institutions—the state and the market. Although similar developments have occurred elsewhere, none have the depth and influence of the Chinese experience. As impressive as China's development has been, significant weight for civil society is missing. The courts and justice system are controlled by the Party with almost no transparency. No matter if you're a worker arrested in a labor dispute, or a high Party official charged with corruption, once in court chances of acquittal are miniscule. The media has little leeway to go outside the bounds of Party approval. The blogosphere and internet face constant limitations. Labor lawyers are arrested, feminist protestors put in jail, and the campaign against Party corruption is kept tightly controlled by the most elite body of the Party itself. The Party's ruling policy offers a trade-off between material well-being and political participation.

Some believe social conflicts will push China back onto the road of socialism. But with no national political autonomy for working class organizations, pressure from below can be kept in check. More likely is a Russian scenario in which capitalist forces within the CCP decide to rid themselves of the Party's statist fraction because it inhibits their growth and wealth. Such internal conflict may develop over anti-corruption campaigns, limits on managerial salaries, and too much capital devoted to social spending.

Wang Huning, an influential advisor to Xi, has been an ardent advocate for strong central leadership during modernization, based on the success of South Korea, Singapore, and other countries. But Wang admits that such a system lacks public participation, and could end up developing a technocracy impervious to popular will. Wang argues that during modernization independent activists in civil society can cause major disruptions that need "forceful action." But he goes on to state that once a developed economy is achieved ignoring popular demands would "cause political instability (and) when the social development enters this stage, political reform would be imperative."[67] But would a ruling class embedded in an authoritarian state be able to make fundamental democratic reforms empowering the working class? By the time economic modernization reaches what Wang perceives to be the right stage, capitalist class interests will be so strong that intense class struggle may well be necessary.

To be sure, many localized demonstrations already take place. Close to 200,000 are recorded by the government each year.

These involve a spectrum of grievances from low wages, poor working conditions, environmental pollution, official corruption, and unjust land seizures. But the question for democracy, no less for socialism, is whether workers, peasants, and the new middle class can create room for autonomous political organizations, not only on a local level, but regional and national as well. This doesn't have to be in the form of oppositional political parties but independent unions, feminist organizations, and environmental advocacy groups that go beyond today's limited arena are necessary. Such developments rarely wait for government to designate the right time to address them.

The Party's fears of mass mobilization, protests, and social upheaval are easy to understand. The Great Leap Forward, the Cultural Revolution and Tiananmen Square all ended with disastrous results. Stability and social harmony achieved through greater material wealth are goals any ruling party with a sense of social responsibility would hope to accomplish. From the point-of-view of the government, class struggle is disruptive and something to be avoided. Mao had the opposite view, that it was class struggle that pushed forward development. This is also easy to understand. Under his leadership the Party went from near annihilation to victory over 25 years of revolutionary armed struggle. Mass mobilization and class struggle were the constant lessons of those years, and Mao continued on that path once in power.

Can the Party move beyond these defining historic experiences, and establish institutions that provide space for independent political expressions of class contradictions? This is no easy task, particularly given the heavy weight of the past and the success of the last 30 years. But underneath that success vast inequality and anger has grown. If class contradictions are not allowed to be fully expressed in a manner that channels social struggles into democratic resolutions, those contradictions will result in disruptive political explosions. If the Party hopes to avoid mass and bloody disorder and repression, as took place in the Cultural Revolution and Tiananmen Square, it must make room for broader institutional forms outside its own political monopoly. A harmonious society can't be built through the artificial suppression of conflict. Whether or not China continues to join with authoritarian global capitalism, or renews its socialist path, depends not only on the Party, but more so on the working class and its independent entry onto the political stage.

Endnotes

1   Jerry Harris, "Statism and the transnational capitalist class in China," in Jeb Sprague, Editor, *Globalization and Transnational Capitalism in Asia and Oceana* (Routledge: London and New York, 2015).

2   Kevin Lin, "Global capitalism and the transformation of China's working class," in Jeb Sprague, Editor, *Globalization and Transnational Capitalism in Asia and Oceana* (Routledge: London and New York, 2015).

3   Julian Snelder, "The Truth about China SOEs," <http://www.businessspectator.com.au/article/2014/12/2/china/truth-about-china-soes> (December 2, 2014).

4   Sun Yingshuai, "'Recurrence' and 'Reconstitution': The Rise of 'New Workers' and the Transition of China's Social Structure—Marxist Class Theory and the new Changes in the Contemporary Working Class," International Critical Thought, Vol. 5, No. 2 (2015): 148-163.

5   Guy Standing, *The Precariat: The New Dangerous Class* (Bloomsbury: London, 2011).

6   Zemin Jiang, "Speech on the 80th Anniversary Celebration of the CPC," *Peoples Daily,* (July 2, 2001).

7   Zhong Nan, "Chinese consumers buy nearly half of world's luxury products," *China Daily*, (February 2, 2016).

8   Tong Bao, "How Deng Xiaoping Helped Create a Corrupt China," *The New York Times*, (June 3, 2015).

9   Edward S. Steinfeld, "China, high tech, and the 'high tempo cost out' revolution," <http://www.brookings.edu/blogs/techtank/posts/2015/05/12-china-high-tempo-revolution> (May 12, 2015).

10   Antony Dapiran, "Green light flashes for foreign investments in China," <http://www.businessspectator.com.au/article/2015/1/22/china/green-light-flashes-foreign-investment-china?utm_source=exact&utm_medium=email&utm_content=1102751&utm_campaign=chs_daily&modapt=> (January 22, 2015).

11   Helen Wong, "China's free trade zones will accelerate reform," <http://www.businessspectator.com.au/article/2015/4/2/china/chinas-free-trade-zones-will-accelerate-reform?utm_source=exact&utm_medium=email&utm_content=1269474&utm_campaign=chs_daily&modapt> (April 2, 2015).

12   Xinhua, "Foreign investment in China hits record in 2015," English. news.cn, (January 5, 2016).

13   Reuters, "China Demands Wall Around Wealth Management Sector to Cut Risk," Reuters, (July 12, 2014).

14   David Barboza, "Lobbying, a Windfall and a Leader's Family," *The New York Times*, (November 24, 2012); David Barboza, "Family of Chinese Regulator Profits in Insurance Firm's Rise," *The New York Times*, (December 30, 2012).

15   David Barboza, "For One Tiananmen-Era Student a Very Different Path to Power," *The New York Times*, (June 3, 2014).

16   David Cai, "The bitter medicine China will be forced to swallow," <http://www.businessspectator.com.au/article/2015/4/29/china/bitter-medicine-china-will-be-forced-swallow?utm_source=exact&utm_medium=email&utm_content=1316491&utm_campaign=chs_daily&mod> (April 29, 2015).

17   David Cai, "Hard truths for a soft landing in China," Business Spectator, (May 5, 2015).

18   Chris Buckley, "Xi Jinping's Remedy for China's Economic Gloom Has Echoes of Reaganomics," *The New York Times*, (March 3, 2016).

19   David Barboza, and Chris Buckley, "Beijing Signals a Shift on Economic Policy," *The New York Times*, (May 24, 2013).

20   John Lee, "The real picture on China's state-owned enterprises," <http://www.businessspectator.com.au/article/2014/12/12/china/real-picture-chinas-state-owned-enterprises?utm_source=exact&utm_medium=email&utm_content=1042502&utm_campaign=chs_daily&modapt=> (December 12, 2014).

21   Barboza and Buckley, "Beijing Signals a Shift on Economic Policy".

22   Peter Cai, "Learning from Singapore: the great Chinese Experiment," <http://www.businessspectator.com.au/article/2015/3/26/china/learning-singapore-great-chinese-experiment?utm_source=exact&utm_medium=email&utm_content=1235763&utm_campaign=chs_daily&modapt=> (March 26, 2015).

23   He fan, "The state and economic enterprise," *East Asia Forum Quarterly*, (February 2015).

24   Reuters, "Record Turnover for Inter-Exchange Trading From Mainland China to Hong Kong," *Reuters*, (April 8, 2015).

25   UCTD, *World Investment Report 2009: Transitional Corporations,*

Agricultural Production and Development, (United Nations: New York, 2009).

26   OECD, "FDI in Figures: International investment struggles," <http://www.oecd.org/daf/inv/FDI-in-Figures-Dec-2014.pdf> (February 2014).

27   Niu Yue, "China top spot for FDI in world in 2014," <http://usa.chinadaily.com.cn/business/2015-02/02/content_19471524.htm> (February 2, 2015). Figures include Hong Kong.

28   David Peetz, and Georgina Murray, "Global 2009 shareholding unit database," Osiris database, Bureau van Dyk, Amsterdam, 2010.

29   Neal Gough, "Citic in Deal to Sell $10 Billion Stake," *The New York Times*, (January 20, 2015).

30   Reuters, "China International Capital Off to a Strong Start," (November 9, 2015).

31   Henny Sander, and Simon Rabinovitch, "Chinese bank takes early step towards IPO," Financial Times, (August 8, 2013).

32   Michael Forsythe, "Alibaba's I.P.O. Could Be a bonanza for the Scions of Chinese Leaders," *The New York Times*, (July 20, 2014).

33   David Barboza, "A Loophole Poses Risks to Investors in Chinese Companies," *The New York Times*, (January 23, 2012).

34   Forsythe, "Alibaba's I.P.O. Could Be a bonanza for the Scions of Chinese Leaders".

35   Ned Levin, "J.P. Morgan Hired Friends, Family of Leaders at 75% of Major Chinese Firms it Took Public in Hong Kong." <http://www.wsj.com/articles/j-p-morgan-hires-were-referred-by-china-ipo-clients-1448910715> (November 30, 2015).

36   Gerry Shih, "China's Unigroup says wins bid to buy 51 percent stake in HP unit," <http://www.reuters.com/article/2015/05/19/ctech-us-hp-m-a-tsinghuaunigroup-idCAKBN0O40ZA20150519> (May 19, 2015).

37   Forbes, "Shanghai Scores As Top New Tech Hub In The World As Silicon Valley Gap Grows," <http://www.forbes.com/sites/rebeccafannin/2014/09/16/shanghai-scores-as-top-tech-hub-in-the-world-as-silicon-valley-gap-grows/> (September 16, 2014).

38   Jack Freifelder, "China, US propel global demand for technology share offerings," <http://www.chinadaily.com.cn/business/tech/2014-12/09/content_19050720.htm> (September 12, 2014).

39   David Barboza, "Red-Hot Web in China Richly Rewards Foreign Investors," *The New York Times*, (May 8, 2014).

40   Xinhua, "Chin's int'l investment balance hits plus 1.8 trln. USD," <http://news.xinhuanet.com/english/china/2014-12/29/c_133885907.htm> (December 29, 2014).

41   Thilo Hanemann, and Mikko Huotari, "Chinese FDI in Europe and Germany: Preparing for a New Era of Chinese Capital," Mercator Institute for China Studies and Rhodium Group, (June 2015).

42   United Nations Conference on Trade and Development, "FDI Outward Stock, by region and economy, 1990-2014," <http://unctad.org/en/Pages/DIAE/World%20Investment%20Report/Annex-Tables.aspx> (2015).

43   Matthew Monks and Annie Massa, "Chicago Stock Exchange Says It's Being Sold to Chinese-Led Group," <http://www.bloomberg.com/news/articles/2016-02-05/chicago-stock-exchange-says-it-s-selling-to-chinese-led-group> (February 5, 2016).

44   Thilo Hanemann, and Cassie Gao, "China's global Outbound M&A in 2015," <http://rhg.com/notes/chinas-global-outbound-ma-in-2015> (January 4, 2016).

45   Anjuli Davies, "China M&A flurry drives cross-border activity to 11-year high," <http://www.reuters.com/articles/us-m-a-data-idUSKCNOVEOZZ> (February 5, 2016).

46   Chen Jia, "Nation to become net capital exporter," <http://news.xinhuanet.com/english/business/2014-12/22/c_133870132.htm> (December 22, 2014).

47   David Barboza, and Keith Bradsher, "After Buying Spree, China Owns Stakes in Top U.S. Firms," *The New York Times*, (February 9, 2010).

48   Heriberto Araugo, and Juan Pablo Cardenal, "China's Economic Empire," *Financial Times*, (June 1, 2013).

49   Barboza, "Red-Hot Web in China Richly Rewards Foreign Investors".

50   Dow Jones, "Hank Paulson plays down China infrastructure bank," Dow Jones Newswires, (May 12, 2015).

51   Elizabeth Matsangou, <http://www.europeanceo.com/home/china-joins-the-european-bank-for-reconstruction-and-development> (December 15, 2015).

52   Kevin Rafferty, "U.S. forfeiting its leadership in global finance to China," *Japan Times*, (March 23, 2015).

53   Jane Peerlez, "China Creates a World Bank of Its Own, and the U.S. Balks," *The New York Times*, (December 4, 2015).

54   Xinhua, "China introduces guidelines on accelerating FTAs," <http://www.chinadaily.com.cn/business/2015-12/17/content_22734215.htm> (December 17, 2015).

55   Brianna Lee, "China, Brazil, Peru Eye Transcontinental Railway Megaproject," *The New York Times*, (May 19, 2015).

56   Rebecca Ray, and Keven Gallagher, "China-Latin America Economic Bulletin 2015 Edition," Boston University, Global Economic

Governance Initiative 2015, p.14.

57   Ibid.

58   Rebecca Ray, Keven Gallagher, Andres Lopez, and Cynthia Sanborn, "China in Latin America: Lessons for South-South Cooperation and Sustainable Development," Boston University, Global Economic Governance Initiative 2015.

59   "Chinese FDI in Europe and Germany: Preparing for a New Era of Chinese Capital", 6, 24.

60   Ibid.

61   Robin Emmott, and Paul Taylor, "Exclusive: China to extend economic diplomacy to EU infrastructure fund," (June 14, 2015).

62   Robert D. Blackwill, and Ashley J. Tellis, "Revising U.S. Grand Strategy Toward China," Council on Foreign Relations, (March 2015).

63   Sara Hsu, "China and the Trans-Pacific Partnership." <http://thediplomat.com/2015/10/china-and-the-trans-pacific-partnership/> (Ocotber 14, 2015).

64   Tom Mitchell, Geoff Dyer, and John Aglionby, "China warns US 'clock is ticking' on shutdown," *Financial Times,* (October 7, 2013).

65   David Barboza, "Chinese Bid for U.S. Pork Had Links to Wall Street," *The New York Times,* (June 2, 2013).

66   Hiroko Tabuchi, "Chinese Textile Mills Are Now Hiring in Places Where Cotton Was King," *The New York Times,* (August 2, 2015).

67   Yufan Huang, "Xi Jinping Adviser Has Long Pushed for Powerful Leadership," *The New York Times*, (September 29, 2015).

Chapter Six

THE FAILED
ALTERNATIVES

"Without general elections, without unrestricted freedom
of press and assembly, without a free struggle of opinion,
life dies out in every public institution, becomes a mere
semblance of life, in which only the bureaucracy remains as
the active element ...not the dictatorship of the proletariat
but only the dictatorship of a handful of politicians. "
Rosa Luxemburg

The Socialist Experience

Shortly after taking power, Russian Bolsheviks began to debate the relationship between the state, market and civil society. But debates were cut short by the brutal civil war and foreign intervention, resulting in a desperate struggle for survival. War communism led to eliminating private property and wage labor. It also resulted in the rapid growth of state bureaucrats, and the expulsion of other socialist parties from the Soviets, measures that essentially abolished the market and civil society.

But following the Red victory in 1921 a renewed debate emerged over the economy, and the relationship between the state and market. The New Economic Policy (NEP) was proposed by Lenin and Bukharin, not only to recover from the devastation of the civil war, but as a strategic policy to develop a modern economy. Bukharin would see this in terms of "dynamic equilibrium," a period of non-antagonistic contradictions in which the economic and social tensions between the peasantry and proletariat could be resolved without a brutal forced march into modernization.

The first step of the NEP was replacing grain requisitioning with a tax, leaving the surplus grain for peasants to sell. This led to the acquisition of private capital, the creation of exchange value between commodities and the denationalization of many enterprises. By 1923 the Soviet Union was a mixed economy with small businesses employing 12.4 percent of industrial labor, but constituting 88.5 percent of Russian enterprises. A much larger private sector existed in the countryside, where 25 million small peasant farms produced almost all agricultural goods and the majority of consumer products. Alongside these were small artisans supplying about 28 percent of all manufactured commodities.[1]

Both Lenin and Bukharin were concerned with cementing social unity between the peasantry and proletariat as a foundation for socialist development. Within this strategy rural marketing cooperatives played an important role, setting up a relationship between private interests and state regulations. According to Lenin this stage was to be established for ten to 20 years and eventually encompass the entire peasantry. This was projected to be a peaceful transformational period that would bring peasants into the culture and economic structures of socialism. Lenin stressed the importance of cooperatives in one of his last essays, "On Co-operation, Our Revolution" written in 1923. As he stated, "If the whole of the peasantry had been organized in co-operatives, we would by now have been standing with both feet on the soil of socialism."[2]

After Lenin's death in 1924 Bukharin become the main proponent of the NEP. Lenin had raised concerns over the growing bureaucratic organization of the Soviet state, and Bukharin shared his apprehension. The centralization of economic management during war communism was accompanied by the large and rapid expansion of state officials. Now Bukharin feared the Party was creating "a colossal administrative apparatus" in which functionaries were "in fact ...state chinovniki[3]."[4] He put his hope in an expansion of civil society as a counterweight to "statization," in a "decentralized initiative" that would include "hundreds and thousands of small and large rapidly expanding voluntary societies, circles and association."[5]

The Soviet Union in the 1920s produced some of the most important artistic movements of the twentieth century. Academic and scholarly publishing were filled with political debates. There was no one Party doctrine, but a proliferation of journals and salons that included non-party thinkers. Communists consisted of 12 percent of state employees and only three percent of the country's teachers.[6] The Party still dominated the political life of the country and commanded the heights of the economy, but overall it was a diverse and pluralistic society.

But the NEP faced a Left Opposition led by Leon Trotsky and the economist Evgenii Preobazhenskii. They argued for stronger state intervention and rapid industrialization based on the exploitation of value created in the rural economy. Bukharin answered, arguing that, "We do not want to drive the middle peasant into communism with an iron broom, pushing him with the kicks of war communism."[7] In some ways Bukharin's plan was similar to demand side economics. Bukharin argued that as peasant income grew demands for consumer goods would expand. As light industry expanded, heavy industrial goods would be brought into the chain of production. In this manner the private sector would objectively serve to enlarge the industrialized state sector. Each side of the economy was tied to the other, not only in exchange, but in creating a solid foundation for a united front of class interests. Viewed from the relationship of the state, market and civil society the NEP sought a balanced interdependence that could guide the inherent contradictions towards socialist modernization.

The slow pace of the NEP, alongside its problems of economic class distinctions, created growing concern among many Bolsheviks. Stalin had supported the NEP and helped to defeat the Left Opposition. But beginning in 1928 he now turned on Bukharin and called for rapid industrialization and mass collectivization in the countryside. At first Stalin posed as the pragmatic middle to Trotsky's left and Bukharin's right. Bukharin himself recognized that he had underestimated the need for state intervention in both the urban and rural economies. But his policy adjustments came nowhere near Stalin's coming revolution.

Stalin insisted that internal enemies were increasingly opposed to socialism and had to be met with "extraordinary measures." This meant an intensified class struggle. By 1929 the Party called for a 400-percent increase in state sector investments, with 78 percent of the total going to heavy industry. In order to achieve the work necessary for rapid industrialization the union's role in defending the interests of factory workers was changed to advocating production quotas. Mikhail Tomskii, a founder of Russia's trade union movement and politburo member, was removed from his office alongside almost the entire national union leadership. This was followed by the reconstruction of factory committees with up to 85 percent of their membership replaced in the major industrial centers. Tomskii stated that unions had been turned into "houses of detention." Stalin's close associate, Lazar Kaganovich, countered, "It could be said that this was a violation of proletarian democracy; but, comrades, it has long been known that for us Bolsheviks democracy is no fetish."[8] Although trade unions were never fully independent of the Party, neither were they official organs; they still could be considered part of civil society. These changes effectively ended that role, and even stricter measures were taken in cultural and academic institutions. As a result, civil society no longer played a significant, nor independent, role in Soviet life.

By the end of 1929 forced collectivization of the country's 125 million peasants began in earnest, ending with the state's overwhelming domination of the economy. As a result, the market as part of socialist economics would disappear, not only in the Soviet Union, but as part of socialist thought world-wide. Collectivization was met with widespread resistance, leading

218 | GLOBAL CAPITALISM AND THE CRISIS OF DEMOCRACY

to prisons and work camps holding nine million people. Grain harvests dropped, creating the worst famine in Soviet history, and over 250 million livestock animals perished. In the city both wages and food consumption fell, and consumer goods largely disappeared.[9] The over emphasis on heavy industry, a weak agricultural sector, and shoddy consumer goods were problems that plagued the Soviet Union until its demise.

With the advent of mass and rapid industrialization another important aspect of Bukharin's thinking was suppressed. Bukharin had been deeply influenced by the environmental work of V.I. Vernadsky, and saw human history within the context of the world's biosphere. His concern for ecological destruction was part of his opposition to the radical rush to industrialization. John Bellamy Foster characterized Bukharin's thinking as a "dialectical naturalism," and writes that his execution was "accompanied by the purge of some of the greatest Russian ecologists. Hence, Bukharin's fate can be taken as symbolic of the grand tragedy that befell Marxist ecological thinking after Marx."[10]

The elimination of the market, civil society and internal Party democracy didn't occur all at once. It took Stalin ten years to consolidate his power, culminating in 1938-39 when terrible political purges swept the country. In 1921 during the heated debates over trade unions with the Left Opposition, Lenin stated, "It is, of course, quite permissible (especially before a congress) for various groups to form blocs, and also to go vote chasing."[11] By 1930 such activity could put you in jail, or worse. At the end of the decade the old Bolsheviks were largely gone, and 70 percent of Party members had less than ten years' experience.

Nevertheless, statization of the economy also had significant successes. Industrial modernization was achieved, technology and education made great strides, as did health care. For example, *Fortune* magazine in March 1932 ran a featured article on the Soviet Union just as the monumental changes above were beginning. Significant advances had been made under the NEP and should be seen as democratic rights within the social sphere. Below are the magazine's observations on health care and the rights of women.

The Soviet has made it easy for either man or women to escape from family ties by making them all but unnecessary from the standpoint of prudence. Today if a young girl 'gets into trouble,' she can seldom be found in the gutter to be pointed at as an example of what girls come to who do not obey their fathers. 'Getting into trouble' is almost a cash asset, because if she can prove the father of her child, she can obtain alimony just as if she had been married. What is more, there is no social stigma put upon her... But once the Soviet child is born, there is no objective for which Joseph Stalin strives more earnestly (in addition to the maximum care of pregnant mothers) than for maximum care and proper feeding of infants, and maximum healthy upbringing and education of Russian children into robust Reds... Fourteen new day nurseries were open in Moscow alone last year... As to the Soviet child, he is not born at all unless actually wanted by his parents, for the State maintains free abortion clinics in Russian cities.[12]

You may be thinking the *Fortune* reporter saw all this as positive social developments. But the article also commented on the "baboon-like mating of a few psychopathic Reds to whom easy divorce is the Open Sesame to lust."[13] Evidently free love and women's rights had gone too far in red Russia.

Not all problems (and for some still, all successes) can be laid at the feet of Stalin. The vanguard party, so necessary for survival and victory, contained its own contradictions. A party of dedicated, smart and tough cadre, fired by their own heroics in overcoming seemingly impossible odds, could too easily be transformed into bureaucratic elites convinced of their mission and correctness. The Party's self-perceived wisdom and leadership downplayed the role of workers in defining the terms of their own liberation. Their view of the masses as a body to be mobilized undercut democratic participation in determining the means and ends of that mobilization. One of Lenin's most highly regarded contributions was his conception and organization of a vanguard party. He intended it as a party that "leads the non-Party workers, educating, preparing, teaching and training the masses...to enable them eventually to concentrate in their hands the administration of the whole national economy."[14]

But that day never came. If the Party merges with the state, and members become an elite class, unions and other civil institutions without democratic independence are reduced to carrying out the policy of those entrenched in power. Lenin was well aware of these dangers. Charles Bettelheim refers to Lenin's resolution to the Central Committee in 1922 on trade union functions under the NEP. As Bettelheim writes, "The resolution pointed out that there could be an 'antagonism of interest' between the working class and the management of Soviet state enterprises, and that 'strike struggle' might be justified by the necessity facing the workers of combating bureaucratic distortions and survivals from the capitalist past."[15]

Moreover, in debating Leon Trotsky two years prior, Lenin had advocated worker organizations having the independence to "protect the workers from their own state."[16] This was in opposition to Trotsky's position that unions should be brought under state control and turned into organizations that would oversee increasing production—a position that was widely adopted throughout the socialist world, although ironically not in Trotsky's name, but in Stalin's.

Lenin's position on civil society and independent working class organizations was tempered by his belief that the cultural and educational level of workers needed to develop over years of Party guidance. In the debate over unions and "industrial democracy" Lenin stated, "Industry is indispensable. Democracy is a category proper only to the political sphere."[17] This awkward dichotomy made workplace democracy secondary to production. Lenin did advocate workers participating in management and in developing production plans. This was to counterbalance the state's planning bureaucracy. Yet limiting workers and peasants to a long transformational period of education and training curtailed a more active democratic space in civil society. That may have been necessary in 1921, but Lenin's narrow view of democracy was easily distorted and made to serve Stalin's purpose a decade later. Particularly so as the political sphere became limited to the Party.

The debate over industrial democracy must be understood in its historic context. The civil war had left urban and rural production in near ruin, and democracy and civil society woefully underdeveloped. In this context Lenin's argument for a transitional period of education and training can be understood. But time was in short supply for the Bolsheviks. By the end of the decade the NEP was over, the purges had begun, and WWII loomed in the near distance.

A legacy of Stalinism is that communists in the twentieth century had little appreciation for what they labeled "bourgeois democracy." This was a pejorative term, used to dismiss the shortcomings, manipulation, and class nature of democracy under capitalism. Democracy in the underdeveloped socialist countries came to mean health care, employment, housing, and free education. Freedom of speech, press, assembly, and transparent trials were criticized as false freedoms, meaningless under the true nature of class dictatorship. Since the Party represented the working class, what the Party said, wrote, organized or who it put on trial was an expression of socialist democracy.

But this ideological stance is a misreading of democratic history. Formal democratic rights, alongside the right of labor to organize, civil rights for minorities and women, universal suffrage, and the social contract are deeply rooted victories of the working class, albeit won in capitalist countries. Such rights were compromises forced on the capitalist class over many decades of struggle, often won under the leadership of communist and socialist organizers. As pointed out in the *Communist Manifesto*, "The political freedoms, the right of assembly and association and the freedom of the press, these are our weapons."[18] These victories are now being undone by global capitalism. In response people the world over are fighting to defend their democratic and economic rights. It would be ironic if socialist countries or movements rejected these historic working class victories as "Western or bourgeois ideas and values."

Is Socialism Dead?

With the fall of the Soviet Union, the jubilant destruction of the Berlin Wall and China's embrace of the market, it seemed socialism was dead. Francis Fukuyama declared, "history is over" and liberal capitalism had won. But as often happens, winners push their victory too far, revealing their own weakness. With the spread of neoliberal austerity punishing millions, climaxed by the financial collapse of 2008, there erupted renewed interest in socialism.

The advent of a new generation thinking favorably about socialism came as a surprise to many, including myself. Having grown up in the teeth of the McCarthy-era Red scares, I witnessed how the 1960s blew open a whole new reality my parents had always told me lay buried somewhere deep below the surface. But socialism was never able to make a real comeback in the minds of the majority. The Soviet bureaucracy offered little attraction, and Maoism had a lively but short life. Che's image appeared everywhere, only to be drained of meaning, drowned in the manipulation of his Hollywood looks.

But as time moved on capitalism offered millions little more than part-time work at minimum wage. Living large, the one percent crassly paraded their imaginative and spiritual poverty by showing they have nothing to offer but money. When conservatives attacked Obama as a socialist many youth suddenly started to reconsider the concept, opening the door for Bernie Sanders' socialist campaign. On the international stage new socialist mass organizations appeared that had a deeper and historic appreciation for democracy. As the Workers Party in

Brazil wrote in their founding documents in 1980, "Democracy understood as the wide aggregate of citizens' rights to political participation and representation cannot be seen as a bourgeois value... (for) democracy became a universal ideal when it was taken by the working class."[19]

Encouraged by events I decided to use my classroom as an experiment, something not uncommon among teachers. I worked at a baccalaureate university in Chicago attended by working and middle class students of diverse racial and ethnic backgrounds. I always found their politics to be an unconscious, left-wing social democracy. None of these students were majors in the humanities, they were earning degrees in nursing, business, and computer engineering. My courses were history, philosophy, and ethics and the social and environmental impact of technology. I was always openly leftist and during one or two weeks I would cover such topics as Marxism, the revolution in Venezuela, and cooperative ownership at Mondragon in Spain. I kept comments from homework and on-line chat rooms, and it's worthwhile, here, to offer some views on socialism, capitalism, and inequality written by students in 2013-2014:

- Socialism to me is basically that the power belongs to the people not the rich 1% nor the corporation, and that we should not be forced into using our life as a labor source to feed the capitalist, [a very beautiful and empathetic idea].

- I see socialism as the belief that individuals should be judged on how they treat other people rather than on their job/race/ sexuality, that people should have equality of opportunity, that in principle wealth should be distributed fairly to everyone who works rather than the minority who own most of the economy and most of the wealth. And that an economy owned by a few individuals without a strong public sector to balance it, is undemocratic and unjust.

- I see socialism as a power of people to make decisions and to control government in all aspects of life in America. Socialist government is not state government. It would not rule over people and places, but would empower the people to rule over things. Socialism means a government in which the people collectively own and democratically operate the industries and social services through an economic democracy.

• Socialism is a system where basic needs—food, shelter, education, health care are provided to all, whether they can afford it or not. It also involves the concept that everyone is responsible for the success of society and that society does better when we all work together to lift us all up, instead of insisting everyone struggle on their own.

• I think that protest and conflict go hand in hand. In much of our history situations that start off as peaceful protest often end in violent conflict. I feel like protest is used to make our voices heard. It's all about the numbers, in a protest the oppressors will see firsthand how many people are against them. You can ignore one person, but it's a lot harder to avoid thousands. This usually causes much tension between the people and the government which leads to government using military or local law enforcement to try and control the masses, which only leads to more violent conflict. In history we've seen this happen many times during the civil rights movement or in any real protest such as the Division Street riots that took place in Chicago's Puerto Rican community. Protest and conflict are going to be a huge part of our future. With the world in chaos and the governments working the way they are, I'm sure before my generation dies off we will have seen massive revolutions take place throughout the whole world. It already feels, in America, that frustrations are building up and soon enough protest and conflict will be a reality all of us are forced to face.

• I would definitely work for a company owned by all the

employees where production is for use instead of for profit, and keeps the greedy capitalist out of the picture. I would like for it to have a combination of both a socialist and democratic economy whereby the decision making power goes to the public stakeholders, regular people like us, instead of the corporate shareholders, greedy Wall Street CEO's. I would also like for it to represent a socialist economy in the sense that it would be a worker cooperative enhancing self-management and self-governance. Think about it, there are 99% of us regular people struggling day in and day out, and only 1% of the rich people who don't struggle at all. Can we the 99% create such an economy by pooling our assets together to make it happen? "One for All, and All for One!" Who's with me...

• I think every human being who cares about others and strives towards the equality among people would like to work in a company owned by all the employees. Everyone's life would be so much easier without running after money and with the awareness that people don't have to struggle in their lives. People who are not willing to work in a company where profits are equally shared are simply egoistic to me, because they see money as the priority in their lives. I would never have satisfaction in making more money than others, and at the same time have friends who can barely make a living from check to check. I would define a democratic economy as a socialist economy. The goal of both is striving for the common good of society, promoting equal rules for everybody, and a conflict-free environment.

• I would definitely like to work in a company owned by all the employees. Sharing profits and responsibility eliminates the inequality and creates a more trusting and comfortable environment. My mother has always told me that two heads are better than one when it comes to opinions and decision making, and I stick by the idea that to make a world a better place and to satisfy people we must unite. In my opinion, a capitalist economy is when the few dictate what to do and what people can earn, while everyone underneath those who dictate are collectively working whether they like it or not. A socialist economy has people like you, me, neighbors, etc. that come together and make decisions. Every vote counts and everyone is solving problems together. The socialist economy doesn't choose the leader; everyone is a leader. It takes each individual to succeed, and each should be rewarded equally.

- The Wall Street bankers are a bunch of greedy bastards; my opinion of them cannot be written on this paper because I'm trying to stay professional. Imagine every curse word in the English language on steroids.

- I consider myself a socialist. When taught socialism in prior history classes, it was taught as a very evil thing. With the fear that if USSR did it then we should not support that system. Now, reading the articles of Mondragon and how companies can be completely functional and more beneficiary, I go with socialism.

It seems socialism has survived Stalinism. The above comments, so open, straightforward and plainly spoken reflect a growing consciousness among urban, working-class youth. Such insightful statements, after only a short exposure to a left worldview, suggest that socialist ideas reflect their own experiences and hopes, and what that world should look like. Perhaps then the popularity of the Bernie Sanders' campaign should come as no surprise. Democratic socialism, embedded in cooperative ownership and social equality, still finds a home in its traditional and historic community, the urban proletariat. It may be a class remade and molded to fit the globalized economy, but it remains the working class. And so as class inequality grows and racism continues to oppress, people discover that socialism can still expresses their dream for a better world.

The Anarchist Vision

Michael Albert is one of the most prominent anarchists in the US, developing Z magazine and ZNet as major platforms for anarchist thinking and analysis. His book, *Parecon,* is an influential and important work of anarchist theory. Translated into 15 languages it was praised by major anarchist thinkers such as Noam Chomsky, Howard Zinn, and others. The word 'parecon' stands for 'participatory economics' and offers a broad and detailed vision of horizontal democracy. If the World Social Forum has raised the slogan, "another world is possible," Albert has given us a version of that world. Historical anarchism has sought to do away with any central government. Albert stays true to this vision, and also positions civil society to govern over the economy and production. Because Albert presents us with the most complete articulation of a possible anarchist society it's important to analyze his effort.

Albert creates various levels of worker and consumer councils to determine all aspects of consumption and labor. This is done in such detail that a plan of overlapping complexity is designed to insure equality in every phrase of social interactions. Albert seeks to ascertain how each individual act of consumption and production affects the quality of life of everyone else to insure fairness for all. Basic to the anarchist philosophy is a society based on total equalitarian principals, and to Albert's credit he articulates this with attention to a great many particularities.

In determining production Albert is interested in analyzing the "costs of every single choice among the totality of possibilities."[20] This means every choice must be judged against all other possible choices. Therefore, the amount of "shoes, autos, peanuts, and everything else and how they are apportioned will determine the value of each particular item." Consequently, if we produce too many pencils we may not be able to produce enough milk, "so that, by not producing that item (pencils) we can use our productive capability to produce something else (milk) that benefits us more."[21] Of course the technology and inputs for pencils and milk have no actual relationship except in the abstract sense of total labor and total costs in the entire economy. So there is no real "productive capability" being lost or gained. But such a decision within one industry may make perfect sense. For example, how many cars do we want in comparison to buses?

But Albert's reference to pencils and milk is no mistake; as he explains, "the decisions have to be made globally for a whole economy with each decision affecting the basis upon which all others should be made."[22] Yet in an economy with millions of products such articulation of interrelations is never ending and impossible to accomplish. But Albert is insistent that production, consumption, and work must be socially balanced and equal, which can only be accomplish if everything is calculated against each other.

When linking consumption and production Albert replaces the market with decisions made in a complex layer of consumer councils. This includes seven layers starting with family and individual consumer choices, to be collated and reviewed by neighborhood councils, on up to the ward level, city, state, regional, and finally, national consumer councils. In addition there are facilitation boards, which help determine prices and revise plans. To begin, each individual or family is to make a list of all the products and services to be consumed over the coming year. This is balanced with the credit they will earn by the amount they wish to work. This not only includes such items as clothes, toilet paper, and video games, but how many times you'll eat out and the types of entertainment you plan to enjoy. Additionally you'll need to make notes and descriptions of your choices. When the neighborhood gets together everyone gets to review everyone's annual plan. If selections seem unfair or immoral you'll have to justify your preference or have it removed. For example, if someone thinks you plan on drinking too much wine, ordered too many condoms, or an unnecessary pair of shoes, their objections can be aired at the local neighborhood meeting. Once the entire list is decided upon it proceeds to the community or ward level, where additional choices can be made, like a park swimming pool.

And on up the chain, each level approving the lower level and adding items appropriate to its territorial jurisdiction.

But the process has only begun. Albert admits prices in the initial plan will not be exact, in fact real pricing won't be accomplished until this entire routine is done five times. This task is helped by the facilitation boards, which look at the plans and adjust costs based on the collected data. Albert insists all this will be relatively simple, "it is only necessary to collect all proposals and compare total demand and total supply for every class of final good and service, for every intermediate good and for every primary input."[23] For Albert this is participatory democracy in action, everyone has a say while working in social solidarity with each other. No need for the market, no need for government, just anarchist equalitarianism working its way through civil society.

But let's break down the time this process may take. Starting with the family, there may be some arguments over how mom and dad calculate their needs, let alone how they want to spend their credit, and then there is the discussion with your kids on what they can expect to receive over the next year. Moving up the chain at each stage all the data needs to be collected, translated into various languages for equal access, read and analyzed, then collectively discussed, voted on and then posted for the next council. And remember we want to account for every product to be produced for the year plus its individual impact on all other inputs and costs. Let's say each link in the chain takes ten days to complete (hopefully no one will be late), that's ten days multiplied by seven councils. So the first round would take 70 days. But wait, there is to be five rounds, so now we're at 350 days and this is supposed to be the plan for the current year. Well let's make it the plan for next year. Now we have 12 days to relax, (perhaps we should declare it a national holiday), before the whole process begins again. As the saying goes, the road to hell is paved with good intentions.

One might find it ironic that Albert's anarchism makes consumption the center of civil society in much the same way as capitalism. Instead of spending time at the mall, we get to spend time in meetings in which social solidarity is defined as reviewing your neighbor's balance between bottles of wine, number of shirts, and rolls of toilet paper. Albert even states that "parecon does not have capitalists and coordinators and workers, but only economic actors."[24] Paradoxically, defining humans solely as economic actors would find a sympathetic audience among neoliberals. Albert also limits the definition of social minorities simply to those whose consumption choices are rejected.

In Albert's world solidarity is so complete there seems to be no place for political debate and conflict. In 300 pages there is no mention of differences outside of choices over allocation and consumption. It's a mystery as to how laws and regulations might be agreed to. Should abortion, bioengineering of food, or gun ownership be legal? How should pollution standards be established, or enforceable speed limits for cars? With consumer councils replacing government at every level, questions outside of consumption don't seem to fit into Albert's anarchist society. Neither does Albert bother to explain how people are chosen to serve on higher levels of decision-making councils. Not only do they decide prices and balance supply and demand, national and regional projects are chosen and funded by these councils. How much should be spent on the military versus infrastructure versus national health care? The power to make those decisions touches everyone in the country. Yet there are no elections mentioned, nor even a system of voluntary rotation. We are left to assume in a system of equalitarianism disagreements will work themselves out based on solidarity without the need for political representation.

The anarchist compulsion for complete equalitarianism is pursued into the workplace. Albert establishes a system of "balance job complexes." This means every job in the country will be assigned a number based on how "unpleasant and disempowering" it is compared to "pleasant and empowering tasks."[25] If you work at a job with a low number on the unpleasant scale, you will be transferred up to a more empowering job for part of the year. The reverse happens if your job is pleasant, then you move down the scale. This may be at your current job site, or a completely different workplace. At the end of the year everyone should be in balance with each other with an average national number. The ratings are done by committees balancing jobs "within each workplace and for the economy as a whole."[26] In other words, every job in the country must be rated, and then balanced in relationship to every other job.

Besides the chaos of moving millions of people from job to job every year, each work group has the right to reject a new hire. It only takes one person to reject another from joining the group. So you better have a plan B in case your first move doesn't work out. Of course your second job may be filled by then, so on to plan C, and so on. Additionally, Albert seems to have no appreciation for the stress of moving to a new job environment, learning new skills, meeting new people, adjusting to a new rhythm of work, and so on. Even a more rewarding job can still be stressful.

Such logistical problems are matched by the confusion Albert exhibits in judging what constitutes unpleasant jobs. His concept revolves around differences in effort, which constitute "the only reason people would have different levels of consumption."[27] Therefore increased effort, rather than skill, education or output, is virtually the only way to obtain more pay. By effort Albert means "anything that constitutes a personal sacrifice for the purpose of providing socially useful goods and services."[28] Albert returns again and again to the idea of sacrifice, posing it almost as a form of suffering, whether at work, in training or school. Sacrifice is described as anything disempowering, boring, unpleasant, and disagreeable. This lays the basis for anarchist-driven equalitarianism. Sacrifice must be equalized, because no one should suffer or be bored more than the next. Thus we have the balanced job complex.

Let's unpack this concept further. I was a machinist apprentice at U.S. Steel in Chicago. Besides learning to run complex machines on the shop floor, we also went to school for 40 hours every six months, ongoing for five years. Among other things, I learned three-dimensional blueprint reading and trigonometry. I found the visualization of spatial relationships in blueprints much easier than their abstraction into numbers and letters. I was easily the worst math student, putting out more time and effort than any of my fellow apprentices to learn the basics of trigonometry, which I found unpleasant and boring. In an anarchist steel mill I now would deserve time in a more empowering job doing intellectual work, Albert's definition of a more pleasurable job. On the other hand, my fellow workers might be sent to labor in the blast furnace for two or three months because they spent less "effort" learning trigonometry. This wouldn't make me very popular among my fellow workers, nor would I have found it necessary to be compensated for my "sacrifice". It was just part of learning the job. Solidarity was expressed daily in friendships, standing up to supervisors, and helping each other out when needed. Albert's idea of equality is an idealized abstraction that would find little sympathy among steelworkers. There were many hard jobs that needed greater compensation, but given the choice, more pay and time off would be the first options workers would choose.

Another complication occurs around the question of seniority. Again, let me return to my days in the mill, this time the two years I spent working in the blast furnace. All the jobs in the furnace are physically draining and dangerous. We worked in five-man crews, each with a different job. The more years you spent on the blast furnace floor, the more you would move up that five-man crew to jobs that were a bit better and less physically brutal. The youngest worker on the crew put out more effort and made a greater sacrifice to keep the "mud gun" working. I won't go into details about this job, but by the time you hit 40 you don't want to be doing it. In Albert's world I now deserve a few months at a more rewarding job. That would have been a change I would have welcomed. The problem is who would replace me? It would have to be someone doing highly rewarding and pleasurable work. Since such labor is usually skilled or takes years of education, this would most likely be a worker somewhat older who needs a few months of unskilled physically challenging work to make his annual "job balance" come out right. But any individual in such circumstances would simply not be prepared to work in the furnace. In fact, it would be a dangerous threat to their health, endanger others on the crew, and lower productivity. The other option is to just move around the crew jobs, throwing older and senior members back to the bottom of the ladder, and letting me work a job it took someone 15 years to obtain. Would this create worker solidarity or discord and anger? Only in Albert's idealized utopia are such arrangements possible and desirable.

Albert approaches education in the same manner, although he most often uses the word training instead. This serves to link all education to work, another area where his anarchism meets neoliberalism. For Albert, education would only lead to more compensation if you disliked school. As he states, "Only if schooling is more disagreeable than working does it constitute a greater sacrifice than others make and thereby deserve greater reward...if one's education is onerous and demanding compared to working, that difference marks the extra compensation."[29] Here let me refer to my 20 years as a professor at a working-class college. Most of my students worked. Morning classes often had students coming off night shifts, and afternoon students often left to go to their job. This was certainly a sacrifice, yet school was not "disagreeable." In fact, most students enjoyed their education. But for Albert, the "personal sacrifice the student makes consists only of his or her discomfort during the time spent in school."[30] Not the sacrifice of less time with the family, less sleep, and rushed meals. Albert allows comparisons only between work and education, not the totality of a person's life. So how do we compare students who must work to go to school, but find education more pleasurable than work; to students who don't have to work but find school "disagreeable?"

I always offered extra credit assignments in my classes. These were readings and questions meant to extend a student's understanding of course themes. Half the students who did extra credit were at the top of the class, they wanted more and enjoyed putting out extra effort to increase their knowledge. The other half were students who were failing and needed the points to pass.

I'm sure for these students the assignments were "disagreeable," more "onerous" and soon forgotten. According to Albert those failing students would have "sacrificed" more and therefore been deserving of higher pay. Those who put out greater effort because they took pleasure in education deserve less because they sacrificed less. Such wrenching abstractions of effort and sacrifice spring from the false equalitarianism so fundamental to anarchist ideology. In the real world it means punishing students who love learning, excelled in their education, and were prepared to contribute more to society. Furthermore, what is the basis of a student feeling his or her education is "disagreeable" and "onerous"? Perhaps it was disagreeable because it took time away from texting friends and other more enjoyable activities. Albert sets out no criteria for judgment other than what a student declares.

Lastly, Albert's presumptive anarchist classic departs from historical materialism. Although he briefly mentions there is plenty of historical and current experience in self-management he refers to none of it. He simply creates castles out of intellectual argumentation, writing a book of anarchist science fiction for some future society. A worthy effort would have analyzed the truly significant experiences at Mondragon in Spain, the cooperative history in northern Italy, and more recent events in Latin America. Instead Albert has achieved the seemingly impossible task of detailing a bureaucratic panoptic anarchism: the exact opposite of what anarchists have historically hoped to achieve. By specifying a predesigned society Albert goes against the very spirit of anarchism, departing from the open-ended humanism of traditional anarchist thought.

Anarchism and the Occupy Movement

What about the actual practice of anarchists in some of the major contemporary social movements? Here we can investigate the Occupy Movement in New York, the epicenter for an upsurge of global protests that focused widespread public attention on growing inequality and created the narrative of the one percent.

Many of the core activists in New York were self-identified anarchists and influential in creating the horizontal organizational structure that ran the occupation of Zuccotti Park in the heart of Wall Street. Moreover, anarchists pointed to a number of common practices during the Occupy movement that they identified as important characteristics of their theory and practice including— prefiguration, autonomy, mutual aid, and defiance.[31]

Mutual aid has no particular anarchist identity; it has long been a pillar of all social movements. Much was made of how medical aid, food, and solidarity were part of the daily life in Zuccotti Park. But such activity was common in the 1960s. For example, the Black Panther Party offered free legal advice, free breakfast for children, and various "survival programs." But their ideological influence was Maoism and Third World revolutionary nationalism. Their popular survival programs were based on Chinese communist slogan to "serve the people," advocated by Huey Newton after his return from China and a meeting with Mao Tse-Tung. Other organizations such as the Brown Berets, Young Lords, and Rising Up Angry created similar programs. My own political collective in Long Beach, California maintained a large community center that had a food cooperative, free child care, hosted political discussions, and provided space for various groups including Viet-Nam Veterans Against the War and the Movement for a Democratic Military. Nobody was interested in anarchism in any of the above organizations. Rather third-world Marxism was the main influence, and this was largely true throughout the US in the latter 1960s. Mutual aid also played an important part in the non-violent movement, for example the Freedom Schools in Mississippi formed by a coalition of civil rights organizations.

As for defiance, or the act of breaking the law and defying governmental authority, what social movement hasn't used this tactic? The labor movement, civil rights movement, and anti-war protests were built around such acts of defiance. Dr. King constructed his non-violent strategy around breaking laws and mass arrests that created a social crisis and moral confrontations. Anti-war protestors burnt draft records, blockaded streets, and engaged in battles with the police. No social movement exists without forms of defiance.

Prefiguration—the attempt to create a culture that reflects the values activists advocate as a moral basis for a new society—is also a common characteristic of social movements. As Gandhi stated, "Be the change you wish to see in the world." Again we can reference the many social movements that existed in the 1960s. The language of love, caring, solidarity, and mutual support was in everything from The Beatles' songs to anti-war slogans urging people to "make love not war." It was the women's movement which pointed out that "the personal is political." Such a culture creates a womb of support that sustains activists, making them feel they belong to a special community that is in the forefront of wider social change. Religious communities also provide the same structure whether based on liberation theology or right-wing fundamentalism.

What was different for the anarchists in Occupy was defining prefiguration as political strategy. Rather than doing outreach and building a broad based alliance, they became consumed in activities within their occupied space. Consequently, horizontalism became an organizational principle. This resulted in no recognized leadership and mass meetings in which consensus was mandatory, yet where one person could block agreement. Jackie Disalvo, a Marxist activist involved in the New York Occupy movement, points out that, "horizontalists didn't do much outreach beyond their own demographic, and in requiring the freedom to attend countless, time-consuming, often daytime meetings, horizontalism was profoundly elitist and undemocratic."[32]

David Graeber, a leading anarchist analyst active in Occupy, describes how a commitment to autonomy and prefiguration defined their understanding of the protest movement. As Graber writes,

> By gathering together in the full sight of Wall Street, and creating a community without money, based on principles of not just democracy but of

mutual caring, solidarity, and support, we were
proposing a revolutionary challenge not just to
the power of money, but to the power of money
to determine what life itself was supposed to be
about.[33]

All very well to create an iconic image, but where is this
revolutionary challenge today? Graber's minimalist focus on
the internal functioning of activity inside occupied park space,
presented as some revolutionary precursor to a new world, only
serves to expose anarchist illusions. This explains the anarchist
aversion to any programmatic demands, which they saw only as
concessions to reformism. No need to relate to the everyday needs
of the 99 percent when your own heroic example of temporary
autonomy illuminates the path to human liberation. Consequently,
no leaders and no program resulted in no organization. The
anarchist of Occupy could take a lesson from their Chicago
anarchist ancestors who led the national movement for an eight-
hour day in 1886. Their demand on capitalism was very specific
and reformist, "eight hours to work, eight hours to sleep, eight
hours to do as you please." Although the Occupy movement
made inequality a topic of mainstream discussion, and scattered
remnants of activity remain, it squandered the rare opportunity to
form a national organization of broad unity. Some 300 cities saw
people join Occupy protests, most of whom were new activists
that belonged to no organization. In reality anarchist "leaderless"
activity is leadership that hides behind a veil of participatory
rhetoric, while creating a distinct form of political culture.
　　Some of those involved in the leadership of the New
York Occupy movement have come to similar conclusions. Yotam
Marom, now Director of the Wildfire Project, has written a number
of critiques of the Occupy experience. He notes the general
assembly was more "performance art than a decision-making
forum," and that there was "an infatuation with public space, a
confusion of tactic for strategy (and) a palpable disdain for people
who weren't radical...the mantra of leaderlessness came from a

genuine desire to avoid classic pitfalls into hierarchy, but it was, at the same time, a farce, and divorced from any sense of collective structure." On Occupy's well known lack of demands he says,

> The refusal to articulate demands was brilliant in opening radical possibilities and sparking the popular imagination, but it also meant we didn't have a shared goal, meant the word winning wasn't even part of the movement's lexicon. In many ways, it was an expression of a fear of actually saying something and taking responsibility for it... We could have lasted longer, brought more people into the movement, established more powerful institutions, won more material gains.[34]

The experience of Occupy does not stand alone. The lack of organizational cohesions and leadership training is a recurring problem with anarchist politics. This experience was repeated with cyber activism. Tom Wolfson made an extensive study of the use of alternative media in his book, *Digital Rebellion: The Birth of the Cyber Left*. Wolfson notes how decentralization, autonomy, and participatory democracy characterized a broad network of media activists. But he also writes that the movement was plagued by an "inability to make proactive decisions and build long-term powerful social movement organizations (and) lacked a shared strategy and political-education program to build clear and committed leaders."[35]

Beyond the organizational failures of anarchism David Harvey has questioned the failure of anarchists to engage the state. Harvey begins with comments on social theorist Murray Bookchin,

> Bookchin, in his last book, says that the problem with the anarchists is their denial of the significance of power and their inability to take it. Bookchin doesn't go this far, but I think it is

the refusal to see the state as a possible partner to radical transformation...How will the left build the Brooklyn bridge, for example? Any society relies on big infrastructures...like the water supply, electricity and so on. There are wings of the state apparatus, even of the neoliberal state apparatus, which are therefore terribly important—the center of disease control, for example. How do we respond to global epidemics such as Ebola and the like? You can't do it in the anarchist way of DIY-organization. There are many instances where you need some state-like forms of infrastructure. We can't confront the problem of global warming through decentralized forms of confrontations and activities alone.[36]

Harvey's points hit home, but there is another side to anarchist criticism of the state that has proven correct. Anarchism has always warned of the hierarchical and bureaucratic nature of government. As P.A. Kropotkin noted, "A highly complex state machine...leads to the formation of class especially concerned with state management, which, using its acquired experience, begins to deceive the rest for its personal advantage."[37] Experiences in post-revolutionary Russia and China lend strength to Kropotkin's argument. Additionally, current problems of corruption have undermined a number of left-wing parties holding governmental power, including the ANC in South Africa, the Workers Party in Brazil, and the United Socialist Party in Venezuela.

Although anarchism has significant problems, its emphasis on horizontalism has made important contributions, such as its insistence on participatory democracy. While socialism veered to bureaucratic state hierarchy, anarchism remained dedicated to worker control, collective ownership, and self-management. Twenty-first century socialism has now accepted these long-held anarchist principles, affirming the central importance of mass democracy and returning to the radical origins of socialist thought. Just what vision of participatory democracy will best serve the building of an alternative society will be determined in the crucible of social practice as the years unfold. In the next chapter we will explore how key ideas of both anarchism and socialism have begun to merge to create a revitalized left.

Endnotes

1   Stephen E. Cohen, *Bukharin and the Bolshevik Revolution* (Wildwood House: London, 1971).

2   V.I. Lenin, *Collected Works of V.I. Lenin* (International Publishers: New York, 1927), 474.

3   The word 'chinovnik' was a term for czarist bureaucrats, and for Russian communist it had an extremely pejorative meaning.

4   Cohen, *Bukharin and the Bolshevik Revolution*, 138.

5   Ibid, 145.

6   Ibid, 127.

7   Nikolai Bukharin, and Evgenii Preobrazhenskii, *The Alphabet of Communism* (Kharkov, 1925), 8.

8   Cohen, *Bukharin and the Bolshevik Revolution*, 301.

9   Ibid, 338-39.

10   John Bellamy Foster, *Marx's Ecology: Materialism and Nature* (MR Press: New York, 2000), 228.

11   V.I. Lenin, *On Trade Unions* (Progress Publishers: Moscow, 1970), 407.

12   Fortune Magazine, "The Soviet State," *Fortune Magazine*, March (1932), 86-87.

13   Ibid, 85.

14   Lenin, *On Trade Unions*, 405.

15   Charles Bettelheim, *Class Struggles in the USSR Second Period: 1923-1930* (Monthly Review Press: New York and London, 1978), 391.

16   V.I. Lenin, *V.I. Lenin Collected Works, Vol. 32, December 1920-August 1921* (Progress Publishers: Moscow, 1975), 25.

17   Lenin, *On Trade Unions*, 382.

18   Karl Marx, and Fredrick Engels, *Communist Manifesto* (1848), <https://www.marxists.org/subject/quotes/miscellaneous.htm>.

19   Emir Sader, and Ken Silverstein, *Without Fear of Being Happy: Lula, the Workers Party and Brazil*, (Verso: London, 1991), 106.

20   Michael Albert, *Parecon* (Verso: London & New York, 2003), 124.

21   Ibid.

22   Ibid.

23   Ibid, 131.

24   Ibid, 160.

25   Ibid, 104.

26   Ibid, 109.

27   Ibid, 152.

28   Ibid.

29   Ibid, 36.

30   Ibid.

31   John L. Hammond, "The Anarchism of Occupy Wall Street," *Science & Society*, Vol. 79, No. 2 (April 2015).

32   Jackie DiSalvo, "Occupy Wall Street: Creating a Strategy for a Spontaneous Movement," *Science & Society*, Vol. 79, No. 2 (April 2015).

33   David Graber, *The Democracy Project: A History, a Crisis, a Movement* (Spiegel and Grau: New York, 2013).

34   Yotam Marom, "Undoing the Politics of Powerlessness," *Medium*, (December 17, 2015).

35   David Love, "Technology and Social Media Spawn New Civil Rights Movements," <http://blackcommentator.com/608/608_cover_col_technology_civil_rights_movement.html> (2015).

36   David Harvey, "Consolidating Power," <https://roarmag.org/magazine/david-harvey-consolidating-power/>

37   P. A. Kropotkin, edited by Martin A. Miller, *Selected Writings on Anarchism and Revolution* (M.I.T. Press: Cambridge, Massachusetts, 1970), 61.

Chapter Seven

DEMOCRACY BEYOND CAPITALISM

*"The economic model upholding the financial
architecture and war politics has as its nucleus the
politics of the free market, that is, the voracious
capitalist policy that pays no attention to anything
other than profit, luxury, and consumerism... People are
treated as things, and Mother Earth as a commodity.
Either we change global capitalist society or it
annihilates the world's peoples and nature itself."*
Evo Morales

In 1989 the fall of the Berlin Wall and the repression of
protestors in Tiananmen Square marked the end of the twentieth
century model of socialism. While the Soviet Union and China had
long split into opposing camps, their state-centric structures were
essentially similar. State-owned enterprises and state-directed
economies dominated both countries. The Party held hegemonic
power over civil society, and promoted its own ideology as the
only correct view of the world. China may still hold onto important
aspects of this model, but its turn towards market socialism
alongside Russia's rush to capitalism ended the social structures
built by the Bolsheviks and Mao's peasant revolution.

These events not only affected Russia and China, but

the entire socialist world. The reevaluation of history, practice, and ideology swept through Communist countries as well as communist and socialist activists in every continent. For the past quarter century the left has been looking for a new vision and practice. If not the Soviet model or Maoism, then what? One of the most important conclusions is that the content and practice of democracy is central for modern society. But how is democracy to be defined and carried out?

All ruling parties seek to create a stable functioning social order, a society in which production runs smoothly, where political differences are benign, and social differences well managed. But such equilibrium is an idealized state of being. Governmental policies and economic practices may establish equilibrium for a time, but the complexity of existence can't be contained in economic plans, presidential decrees, or legislative bills. Inevitably disequilibrium reemerges because society is in a constant state of flux. Harmony is an illusion resulting from static social categories.

Dialectical and historical materialism helps to clarify the underlining process that defines social contradictions. Nikolai Bukharin's *Historical Materialism* was a classic of Marxist thought in the 1920s. Here he writes of the tensions in dialectical relationships,

> The world consists of forces, acting in many ways, opposing each other. These forces are balanced for a moment in exceptional cases only. We then have a state of 'rest,' i.e., their actual 'conflict' is concealed. But if we change only one of these forces, immediately the 'internal contradictions' will be revealed, equilibrium will be disturbed... It follows that the 'conflict,' the 'contradiction,' i.e. the antagonism of forces acting in various directions, determines the motion of the system.[1]

Lenin understood dialectics along the same lines, writing,

"Dialectics in the proper sense is the study of contradictions *in the very essence of objects*."[2] Mao also focused his writings on dialectics on the constant presence of contradictions.[3]

If we view the contradictory relationships as a basic condition of being, we can then understand the relationships between the state, market, and civil society as mediated by conflicts. The balance of influence and power between the social forces that inhabit these institutional spaces is always changing. Stability is only a temporary stage before disequilibrium emerges once again. Each of these institutions is internally dynamic and linked to the other. When problems arise, and solutions are formulated and applied, that very act creates new dynamics, which eventually produce another set of contradictions. This is a never-ending dialectical process. Fundamentalist ideologies have sought to resolve the dialectic through the suppression of one or another aspect, but the solution lies in accepting the underlying tensions that define human society. Ideas of permanent social harmony without contradictions is a left religious vision of earthly heaven, a socialist opiate for a cruel and unforgiving world.

If we accept the permanence of contradictions the question then becomes, how does society manage conflict without violence or the suppression of basic human rights? This is where democracy plays the determining role. It creates a structural process for the internal functioning of the state, market, and civil society, as well as for the interaction of the social forces existing within these institutions. Democracy is the political practice that resolves contradictions in a social system constantly veering to disequilibrium. It recognizes the dialectical interpenetration of economic, social, and political existence that co-exist and constantly redefine each other. Consequently, conflicts are managed as non-antagonistic contradictions needing constant quantitative adjustment.

At times contradictions necessitate a decisive break with the chains of current conditions. But states of *revolutionary disequilibrium* demanding a qualitative and revolutionary leap forward are historically rare. The ultimate expression of such dialectical ruptures are the shattering social revolutions experienced in France, the US, Russia, and China. But most social struggles are resolved as non-antagonistic contradictions, what Mao termed contradictions among the people.[4] Such contradictions can still produce intense conflicts, and may veer towards violence if not handled correctly. Therefore, recognizing dynamic *democratic disequilibrium* as a normative social state of being that encompasses political conflict, would allow sharp contradictions to be encompassed in a constantly evolving ecosocialist society. Contradictions solved through democratic competition, preventing destructive upheavals that carry out the struggle in ruthless terms.

Such an approach seeks to avoid an idealized quest for static equilibrium, a harmonious utopia without social conflict. Both static equilibrium and revolutionary leaps are often pursued through repressive measures. It's either a state-imposed peace with the gagged silence of oppositional views, or the cacophony of heroic acts and unending sacrifice that end in social and economic regression. Instead dynamic democracy accepts conflict, constantly seeking resolution through institutionalized democratic practices, as a normative functioning society. This entails accepting protest, direct action, and degrees of social disruption as positive acts of political involvement and concern.

Dynamic democracy, once made possible, may help avoid the impulse for revolutionary leaps deeply ingrained in socialist practice. The Cuban mass campaign to produce ten million tons of sugar cane resulted in failure, and China's Great Leap Forward produced famine instead of modernization. Stalin's forced collectivization and rapid industrialization was rationalized as a revolutionary transformation that would smash all opposition to building socialism, while the Cultural Revolution was yet another endeavor to make a revolutionary leap using antagonistic class struggle as a tool for change. Mao mobilized a massive social rebellion outside of traditional Party channels to overthrow what he saw as bureaucratic threats to socialism. Stalin's methods were the opposite, the creation of oppressive state machinery that drove peasants into collectives and executed opponents, many of whom were members of the Communist Party. While the methodologies were very different, the underlying belief in the necessity of radical ruptures and transformations were similar. The Khmer Rouge were the ultimate expression of such errors. Without institutional democratic practices that protect oppositional views, intense debates and radical shifts in policy can become antagonistic life and death struggles for control.

But how do we model our thinking around a future social system? Most answers lie in historic developments because concrete questions only generate possible solutions as problems arise and are recognized. But we don't have to wait for future history. Past and present experiences can help develop the next steps forward. This was the basic methodology used by Marx and Engels. They laid out fundamental principles such as, "From each according to their ability, to each according to their need." But there was no blueprint offered for revolutionaries to follow. When the Paris Commune wrote its short but courageous page in history, Marx look at the concrete experience of the insurgent working class and urged the intelligentsia to put forward more detailed thinking on how a communist society might function. For Marx the Communal Constitution was a historic document that eliminated the bourgeois state and replaced it with "a working-class government... the political form at last discovered under which to work out the economic emancipation of labour."[5]

Protagonistic Democracy

This same methodology is used by Marta Harnecker, one of the most insightful Marxists produced by contemporary Latin American society. In *A World to Build: New Paths toward Twenty-First Century Socialism*, Harnecker's thinking is based solidly in the experiences of Venezuela, Bolivia, Ecuador, Cuba, and Chile as well as Kerala, India. Consequently her extrapolations are not flights of fancy, but carefully considered roads forward looking at innovative and revolutionary democratic struggles today.

Along with many others on the left, Harnecker is critical of the Soviet Union's lack of democracy and bureaucratic centralization. These problems are positioned as key elements in the failure of twentieth century socialism. Consequently, her approach begins with constructing institutions and methods that ensure the active participation of the broad masses, or what is termed 'protagonistic democracy.'

As Harnecker explains,

> This participatory and protagonistic democracy is not democracy solely for the elites, as bourgeois representative democracy is; it is a democracy for the great majority of the people. Within it, the common citizen can participate in a variety of matters, not only in the formulating demands and supervision, but more fundamentally in the making decisions and ensuring they are carried out.[6]

Harnecker is trying to solve one of the central questions facing the left: the relationship between the state and social movements. Although some social movement activists reject electoral engagement, popular left governments have nonetheless come to power as part of the social awakening that movements generate. Social movements in Spain, Greece, Portugal, Venezuela, Bolivia, Ecuador, Argentina, and Brazil all led to radical and socialist gains in the voting booth. Once in power left parties find the critical support of social movements essential, but are often uncomfortable with the critical aspect of that support as they struggle against conservative opposition. In turn the same is true for the movements, which are often unhappy with the slow pace of reforms, or concessions to global capitalism made by left governments. Such pressures are the necessary contradictions of democratic disequilibrium, essential for creating a dynamic political society. That such tensions exist today between left governments and left movements, is a good indication they such contradictions will continue in ecosocialist societies, and moreover, that such relationships are key to building a viable alternative.

Harnecker addresses this question by drawing the state down into civil society, and civil society up into the state. Her ideas are based on the creation of communal councils in Venezuela with the accent on decentralization to the grassroots where power is rooted in mass participation. These councils are community forms of governance encompassing 200 to 400 families discussing, deciding, and supervising local projects. But Harnecker wants to expand the experience to a country-wide form of popular self-governance, with elected spokespersons who would be representatives to regional assemblies. Proceeding from there she moves to national governance bodies, which would be responsible for country-wide strategic plans based on a synthesis of ideas and programs coming from the assemblies.

Class and social conflict is accepted as part of this system. But what Harnecker fails to address is the role of different political parties. Competitive parties exist in all the countries Harnecker is examining with the exception of Cuba. She does vigorously argue for a "political instrument," whose function would be to coordinate diverse revolutionary forces and carry out popular political education.[7] This argument is directed mainly at anarchist-defined horizontalism, popular among social movement activists who reject political parties. But the argument also indirectly suggests that elections between diverse parties is a fetish of bourgeois republicanism, designed to separate governing power from any meaningful direct mass participation. Instead protagonistic democracy is offered as a deeper, more direct, and more true democratic practice.

But in countries where multi-party systems have deep historic roots there would most likely be competition for political and social leadership within participatory institutions at the local, regional, and national level. The idea of the central governing body acting as a harmonizer seems too simplistic. Harnecker is taking an important idea first popularized by the Zapatistas in Mexico, that one leads by obeying popular will. But what happens when there are diverse popular wills? Then coordinating various demands is subject to political conflict. What is prioritized, what gets the most funding, whose needs come first within a pact of social solidarity under conditions of limited resources?

In a diverse society with perhaps tens of thousands of community assemblies there will exist contradictions in perceived needs and demands. Political instruments or parties organized by workplace cooperatives may also exist that argue for resources consistent with the needs of their sector. With an increase in popular democracy more advocates, activists, and militants will arise to organize and serve their base. It would be a natural tendency for this activity to take on political forms of organized groups. Furthermore, as contradictions erupt between different social sectors won't such groups compete for influence over spending priorities and resource allocations that are determined by governmental forms of participation and representation? Protagonistic democracy leaves plenty of room for such activity and debate. But Harnecker's description may underestimate the level of conflict, and the need for organized political expressions outside of her single "political instrument."

Abdullah Ocalan, leader of the Kurdish Workers Party, advocates a democratic confederalism "where all kinds of social and political groups, religious communities, or intellectual tendencies can express themselves directly in all local decision-making process." As he further explains, "This understanding of democracy opens the political space to all strata of the society and allows for the formation of different and diverse political groups."[8] Ocalan's concern is with the guarantee of self-determination of cultural and ethnic groups that have suffered national oppression. He sees these groups as having their own political instruments in a decentralized political and economic configuration, built upon self-administration of an alternative economy, ecological sustainability, and feminism. Ocalan's thinking is concerned with conditions in the Middle East, but the question of political autonomy and self-determination within any democratic multi-racial and multi-ethnic state is essential to recognize.

On the question of competitive political parties a further example, this time from El Salvador, is instructive. Estela Hernandez is a representative to the national legislature and a leader of La Coordinadora, a participatory community-based organization that encompasses 27,000 people. The organization functions along the lines that Harnecker proposes: protagonistic democracy at the local level whose body elects representatives to an assembly that decides on priorities. These are taken back to a full assembly of the communities for approval, and then leaders take a single strategic plan to the municipal and national government. But these activities take place in the context of fierce opposition by the traditional oligarchy. So as Hernandez explains,

> We've also been part of political parties that are in sync with us, representing the great majorities in our country. We have the FMLN party (the Farabundo Marti National Liberation Front) that took office in 2009, with the support of the whole (grassroots) population. They realized that it was necessary to change the economic model because all the wealth in our country was concentrated in a few hands. So La Coordinadora started to take our proposals to a public level. That's people's power: democratic power coming from the social movement, and giving the local and national governments alternatives which we already know work."[9]

As in Venezuela, here we have a living model of social movements in civil society entering the state through grassroots participatory democracy. In both countries such bodies have been built in environments of extreme opposition from traditional capitalist groups. If parties can contend under such conditions, why not under conditions of socialist hegemony? Historically even with one hegemonic revolutionary party, other left tendencies have continued to exist either inside or outside the dominant organization. Rather than repress such tendencies democratic political competition can exist and encompass other parties, as long as socialist legal norms are followed. The lack of political parties does not necessarily lessen the democratic content of a system built around protagonistic activism, but their existence within such a system should not be ruled out either. A multi-party system will largely depend on the political culture and history of each country. What is essential is that avenues for broad participation be established, that institutional forms can democratically express differences that naturally arise as an expression of complex societies, and that such expressions can take the form of organized protest at the local and national level.

But what of Harnecker's view of production and the market? Here she is again mainly concerned with worker participation as a means of democratic control. Nationally important industries should be state owned with workers participating in decision making, for example, putting forth a number of different names for the top managerial position from which the government can choose. Smaller units should be responsible to a community of stakeholders that would include not only workers, but also local suppliers and consumers. What Harnecker doesn't address is cooperative enterprise ownership. In the present period she believes the cultural level and knowledge of the workers must develop before they are ready to manage industries. This is similar to Lenin's position in the debates over industrial democracy in the early 1920s. Lenin argued workers could participate in aspects of management, but that their educational and cultural levels needed to develop over a period of years before they could fully manage industrial factories. Venezuela, Cuba, Bolivia, and Argentina are experiencing various forms of worker management, some successful and some not. And so Harnecker understands the process as unfolding historically rather than as an immediate transformational demand. Although Harnecker's distrust of market socialism and multi-party democracy aligns her with orthodox Marxism, her emphasis on protagonistic democracy is an escape from bureaucratic centralist formulations.

But there is perhaps an intellectual bias in Harnecker's vision of workplace democracy typical of the left. She argues that socialist efficiency must allow "workers to develop themselves as rich human beings by combining their thinking and doing through participation in management (where) every workday should involve a determined amount of time, considered an integral part of work, that is dedicated to worker training and education."[10] The problem is not all workers have a deep interest in the type of technological, marketing, and financial education necessary to run a business. Such idealization reflects a fascination with meetings and formal education as central to human development. Most every worker will have interest in freely expressing their ideas and learning key information about their job, but rather than daily meetings they may find a richer experience spending time with their kids in the park, writing poetry, playing soccer with friends, or thousands of other meaningful and enriching activities. This doesn't mean turning your back on social solidarity that comes with engaged participation at work. But do we assume this should define one's main social responsibility and political involvement?

Surely protagonistic democracy must have a broader definition than one focused solely on the economic and political management of the country. If you don't attend a meeting on the environmental needs of the neighborhood, but you volunteer time at the local organic garden, have you failed in some social duty? If you skip the meeting on community budgeting, but spend time coaching youth sports are you lacking in socialist consciousness? We might ask Harnecker if her daily enterprise meetings are required or on a volunteer basis. Of course her book's main concern is the democratization of political and economic power. But given the history of twentieth century socialism, let's be careful to remember the complex human ecology of social interactions that need to be valued as democratic and free functions of any socialist sustainable society.

nomic Democracy

nother social theorist whose main concern is the

intersection between the market and democracy is David Schweickart, a leading advocate of market socialism. Unlike Michael Albert, Schweickart is concerned with developing a path forward that springs out of today's conditions. As Schweickart argues, "It is a tenet of historical materialism that the institutions of new societies often develop within the interstices of the old. Successor-system theory...should specify a set of structural modifications that might become feasible (and) transform a capitalist economy into an economy qualitatively different."[11] Moreover, workers need to live a social and productive reality that changes their consciousness and ideas about how society can function. Taking this approach he pays careful attention to contemporary experiences such as Mondragon, and links the politics and economics of today to a vision of what can be, tomorrow.

Garcia Linera, the vice-president of Bolivia, also considers the question of transformation and how the working class gains experience to build a society beyond capitalism. Linera contends that collective self-directed activity is key in the "historical, long-term movement in which, even long before the political overthrow of the bourgeoisie, labour cracks and erodes the power-relations in economics, politics, culture and technology that maintain capital... This revolutionary process is a decades-long historical process... experiences of autonomy and social self-management, which prepare the proletariat to take responsibility for society's fate into its own collective hands."[12]

Linera's and Schweickart's thinking is consistent with Gramsci's theory on building working-class institutional power within the existing system, what he termed a "war of position." Viewing the establishment of worker cooperatives and horizontal neighborhood assemblies from this perspective seems to open the door to a transformation strategy that can lead to a new society.

Linera's and Schweickart's ideas of building the new within the old are similar to those of Marx, who saw cooperatives as important examples of the coming socialist society. In his inaugural address to the First International Marx said, "But there was in store a still greater victory of the political economy of labour over the political economy of property. We speak of the co-operative movement, especially of the co-operative factories raised by the unassisted efforts of a few bold hands. The value of these great social experiments cannot be over-rated. By deed, instead of by argument, they have shown that production on a large scale, and in accord with the behest of modern science, may be carried on without the existence of a class of masters employing a class of hands..."[13]

In Volume Three of *Capital* Marx reaffirmed the importance of cooperatives as transitional institutions, in much the same fashion that Gramsci would later write about building working-class institutional power as counter hegemonic space within capitalism. Furthermore, Marx understood the problems cooperatives face within capitalism, and yet he underlines their social importance. As Marx wrote, "The co-operative factories run by workers themselves are, within the old form, the first examples of the emergence of a new form, even though they naturally reproduce in all cases, in their present organization, all the defects of the existing system, and must reproduce them... These factories show how, at a certain stage of development of the material forces of production, and of the social forms of production corresponding to them, a new mode of production develops and is formed naturally out of the old."[14]

Schweickart's strategic vision centers on worker-owned cooperatives. He defines capitalism as private ownership of the means of production, the market, and wage labor. He proposes to end private ownership and wage labor through collective ownership and self-management, while maintaining the market. The state would own the means of production, and workers essentially rent these through a tax on the assets of their cooperative enterprise. These taxes are returned to the economy through a network of banks, and considered a national investment fund. Public investment banks operate at the national, regional, and local levels, making loans based on job creation, infrastructure development and responsibility to the community.

Companies would be under worker control, including decisions over investments, working conditions, wages, and management. Schweickart leaves open how cooperatives should be organized since different forms exist, but there is one important principle—one person, one vote. Consequently, inequality can exist if workers choose to have wage differences based on seniority, incentives, or skills. These companies are also subject to market competition where price, supply, and demand act as incentives for efficiency and innovation. This hopefully can avoid the stagnation and corruption that was common in the Soviet command economy. Schweickart terms this "market democracy" where individuals essentially vote on what they want the economy to produce. Schweickart is proposing a dialectical transformation from capitalism, recognizing how all successor systems inherit and use aspects of the old system.

Politically there would be democratically accountable legislative bodies at the local, regional, and national level. Besides traditional political questions these bodies would also have the power to decide how much investment funds should be allocated to the public and market sectors. Open hearings would be held where representatives of enterprises may lobby for more funding, and community activists may call for more public investments. This social process to determine budgets is similar to experiences first developed in Brazil. Schweickart leaves open a role for political parties, but says "it is not altogether clear that political parties—as opposed to temporary and shifting voter alliances—would remain a feature of politics in post capitalist society."[15]

Schweickart's system of Economic Democracy is more adept than Albert's or Harnecker's in considering the relationships between the economy, civil society, and the state. He views state functions in three essential ways—as collective owner of the means of production, through investments by state-owned banks, and as promulgator of laws and rules through legislative bodies. The economy is democratized by worker management, giving the market a role, but tied to social investment and innovation rather than speculation and low-wage labor. Civil society is empowered at the work place and politically through social budgeting.

Schweickart's ideas certainly seem to be similar to Engels', who stated that he and Marx had never doubted "that in the case of transition to a communist economy it would be necessary to make extensive use of co-operative enterprises as an intermediate rung, provided that matters were organized in such a way that society (and so, to begin with, the state) retained ownerships of the means of production..."[16]

Yet Schweickart falls into the same trap as Harnecker. All post-capitalist theorists want their system to run smoothly, resulting in a pull towards idealism. There is room for disagreements over allocations, and at times these may be strongly argued. But Schweickart, and I suspect Harnecker, understand political parties as expressions of class interests. Without a capitalist class Schweickart questions the continued existence of parties. Consequently, debates reflect shifting alliances, not differences based in social or institutional sectors. Yet parties also express ideological and social interests. Just look at the many left parties claiming to represent the working class. Schweickart says there will "be no systematic bias" in the debates over market versus public spending.[17] I think the opposite, that sharp debates will erupt and express the viewpoint of various social actors. Parties and differences may not reflect classes per se, but institutional interests based in the state, market, or civil society. Not only will there be differences between public and market investment quotas, but also where those investments should go within each sector. Such differences can easily coalesce into organizational platforms and political parties. Besides battles over money, there will be other issues like energy policy, minority reparations, immigration and borders, foreign policy and so on. At least Schweickart's acknowledgment of broad democratic rights opens the door for a vigorous political society where contradictions can contend and be resolved in an open and non-oppressive manner. Historical dialectical materialism warns us against utopian visions. Yes, society can be made more humane, more just and more equal, but contradictions will always remain.

Workers Cooperatives in Italy and Venezuela

In considering Schweickart's cooperative strategy for post-capitalist society, it's useful to examine the cooperative movement in Italy that has existed for over sixty years. Perhaps the most advanced experience in developing cooperatives as part of a transformative project has been in the Emilia-Romagna area of northern Italy. Although cooperatives had historic roots in the region their expansion and development became a key component in the political strategy of the local Italian Communist Party (PCI). Emilia-Romagna was continuously governed by the PCI from 1945 to 1989, and then for another decade by a center-left coalition. Today there are 7,000 cooperatives in every sector of the economy providing a major source of employment, growth, and innovation. The most developed area is the Imola district where, as described by Matt Hancock, "More than 50 percent of the total population are members of a cooperative, and more than half of the total industrial output comes from the district's 15 industrial cooperatives, three of which are global market leaders and manage multinational networks of private subsidiaries, with sales offices and production on at least four continents...producing more than two billion euros in annual revenues."[18] In fact, a number of cooperatives in the region have become transnational companies, as has Mondragon in Spain. Cooperatives are normally conceived as local or regional companies that mainly serve the internal economy, but if they can develop a democratic corporate model that is competitive on a global scale the transnational market may also become contested political territory.

The idea of globally competitive cooperatives is controversial, but controversy is not new to the movement. There have been many important debates over managerial organization, who has rights of membership, the relationship of the parent company to subsidiaries, the role of profits and inheritance, and the conflict between entrepreneurial functions and social responsibility. Cooperatives have experimented with different models and functioned under different social/political visions, but consistent in their history has been the development of a high-road strategy that pursues democratic management, loyalty to its members and community, competitive innovation, and the protection of productive capacities and long-term value.

The PCI has been part of these debates and evolved a number of different theoretical stands in their approach to the cooperative movement, but overall the PCI has seen cooperatives as part of a mass social bloc laying foundations for the socialist project, in effect, part of Gramsci's "war of position," carving out autonomist space in the counter-hegemonic struggle. The strategy linked cooperatives to an "Italian way to Socialism" that saw a series of economic and political advances that would eventually change the relationships of power. For the CPI the cooperative movement was part of a broad strategy for transformation, a way to bring democracy to the economic field. Because the CPI held governmental power for many years, funding for social services, such as child care, elderly care, and park maintenance, was contracted to cooperatives to carry out the work. This pre-dated similar efforts in Venezuela.

But as Hancock points out, "Today, a shared vision for profound social change is largely absent in the cooperative movement."[19] The left has lost the political and cultural hegemony it once held, and cooperatives are seen in more local terms, as the "patrimony of the local community." As Hancock says, "this is profound and radical. Nonetheless, as a vision, it doesn't imply movement, or a larger context of social change. Instead, the implication is *conservation*, of consolidating the gains of the cooperative and assuring that it endures over time. Both, of course, are essential, but not enough."[20]

Consequently, over the decades the strategy for cooperatives to act as a social and economic base for socialist transition has lost its way. In Gramscian terminology the cooperatives functioned as a war of position, building independent working-class institutional power. Although Italy has had moments of intense class struggle, or as Gramsci put it "wars of maneuver," Communists never captured national state power. Over time the

CPI dissipated into Euro communism and then social democracy, and so cooperatives became an acceptable regional component of the hegemonic capitalist economy.

A more dynamic and contested project is currently occurring in Venezuela where there are over 70,000 cooperatives active in every sector of the economy with some two million members. The Chávez constitution defines cooperatives as essential economic institutions for mass participation and state decentralization. State-run educational missions have trained over 195,000 students in technical and managerial subjects. These students upon graduation have created 7,592 new cooperatives. As part of Endogenous Development Zones cooperatives receive credit, technical support, and physical space. As early as 2005 there were 115 active zones covering 960 cooperatives, 75 percent in agricultural, 15 percent in industrial enterprises, and 10 percent in tourism. Over time the cooperative enterprises are expected to make profits and payoff their loans, with most production geared towards building a stronger internal market. But cooperatives are not cut off from global markets. Through the Ministry of Popular Economy the integration of cooperatives with small and medium size companies is facilitated to create production chains that can contract with foreign buyers.[21]

As in Italy, this is a Gramscian strategy of creating counter-hegemonic institutions based in working-class power that can contest with capitalist structures over a long period of time. There is a dialectic relationship at work between periods of building a war of position to periods of mobilization and intensified class struggle in which the war of maneuver leads to greater occupied social and economic space. For example, when Chávez was kidnapped and his government overthrown, the coup leaders were faced with massive mobilizations that forced them to concede after two days. This led to advances in the popular political and social programs, greater consolidation of the revolutionary forces, and disorganization among the opposition.

In addition to the new cooperatives in the Development Zones, many state-run industries have moved to co-management or cooperative management forms. Additional efforts include 40,000 community councils in the planning and decision-making process over municipal public services. This involves supervision, prioritizing projects, and hiring cooperatives to carry out the work. The Venezuelan government also hands out land titles and work contracts to those who self-organize into cooperatives, promoting collectively-owned production capacity. In this fashion the state helps to support and expand civil society and the independent cooperative economy. Expanding the cooperative movement is an important strategy to counter balance the centralized state economy, which owns the oil industry. Oil production makes up 30 percent of the GDP and 80 percent of national exports. While providing funds for the social missions its massive economic weight may pull Venezuela towards state-centric socialism.

Still, there are many old habits that can undermine the revolutionary process. The state may turn the cooperatives into cliental relationships, trading economic support for political loyalty. Easy credit and poor technical and managerial skills may lead to economic failure, or state support that produces debt and deficits. Additionally, problems of false accounting, undemocratic decision-making, and managers stealing profits have occurred. Such internal contradictions are not uncommon in the history of cooperative movements. The political struggle may also sway back and forth, with capitalist parties again taking over the government. In such a case cooperatives may provide institutional structures from which the working class can relaunch their struggles. For example, during the Progressive Era in the US cooperatives formed an important political base for the Socialist Party of Eugene Debs.

Chávez had a deep theoretical, practical, and strategic commitment to protagonistic democracy. John Bellamy Foster points out, "The complex aspect of the revolution under Chávez, however, was that the constituted state power had as its main objective the creation of a communal state, the shifting of power to the populace through a myriad of structures: constituent assemblies, plebiscites, social missions, cooperatives, socialist workers councils, communal councils, communes, and communal cities."[22] The call for '21st Century Socialism' was more than a political slogan; it was a strategic orientation that recognized the democratic limitations of the Soviet experience. The commitment to popular democracy by Chávez was connected to his appreciation of the revolution led by Simón Bolivar and the writings of Simón Rodriguez, Jean-Jacques Rousseau, and contemporary Marxist theoretician István Mészáros.[23] Therefore, his understanding of revolutionary bourgeois democracy alongside its historic limitations, linked to his grasp of both Soviet failures and the emancipatory tradition of Marxism, led Chávez towards building a new socialist project based in participatory democracy, a project that uses the state to decentralize economic and political power by promoting mass social activity, and the integration between governance, civil society and the market.

Experience indicates that cooperatives have a long and deeply rooted appeal to the working class. An upsurge by social movements becoming producers, rather than just groups marching to demand more services, is evident in Venezuela, as throughout Latin America. The market is now contested territory to develop an alternative cooperative model. Counter-hegemony needs to create labor relations that can challenge capitalist hierarchy and individualism in the here and now. Not only is there a need to build an alternative social vision, but also alternative economic activity that generates new social relations. The response to the crisis of neoliberalism illustrates that social movements have started to go beyond the struggle between civil society and the state to include the market; while state actors have begun to use their institutional power to decentralize economic decision making into a participatory democratic process.

Horizontal Democracy in Argentina

Periods of mass turmoil and mobilization often create forms of popular democracy producing new social visions and relationships. Horizontalism may be the best framework from which to examine and understand such times. Marina Sitrin describes horizontalism as "direct democracy and the striving for consensus, processes in which everyone is heard and new relationships are created."[24] In another passage on horizontal organization in Argentina, Sitrin writes, "They reject hierarchy, bosses, managers and party brokers ...Simply put, they reject the very idea of anyone having power over someone else. They organized themselves in every aspect of their lives, both independently and in solidarity with others: *autogestionandose* in communities, neighborhoods, workplaces, schools, and universities."[25]

In the great 2001 rebellion in Argentina hundreds of neighborhood assemblies were formed encompassing tens of thousands of people. Poverty had risen to 44 percent, and so the majority of activists were the unemployed, particularly women. But many middle-class people also joined and participated, as did those who still held jobs. As part of the uprising over 200 factories were seized and turned into cooperatives. All of these were small to mid-sized enterprises encompassing about 10,000 workers. As mentioned when discussing the Occupy movement, direct action, pre-figuration, mutual aid, and a total delegitimization of political elites were important aspects of the Argentine movement.

But similar problems that affected the organizational structures in Zuccotti Park arose in Argentina. In speaking to Graciela Monteagudo, an activist involved in the neighborhood assemblies, she described meetings that ran long into the night. As time wore on the first to leave were women with children, next were those who still held jobs and needed to rise early the next morning, finally as the night marched on a small group of political militants remained who made the decisions. While participants recognized such problems, the overwhelming feeling was that horizontal and participatory assemblies were a liberating experience, and promoted the self-directed and successful organization of community needs.

But Marina Sitrin refrains from defining this as an anarchist inspired movement. She asks, "What is the name of this revolutionary process? Horizontalidad? Autogestion? Socialism, Anarchism, Autonomy, Politica afectiva? None of these? All of them? Certainly, no single word can describe it."[26] Here Sitrin opens the door to new revolutionary and transformative political practice. As one of the assembly members Sitrin interviewed stated, "It isn't that there was a decision to be horizontal—it's not that there was a decision to use direct democracy as if someone had just thought it up. It wasn't a decision. We simply came together with a powerful rejection of all we knew."[27] This is the same spontaneous democratic impulse that Harnecker connects to in developing her vision of a new society. History shows us that in Argentina, Brazil, Venezuela, in Soviet and Chinese early revolutionary periods, and in the Paris Commune millions of people have sought to create horizontal and direct democratic forms to organize their communities. This broad canvass indicates that such activity is an innate, viable, and desired social structure.

Nevertheless, practice illuminates problems that need to inform our path forward. Horzontalism has often rejected dealing with the state or political parties. A prime example is that the World Social Forum (WSF) is open to social movements, but not political parties. Given the history of manipulations and attempts to control popular movements by parties, one can easily understand the stance taken by the WSF. But when a rejection of parties is transformed into a political principle it embodies the dismissal of a whole set of possibilities. Essentially it is an artificial separation of civil society and government. The upsurge of self-directed action in Argentine civil society has largely faded away, just as the Occupy movement did. This is why Harnecker raises the necessity of a "political instrument." Compare the creation of over 70,000 cooperatives with two million members in Venezuela, to the several hundred workplace and community cooperatives that survive in Argentina. The Venezuelan state, under direction of a socialist political organization, has moved important economic resources into civil society, while the government in Argentina has launched numerous police attacks on occupied factories and social movement activists. Is taking resources from the government being captured by the state? Or the result of mass movements changing the balance of power, electing more responsive politicians, while pressuring others into taking favorable action? It depends on the situation. But when one turns their back on the necessity of a political instrument, the door is closed on a great number of things.

In Argentina a radical rupture took place in which a number of presidents were quickly thrown out of office in the same month. Millions were activated and new social movements created, but in the end no revolutionary leap occurred to a new system. Seizing the state was never the focus and never the strategy. Rather localized efforts in communities and factories, motivated by the necessity to survive an overwhelming economic failure, characterized the movement. These neighborhood efforts that created popular kitchens, clinics, and schools were theorized as creating an alternative social structure that could change the country without taking state power. That's not what happened, though. Capitalism is still hegemonic and functioning in Argentina.

Taking Power in Bolivia and Greece

Bolivia is a country where social movements led to a change in the national balance of power, and the election of the left to state leadership. Bolivia has the advantage of a long history, culture, and practice of autonomous democratic forms that predated the post-colonial Republican state. Alvaro Garcia Linera explains how indigenous communities continue to "have their own practices of deliberation, of accountability, of choosing authorities, of presenting demands, of shaping public opinion, of dissent and consent, of establishing the political equality of its members (and) the management of collective resources, in the management of family-rights tied to political responsibilities."[28]

Bolivia faced the same neoliberal practices that devastated Argentina. The traditional mining working class was broken, and poverty expanded as national production succumbed to transnational accumulation. Campesino communities were compelled to fight against the privatization and marketization of water and land, resources long under collective oversight. Additionally, state-regulated services essential to social reproduction such as health and education needed to be defended. Broad social movements uniting all affected popular sectors arose using assembly-style democracy, demanding greater civic and political rights. This led to what Gramsci termed "wars of maneuver" where sharp class conflicts and mobilizations came into play, contesting power relations between civil society and the state.

It was during the Cochabamba water wars that the social struggle enacted what Linera describes as a "communal-Andean civilizational structure."[29] Through mass organizing and protests a decentralized system of community assemblies tied to traditional family and community territory emerged. Campesino communal democracy was extended to cross regional areas in which assemblies functioned as public bodies of power, based in collective values, open discussions, and local autonomy.[30] As in Argentina, assemblies sought consensus leading to long meetings. But unlike Zuccotti Park where consensus became mandatory, minority dissent was not allowed to bring decision-making to a halt. Eventually assemblies took over management of the Cochabamba water system, replacing traditional state authorities.

Alvaro Garcia Linera's description is similar to the propositions put forward by Harnecker. He states the social organizations "became a government established in a web of assembly-style, deliberative and representative democratic prac-tices that replaced the system of political parties and legislative and judicial power in practice... This allowed shared criteria to be developed among equals at the local level (territorial assembly) and the departmental level...and an executive synthesis of opinions at the departmental level (assembly of local representatives...)."[31]

But unlike the Zapatistas in Mexico, or the autonomous movement in Argentina, the Bolivian social movements became focused on replacing the government. This led the Movement to Socialism to organizing a successful campaign for a parliamentary majority, and the election of Evo Morales to the presidency. As in Venezuela class combat continues between the socialist-led government and powerful capitalist forces inside society. Also as in Venezuela, political debate and competition continues between left political tendencies and groups, and between the state and social movements. If socialist forces in Bolivia are able to complete their transformation of society, why would left groups and tendencies simply disappear? There are organizational forces and theoretical traditions that have continued to be active during the whole process of social and political rebellion. With such traditions it's natural that different political programs and advocacy would continue over questions of how to build the new society. So we return again to the continuation of contradictions, and the institutionalization of democratic forms to contain and direct those tensions.

The experiences of Venezuela, Bolivia, and especially Greece have taught the left the difference between winning government leadership and taking power. Taking governmental positions within the capitalist state opens up certain possibilities of transformation. But it is only one step, although an important one, towards changing the relations of power between capital and labor.

From the start Syriza's victory in Greece was more restrained than the victories in Venezuela and Bolivia. Chávez and Morales had the benefit of rich resources to fund social programs, and the US overlord was focused on debilitating wars in the Middle East. Greece, deeply in debt and with few natural resources, faced a united European elite intent on destroying any viable opposition to neoliberalism. At the time, at least, the main enemy for the left in Venezuela and Bolivia was a weakened local capitalist class. For Greece, the main contradiction was with a powerful external TCC, which had them trapped in economic negotiations.

Andreas Karitzis, former member of the Syriza Central Committee, reflects on democracy, the state and civil society as it pertains to the crisis in Greece. After detailing the attacks on democracy by European elites he states, "In Europe, democracy was openly rejected. I am stressing the fact that this happened openly and not in a disguised way because I believe that this point is of extreme importance. We witnessed a major historical event: democracy is no longer relevant when it comes to serious social, economic and financial issues."[32]

If bourgeois democracy has reached its limits how can a left government function within this tightly restricted political arena? Karitzis calls for a strategy that would use the state to empower people to run the basic economic and social functions of society. This means moving beyond representative government to engage citizens "into collaborative groups embedded in a vast network of democratic decision-making that produces policies of our own logic."[33] Essentially Karitzis is proposing a Gramscian war of position in which popular institutions are built within capitalism to prepare for a deeper seizure of power. This strategy promotes working in and out of the state. Karitzis maintains the state is too important to be left under the domination of neoliberals. But with important decisions controlled by transnational governance bodies a left-led national state is but one center of power facing hostile forces. Under such circumstances there are two paths— the left can succumb to exercising limited influence, or facilitate popular empowerment by using the state to transfer resources to social movements.

Such a relationship between the state and people was a key aspect of the efforts of Chávez and the left in Venezuela. But Karitzis also speaks to the dangers of state patronage and corporatist models of development. In calling for a joint effort between social movements and the state he warns, "Social agents must overcome a corporatist mentality, a partial view on the issues… acting solely to secure from the state the satisfaction of the demands of the groups of people the movements represent."[34]

How is this new relationship between the state and social movements to be achieved? Again Karitzis strikes out against conventional politics,

The institutional framework of representative

democracy marks the traditional relation; people vote and movements demand. This is not viable anymore. The state cannot deliver what people need and want if we do not change the mentality both of the people in public administration and the government, and the people that participate in the movements... This involves the gradual transformation of the state and the movements toward an institutional and social configuration based on a new ideology and logic. It involves widening the logic of cooperation and democracy within the state and society, both in terms of their scope and their functioning, even building new institutions shaped by this new logic and these new principles.[35]

Through his experience in Europe, Karitzis gives us a strategy inline with the lessons emerging from the Latin America left: a dialectical appreciation of the role of the state and civil society in building a more democratic and just economy.

Post-Liberal Democracy

During revolutionary waves, activism that involved millions of people opened vistas that were previous hidden. Such revolutionary upsurges lasted five, ten, or sometimes 15 years. Yet they faded. Even if they achieve revolutionary state power, periods of mass mobilization recede. The question then becomes how do we build and normalize new democratic practices? And can revolutionary enthusiasm and new social relations turn into a permanent new culture? What are the institutional channels that can maintain mass involvement, while preventing stagnation and bureaucracy from expanding? The Soviet, Chinese, and Cuban revolutions all faced these questions.

If we are indeed approaching the end of the national bourgeois democratic era, then the future of democracy needs to be reconstructed into a post-Republican form of popular democracy. Liberal democracy was based on equality under the law, electoral political parties with indirect representation, state defined and administered rights, free markets, the protection of private property, and a monopoly of violence by the state. This was accompanied by freedoms of speech, press, assembly, and religion. A new system of protagonistic democracy must maintain the best and revolutionary content of these original democratic forms, but go beyond them to be rooted in a broader and direct participatory social system.

In considering new forms of democracy Gramsci's ideas are important to consider. Gramsci argued Bolshevik underground activity and the armed overthrow of the old regime was necessitated by the backward character of Czarism,[36] a political system based on repression that lacked channels for democratic challenge. The Bolshevik experience also applied to conditions in China and most Third World countries where dictatorships, often propped up by an imperialist power, ruled through the harsh repression of political groups and social movements. All these countries lacked an experienced bourgeois class, and mature networks of political, social and economic institutions.

Gramsci argued that more developed capitalist states were armed with a sophisticated system of rule in which both consensus and coercion were used. Consensus was the preferred method, channeled through restricted democratic practices, economic incentives, and cultural hegemony. In such societies, with greater social complexity, there was sufficient political democracy for social movements and oppositional socialist parties to arise and function. In considering a system beyond capitalism such complexity should continue, through a dense network of institutions in civil society, developed forms of market exchange, and political competition in government. Highly centralized hegemonic revolutionary parties corresponded to the conditions of their era, conditions in which dictatorships were strong and civil society was weak.

Most communist organizations built around Bolshevik

principles with roots in the twentieth century have diminished in size and authority. During the last century Leninist parties were successful in a number of important revolutions. But it seems history has moved on from the vertical organizational structures that corresponded to the institutional and technological formations of the twentieth century. Socialism built a modern industrial society centered on state planning, run by a professional technocratic bureaucracy, and organized into a hierarchical structure with orders running down the chain of command from the politburo to the factory floor. Everyone was a foot soldier of history marching in unison towards utopia.

But minus the revolutionary vision, the above configuration paralleled capitalist organizational forms, as well as the relationships that developed around large-scale industrial technologies. In both the East and West, factories were organized into a hierarchy of skills and engineering knowledge, in which the centralization of information translated into power. American workers were cogs in a great machine well illustrated by Charlie Chaplin in his movie, *Modern Times*, ever threatened to be consumed by the menacing gears of the assembly line.

Nonetheless, long-term employment helped to develop an evolutionary political outlook of slow but steady improvement through wage and benefit gains. When I worked at U.S. Steel my neighbor had been employed in the same mill job for 42 years, and his sons were expected to follow those footsteps into "good" jobs. The concentration of mill, fabrication, and warehouse workers in south Chicago created a working-class culture and memory, one of both resistance and accommodation, each side played out in union elections between conservative and radical candidates.

Socialist workers were also living in a world defined by coercion and consent, threatened by bureaucrats and managers not to challenge Party power, yet also beneficiaries of job security and a generous economic social contract. Both the socialist and capitalist working class were attached to the fundamental political, social, and cultural bonds born in industrial society, and organized by hierarchical and bureaucratic structures in both economic and political life. Socialism and capitalism were two different social systems, but in the end based on similar organizational principles that justified similar class relations of power.

Can the revolutionary parties of old be redesigned to suit a highly educated society with a fragmented working class, diverse middle class, and multiple organizations existing in civil society? Or does such a society more naturally give birth to multi-tendency left parties such as we see in Brazil, South Africa, El Salvador, Venezuela, Greece, Spain, Germany, and other countries—parties built more along horizontal lines than vertical hierarchy? Such parties have their own set of problems, but have quickly grown in influence. Horizontalism seems to correspond to current conditions in which concentrated, mass, and vertically organized industries have given way to a more diverse and segmented workforce. Huge factories, such as Foxconn in China, are now more the exception than the rule. According to Linera, Taylorism, which entrenched the routinization and deskilling of work, has given way to the intellectual capacity of workers as the "pivotal and final part of the subordination of the labour-process to capital."[37]

In such a society cooperative ownership corresponds with a more knowledge-empowered and individualized population. Digitalized technologies have made information more accessible. At the same time workers have been forced out of stable lifelong employment into developing new ways to constantly survive their precarious social position. Today's conditions and technologies have led to extensive networking and horizontal relationships to navigate the labor market. Such workers don't fit well into a hierarchical machine. But cooperatives are knowledge-rich networks that take advantage of the new forms of social organization, emphasizing individual responsibility within collective efforts. In the same instance, cooperative ownership offers a solution to the instability of a precarious existence.

Communist and anarchist utopias may be nice as aspirations, but aspirations that envisage societies without the political contradictions of daily-lived social and economic differences are flights of fancy, no more than metaphysical dreams in the face of materialist reality. Instead we need to envision a rich democratic political ecology that encompasses different organizational forms, thoughts, and methods. A society in which the dialectic between centralized governance and horizontal democratic practices exist together in a healthy and, at times, disruptive tension, and empowers their further preservation when confronting the pressures to be faced from the external world

All post-capitalist projects face fierce resistance from those who would lose power and privilege. This not only includes economic blackmail as faced by Greece, but economic sabotage as carried out in Venezuela. State power is now protected by the ability to collect massive amounts of data and spy on the daily lives of millions of people. And military violence continues to endanger the world, heightened by drone assassinations and political coups. There is no easy answer to such threats. The ruling class of every age and every empire has fought to keep its place. But as Frederick Douglass reminds us:

> If there is no struggle, there is no progress. Those who profess to favor freedom, and yet depreciate agitation, are men who want crops without plowing up the ground. They want rain without thunder and lightning. They want the ocean without the awful roar of its many waters. This struggle may be a moral one; or it may be a physical one; or it may be both moral and physical; but it must be a struggle. Power concedes nothing without a demand. It never did and it never will."[38]

A number of the theorists reviewed in this chapter are intimately familiar with the face of violence. Harnecker was exiled from Chile after the coup against Allende, Linera was a combatant in a failed guerrilla movement, Ocalan was leader of the Kurdish armed struggle, and Chávez was both the head and victim of armed coups. Having had such experiences is one element that gives weight and authority to their analysis today. The value of

Chávez, Harnecker, Karitzis, Linera, Schweickart, and others in the twenty-first century left is that their ideas are based in the social practice of millions in battle with neoliberal capitalism, even as, at the same time, there is a critical assessment of the achievements and failures of twentieth-century socialism. The strength of the ideas presented in this chapter is that they allow us to see a workable transitional strategy to a society beyond capitalism, one based in today's world, but taking us to tomorrow. These are deas that contemplate the interrelationships of the market, civil society, and the state, grappling with the inner connections, the conflicting demands, and how popular democracy can be the gear that turns them all.

Endnotes

1   Stephen E. Cohen, *Bukharin and the Bolshevik Revolution* (Wildwood House: London, 1971), 116.

2   V.I. Lenin, as quoted in Mao Tse-Tung, *On Contradiction* (Foreign Languages Press: Beijing, 1975).

3   Mao Tse-Tung, *Selected Works of Mao Tse-Tung* (Foreign Languages Press: Beijing, 1975).

4   Mao Tse-Tung, *On the Correct Handling of Contradictions Among the People* (Foreign Languages Press: Beijing, 1977).

5   Karl Marx, Friedrick Engels, and Hal Draper, *Writings on the Paris Commune* (Monthly Review Press: New York, 1971), 75-76.

6   Marta Harnecker, *A World to Build: New Paths toward Twenty-First Century Socialism* (Monthly Review Press: New York, 2015), 69.

7   Ibid, 185.

8   Abdullah Ocalan, *Democratic Confederalism* (Transmedia Publishing Ltd.: London, Cologne, 2011).

9   Beverly Bell, "Transforming Power, Protecting the Environment," <http://otherworldsarepossible.org/transforming-power-protecting-environment-el-salvador> (January 8, 2015).

10   Harnecker, *A World to Build: New Paths toward Twenty-First Century Socialism*, 87.

11   David Schweickart, *After Capitalism* (Rowman & Littlefield, 2011), 13.

12   Alvaro Garcia Linera, *Plebeian Power: Collective Action and*

Indigenous, Working-Class, and Popular Identities in Bolivia (Haymarket Books: Chicago, 2014), 59.

13   Karl Marx, "Inaugural Address of the International Working Men's Association," <https://www.marxists.org/archive/marx/works/1864/10/27.htm> (October 27, 1864).

14   Karl Marx, as quoted by Bruno Jossa in *Producers Cooperatives as a New Mode of Production* (Routledge: New York, 2014), 18.

15   Schweickart, *After Capitalism*, 164.

16   Karl Marx, and Friedrick Engels, as quoted in Charles Bettelheim, *Class Struggle in the USSR: First Period 1917-1923* (Monthly Review Press: New York, 1976), 426.

17   Schweickart, *After Capitalism*, 57.

18   Matt Hancock, "The Cooperative District of Imola, Forging the High Road to Globalization," University of Bologna, Schools of Economics, 2005.

19   Matt Hancock, "The Communist Party in the Land of Cooperation," University of Bologna, School of Economics, 2005.

20   Ibid.

21   Camila Pineiro Harnecker, "The new Cooperative Movement In Venezuela's Bolivarian Process," <http://mrzine.monthlyreview.org/2005/harnecker051205.html> (May 12, 2005).

22   John Bellamy Foster, "Chávez and the Communal State On the Transition to Socialism in Venezuela," Monthly Review, Vol. 66, No. 11. (April 2015).

23   Ibid.

24   Marina Sitrin, *Horizontalism: Voices of Popular Power in Argentina* (AK Press: Oakland, 2006), vi.

25   Ibid, 5

26   Ibid.

27   Ibid, 41.

28   Linera, *Plebeian Power: Collective Action and Indigenous, Working-Class, and Popular Identities in Bolivia*, 203.

29   Ibid, 253.

30   Oscar Olivera, *Cochabamba! Water War in Bolivia* (South End Press: Cambridge, Massachusetts, 2004); Jeffery Webber, *Red October: Left-Indigenous Struggles in Modern Bolivia* (Haymarket Books: Chicago, Illinois, 2011).

31   Linera, *Plebeian Power: Collective Action and Indigenous, Working-Class, and Popular Identities in Bolivia*, 241.

32   Andreas Karitzis, "The Dilemmas and Potentials of the Left: Learning from Syriza," *The 2016 Socialist Register* (July 2015).

33   Ibid.

34   Ibid.

35   Ibid.

36   Antonio Gramsci, *Selections from the Prison Notebooks* (International Publishers: New York, 1971).

37   Linera, *Plebeian Power: Collective Action and Indigenous, Working-Class, and Popular Identities in Bolivia*, 3.

38   Frederick Douglass, Edited by Yuval Taylo Philip S. Foner and Philip S. Foner, *Frederick Douglass: Selected Speeches and Writings* (Chicago Review Press; 1 edition, 2000) Quote retrieved from <https://www.goodreads.com/author/quotes/18943.Frederick_Douglass>.

INDEX